DERBY COUNTY
THE CLOUGH YEARS

Michael Cockayne

The Parrs Wood Press
MANCHESTER

First Published 2003

THE PARRS WOOD PRESS
St Wilfrid's Enterprise Centre
Royce Road, Manchester, M15 5BJ
www.parrswoodpress.com

© **Michael Cockayne 2003**

ISBN: 1 903158 44 3

Printed by Newton Printing Ltd. of London
www.newtonprinting.com

CONTENTS

ABOUT THE AUTHOR

Michael Cockayne was born in September 1958 and spent the first twenty one years of his life living in Belper, Derbyshire. He was educated at the Herbert Strutt Grammar School and Belper High School and represented both at football, rugby and athletics. As a County triple jump champion he also represented Derbyshire and Derby and County Athletics Club for several seasons. Over the Autumn and Winter months he watched Derby County and witnessed many of the games recalled in this book with his late father and other family members. Michael studied accountancy at Newcastle-Upon-Tyne Polytechnic and has worked in America, Canada and the Far East. He has been involved in sports administration and reporting for many years and is a member of the Society of Sports Historians. Now a resident of South Manchester, this is his first book, all royalties from which are being donated in full to the support of renal services in the North West of England.

ACKNOWLEDGEMENTS

IT WOULD NOT have been possible to complete this project without the help and support of a number of people. Firstly.a big thank you to Kirsty Matkin, Carol Seal and Gemma Evans - the photographic and library staff at the Derby Evening Telegraph - for the supply of archive pictures. The Evening Telegraph cannot be mentioned without also making a reference to the magnificent work of Gerald Mortimer and George Edwards for their years of dedication to everything Derby County. Indeed, Gerald's book, "DERBY COUNTY A COMPLETE RECORD 1884-1988", remains a constant inspiration to any serious students of the Rams history. I would also like to express my appreciation to Dave Scranage for the use of the Associated Sports Photographs (ASP) pictures - particularly so as his own allegiance is to another team a bit further along the A52! Thanks also to Nigel Mercer, Neil Hallsworth and Dave Burrows for the images from their own personal websites, and also Ian Hayes for his support on the RAMSMAD website. Jim Sanderson has also provided valuable advice and support throughout. Finally to Andy Searle and the staff at The Parrs Wood Press - the ideas and back up have been tremendous - thanks to you all.

Away from the production side of this book, many people, either in a professional or personal capacity, have offered their support and encouragement. Although space does not permit me to mention you all by name, to those who have kept the faith in both the good times, and the not so good times, thank you - the quotation below has been selected with you all in mind.

"Old friends, they mean much more to me than the new friends. Because they can see where you are, and they know where you've been."

Harry Chapin "Greatest Stories Live" 1975

1.

A Double Decade of Decline
(1946-1967)

IN THE YEARS FOLLOWING the end of the Second World War, sport and leisure activities across the country witnessed a remarkable upturn in popularity. There was a demand to be entertained, the long period of conflict having left people desperate to return to their traditional pre-war pastimes. Attendances at football and cricket grounds, dog and speedway tracks, and indeed sporting events in general were unprecedented, whilst away from the competitive arena the nation flocked back to cinemas and dance halls.

Being the national sport, football was at the very forefront of the increase in spectator numbers. Attendances at Football League games which for the 1946/47 season had totalled 35.6 million, rose by 16% to a staggering 41.2 million the following year, a figure which equated to an average gate of 22,333. The interest in football was not however limited to people watching games, the entire footballing industry was booming; more players started to take up the game as youngsters, whilst figures from the pools companies suggested that in 1946 almost eight million people each week were submitting a coupon. Within four years, the pools and gambling concerns provided work for almost 100,000 people and were the country's seventh largest employers. For the clubs themselves, given that the maximum wage during the playing season was just £12 per week, it was a time to make bumper profits. Crowds regularly filled stadiums which unfortunately, in far too many cases, remained dilapidated and bomb damaged after years of neglect.

For Derby County, the immediate post-war seasons were an opportunity to re-establish themselves as one of the strongest teams in the First Division. In the six years up to the end of the 1938/39 season they had finished in the top six on all but one occasion, thanks in part to having experienced internationals such as Sammy Crooks and Dally Duncan in their line up. For the 1945/46 season, the first after the War, the Rams competed in

Derby County 1932/33.

Football League South, a twenty-two team competition which incorporated a traditional forty-two game schedule. The twenty-four goals of inside forward Peter Doherty helped them clinch 4th place in the table, a performance that was franked by the club's first ever FA Cup Final win at Wembley, Derby beating Charlton Athletic 4-1 after extra time in front of a crowd of 98,215 which included King George VI. With so many fans wanting a glimpse of the returning stars, games up to the semi-final stage of the Cup were contested on a home and away basis to generate additional income. Gates throughout the competition were remarkable. Over 700,000 fans watched the thirty-two 3rd Round first leg games, and 80,407 alone witnessed County's semi-final replay against Birmingham City at Maine Road, Manchester. Sadly, the overall success of the tournament was vastly overshadowed by the events at Burnden Park before the start of the quarter-final game between Bolton Wanderers and Stoke City. Thirty-three people died and over four hundred were injured when a barrier collapsed in a corner of the ground, with it later transpiring that over 85,000 people, 15,000 above the capacity, had gained access to the stadium.

By the end of the decade, County had twice broken the British transfer record in an attempt to maintain their position as a leading side. In June 1947, manager Stuart McMillan paid £15,000 for Morton's abrasive inside left Billy Steel, following that less than two years later with the £24,500 purchase of John Morris from Manchester United. It was hoped that the duo would become the successors to Doherty and Raich Carter, the goalscoring partnership behind the FA Cup triumph. Unfortunately, the terms of the deal that brought Steel to the Baseball Ground were the topic of intense media speculation. As a consequence, the Rams accounts were investigated by the Football League and found to contain "gross irregularities". A fine of £500 was levied

Cover of 1946 FA Cup Final programme.

Jack Nicholas receives the FA Cup from King George VI.

on the Club and the Chairman Mr Robshaw suspended *sine die*. It was not the first time Derby had fallen foul of the game's authorities. Just seven years earlier in 1941, another £500 fine was incurred and five Directors plus manager George Jobey were given life bans for paying illegal bonuses to players dating back to 1925. Although the ban on Jobey was rescinded in 1945, it was another seven years before he returned to management with Mansfield Town.

On the pitch, Steel stayed with the club for just three seasons. In September 1950 after thirty-five goals in 124 appearances, he returned to his native Scotland with a £23,000 move to Dundee. At the time the Rams' fortunes were starting to decline, and by the end of the 1952/53 campaign they had been relegated to the Second Division after winning just eleven games. They found things equally hard at the lower level and after finishing 18th in 1953/54, their ageing side were relegated to the Third Division (North) the following year. It was undoubtedly the lowest point in the club's history, destined for the first time to play outside of the the top two divisions of the English game. Attendances, which in the post-war boom season of 1947/1948 had averaged almost 30,000, fell to an extent that just 7,776 people witnessed their last Second Division game of the season at the Baseball Ground, a 3-0 defeat at the hands of Hull City.

With former 1920s stalwart Harry Storer taking over as manager from Jack Barker, the Rams just missed out on an immediate return to the Second Division. Despite twenty-four goals from Jack Parry and fourteen in twenty-three games from the emerging local player Ray Straw, they finished five points behind Grimsby Town, the East coast team claiming the one available promotion place. It was however a short-lived disappointment the following season; Straw, who had been signed as a teenager from Ilkeston Town in 1951, netted a club record thirty-seven goals, a total which included hat tricks against Halifax Town, Tranmere Rovers and Chesterfield Town. Over their forty-six game schedule the Rams rattled in a remarkable tally of 111 goals - averaging three at every home game. They were promoted back to the Second Division after winning the title with the following playing record:

GP 46   W 26   D 11   L 9   GF 111   GA 53   PTS 63

The composition of the Rams side which had changed dramatically during the early Fifties, continued to do so into the Sixties. Financially, they were no longer able to compete at the top end of the transfer market and instead relied heavily on locally developed talent. The days of them establishing British records for incoming players were certainly long gone, a fact emphasised by the signing of Bill Curry in 1960. The former Newcastle United and Brighton and Hove Albion centre forward cost £12,000, the largest fee Storer spent on a player in his seven years, 1955/56 - 1961/62, as the manager. During that time, County's highest finishing position was 7th in 1959, otherwise they regularly occupied a place in the lower half of the table, their equally disappointing FA Cup fortunes resulting in just one 4th Round appearance. Their performances reflected little on Storer's ability; he had a vast knowledge of the game and very fixed views on the role of a manager. In one of football's strange occurrences, he had also become a mentor for a young player at Middlesbrough, a centre forward named Brian Clough.

When Storer decided to retire at the end of the 1961/62 campaign, the County Directors again chose to install one of their former players as manager. Forty-four year old Tim Ward had made 260 appearances for the Rams between 1938 and 1951, his attacking play from the wing half position having additionally earned him two full England caps. After an 18th place finish in 1962/63, Ward spent £10,000 to bring Alan Durban to the Baseball Ground from Cardiff City, the young inside forward having been one of a number of players transfer listed by the Welsh side in order to finance their purchase of the legendary John Charles from Leeds United. Although Durban was the top scorer in his first season with eleven goals in thirty-five league and cup appearances, a meagre four away victories condemned County to a disappointing 13th place in the table. It was also a season which saw their average league attendance drop to 11,331, with just 5,934 witnessing a 2-1 win over Bury. In readiness for the 1964/65 campaign Ward returned to Wales to find a partner for Durban, shrewdly signing Eddie Thomas from Swansea City for £6,000. Over the two next seasons, the Welsh duo formed an excellent attacking partnership. In the 1964/65 campaign they both netted twenty-two league goals, and then snared thirty between them the following year. Unfortunately, poor defending again cost the Rams dearly, their 9th and 8th places respectively would have been much better had they been able to limit the number of often sloppy goals they conceded.

Alan Durban, scorer of 39 league goals over two seasons, seen here in action against Blackburn, 20th August 1966.

After County failed to win any of their opening six games of the 1966/67 season, Ward undoubtedly made his finest ever signing. Amazingly, in September 1966 he persuaded the Directors to pay Fourth Division Bradford Park Avenue £38,000 for their twenty-one year old striker Kevin Hector. It was a transfer which shook even the most well connected observers of the game. As a mediocre Second Division side, the Rams signings, with the exception of Curry and Durban, had for the best part of two decades been well below the £10,000 mark. Hector though was already a proven goal scorer, whilst with the Yorkshire side he had accumulated 113 league goals in 176 appearances and had netted a staggering forty-four in the season just past. It was certainly a move which excited the Rams long-suffering supporters, who longed for the return of a successful Derby team playing First Division football.

Hector certainly did not let them down. He made his home debut against Huddersfield Town on September 24th 1966 and, in a dream start, netted a well-taken goal in the Rams 4-3 victory. Although Durban scored the second hat trick of his County career in that game, it was Hector who stole the headlines and the applause, the crowd of 15,029 lingering long after the final whistle had sounded in acknowledgement of the newcomer. Sadly, Hector missed the last four games of the season because of a bout of jaundice. He had however by that stage rattled in sixteen goals in thirty games, his tally including braces against Millwall and Bury.

His pacy running with the ball and superb balance quickly led to him being heralded by the Baseball Ground faithful as the "King". Although his goals produced several excellent results, the Rams were again woeful on their travels and after winning just twelve times over the whole campaign the outcome was depressingly familiar: a 17th place finish, nine worse than the previous year.

Having spent the money, the Directors had expected more... much more. It came as no surprise when they subsequently announced that Ward's contract would not be renewed. He had managed the side for five seasons. Under his leadership, County were certainly a team that had the potential to score plenty of goals. On the negative side however, his own penchant for players with flair seemed to be reflected too often in the use of the limited funds at his disposal. During his spell in charge all of his major purchases were attackers, whereas the addition of one or two good defenders might certainly have had a better overall effect on the club's results and standings. He did however leave something for any successor to build on. Besides Hector and Durban, already a Welsh international, the locally born Ron Webster and Peter Daniel, along with experienced goalkeeper Reg Matthews, had regularly displayed enough quality to suggest that they could form the basis of the team for the following year.

Such thoughts were for the future. Before another County side took to the pitch for a competitive fixture, the Directors needed to appoint their sixth post-war manager, someone who hopefully could reverse the club's ailing fortunes.

2.

A Time for Change
(1967/68)

CENTRE FORWARDS SCORE GOALS. . . . Brian Clough, the centre forward, netted goals at a rate that no other player, before or after, has matched. In 274 appearances for Middlesbrough and Sunderland between the 1956 and 1965 seasons, he hit the back of the net on a remarkable 251 occasions. His goal scoring prowess was uncanny. Over his career he accumulated eighteen hat tricks, five four-goal hauls, and against Brighton and Hove Albion on August 23rd 1958 he notched five in Middlesbrough's 9-0 victory. Add to those numbers a five goal tally in a game for the Football League, plus another five in a Football Association fixture and it soon becomes apparent just how good Clough was at his job. The fact that he won only two senior England caps was certainly more to do with Middlesbrough's northern location and Second Division status, rather than any lack of ability on Clough's behalf.

Tragically, a serious knee injury sustained on Boxing Day 1962 ultimately ended his playing career. Although, to Clough's immense credit, he battled his way back to fitness and managed three more games at the start of Sunderland's 1964/65 campaign, the damage to his right leg had however been so severe that a return to regular action proved impossible. A spell coaching the Roker Park youth team followed and, on the evening of his testimonial in October 1965, attended by almost 32,000 people, the thirty year old was appointed manager of Hartlepools United.

The Fourth Division club was at the time in a desperate situation. The Directors had been forced to seek re-election to the Football League in four out of the six previous summers, their struggling side more often than not attracting home crowds of less than 2,000. Clough's first move was to appoint Peter Taylor as his assistant although, as clubs in Hartlepools' circumstances certainly never employed two-man management teams, Taylor's official title was that of trainer. The pair had been close friends since their Middlesbrough playing days, Clough's goalkeeping team mate having already embarked on the managerial ladder at Southern League side Burton Albion.

By the end of the 1965/66 season Hartlepools were a much improved side. They finished in 18th place in the table, a creditable performance given that they had just eight points from thirteen games prior to the duo's arrival. The following season saw them rise to 8th, their highest position since the 1958/59 campaign. By the end of that second year, both men had however become restless. Constant disagreements with Ernie Ord, the Hartlepools chairman, had not helped the situation, and the pair were actively looking for a new challenge. Len Shackleton, a former England player turned journalist, was aware of their circumstances and set up a meeting for Clough with Sam Longson, the Derby County chairman. A deal was soon agreed, Clough being named as the Rams new manager in May 1967, with Taylor second time around officially in the role of assistant manager.

Once installed, Clough seized an early opportunity to demonstrate that he would have little hesitation in challenging what had, over the years, become established Baseball Ground practice. The clubs centre forward Ian Buxton also had a contract with the County cricket team. It meant that the twenty-nine year old, a scorer of ten league goals in 1966/67, fitted his training and early season football appearances around the demands of the County Championship fixture list. The new manager was certainly not going to have any of his team selections disrupted in such a way. With an impressive transfer fund of around £75,000 at his disposal, he immediately returned to Sunderland and paid them £20,000 for John O'Hare, a broad-chested target man, who had been under his charge in the Roker Park youth team. Buxton meanwhile, despite a goal against Rotherham United on August 28th, was sold to Luton Town for a £10,000 fee within a matter of weeks.

Two more major signings had been earmarked. Roy McFarland, a young centre half who had impressed both Clough and Taylor with his domination of Ernie Phythian, the leading forward in their 1965/66 Hartlepools side, was quickly recruited from Tranmere Rovers for £24,000. Then in September 1967 a £30,000 fee secured the services of Alan Hinton, a three times capped England wide man, from local rivals Nottingham Forest. With the trio signed, the foundations of Clough's rebuilding strategy were in place. O'Hare with his vision and excellent close control game would be the ideal

**John O'Hare, Brian Clough's first signing,
seen here later in his Rams career.**

partner for the goal hungry Kevin Hector. Twenty-four year old Hinton, as well as being able to utilise a ferocious shot at free kicks, would, with his pinpoint crosses, be the duo's main provider. When McFarland put pen to paper Clough boldly predicted that he would ultimately also play for England, such was his confidence in the nineteen year old's ability to stem the flow of goals that had become the Rams' Achilles heel.

For the first time in three seasons, the Rams' league campaign got off to a winning start. An own goal, plus markers from O'Hare and Hector gave them a 3-2 home victory against a Charlton Athletic side managed by Bob Stokoe - who later in his career led Sunderland to their famous 1973 FA Cup Final triumph over Leeds United. Although County then slipped to a 1-0 defeat at Crystal Palace, another three goal performance saw Clough's side beat Rotherham United 3-1. Baseball Ground wins over Aston Villa and the previously unbeaten Queens Park Rangers followed, those victories coming either side of a disappointing 3-2 reversal at Norwich City.

In an ironic twist, County were drawn against Hartlepools in the 2nd Round of the League Cup, an excellent hat trick from O'Hare plus a headed goal from Billy Hodgson setting up an easy 4-0 win. Although Hodgson's goal was his 20th for the club in a little over two seasons, he played just two more games before losing his place following the signing of Hinton. It was clear that the thirty-two year old did not feature in Clough's future plans and he was subsequently sold to Rotherham United for a small fee.

After defeating Plymouth Argyle in a scrappy game at the Baseball Ground, the Rams put on a scintillating display of attacking football when they visited Cardiff City on September 23rd. In a comprehensive 5-1 win, Hector followed O'Hare's lead and netted his first hat trick for the club. To emphasise what a good partnership the pair were forming, it was the centre forward who scored the other two goals. The result moved Derby up three positions to 5th place, just three points behind the early leaders Queens Park Rangers who had been promoted the previous year, thanks to a thirty goal tally from their mercurial striker Rodney Marsh. Such an impressive performance, especially away from home, had an immediate effect on attendances at the Baseball Ground. Over 28,000 - double the 1966/67 league average - turned up for the midweek return game against Rotherham. Again the Rams were much too strong for their South Yorkshire rivals; a brace of markers from Hector, goals which took his league total to nine in as many games, set up a comfortable enough 4-1 victory.

On the last Saturday of September the Rams lost at home for the first time. Visitors Portsmouth snatched a 1-0 win, thanks to a 79th minute breakaway goal from George Smith. A 3-3 draw with Millwall followed, a contest which marked the Rams debut of twenty-six year old Pat Wright who had been signed from Third Division Shrewsbury Town for a nominal fee. Wright came into the line up at right back and replaced Peter Daniel who had occupied the position for the first ten league games. Although the home point maintained County's place in the top five, they soon moved into the transfer market again to recruit teenage defender John Robson and forward Ritchie Barker. Both deals were completed thanks to Taylor's almost unique ability to assess a player's potential to cope with the demands of league football. Robson had been spotted playing for North East junior side Birtley, whilst twenty-seven year old Barker had been under Taylor's management at Burton Albion, the Rams paying the non-league side £2,000 for the well built marksman.

At Ipswich Town on October 14th, the County defence fell to pieces and as a consequence the home side strolled to an easy 4-0 win with Scot Frank Brogan netting a pair of goals. It was a particularly sad day for goalkeeper Reg Matthews who was making his 200th league appearance for the club. The nature of the defeat at Portman Road set a trend for the next seven matches. The Rams struggled to beat a poor Huddersfield Town side 1-0, thanks to a debut goal from Barker, although a head injury to John Richardson in the game against the Terriers meant that another reorganised back four travelled to Bolton Wanderers on October 28th. An eight goal contest ensued, but despite markers for Hector, O'Hare and Alan Durban, the bus journey home came on the back of a 5-3 defeat. During November things got worse. Although County picked up a point from their home fixture with Birmingham City, consecutive losses at Bristol City, Carlisle United and Hull City, all without netting a goal, saw them slide down the table to 10th place.

At least the Rams enjoyed a better time in the League Cup competition. After the defeat of Hartlepools, they beat Birmingham City at the Baseball Ground, but then needed a replay at Sincil Bank to overcome a determined Lincoln City side. The 3-0 win against the Fourth Division club set up a home quarter final clash with Darlington, yet another team from the bottom division. That game on November 29th came immediately after the three straight league defeats and provided further evidence of the rut that Clough's side were in. After allowing their lowly visitors to take the lead on the stroke of half time, County came out after the interval and, inspired by two in two minutes from Durban, hit back to lead 5-2 by the 71st minute. Desperately poor defending then allowed the North East side to pull back two quick markers, the Rams eventually winning 5-4 with the 23,631 crowd having seen eight second half goals in thirty-five minutes. It meant that for the first time since the 1947/48 season, Derby were in the semi-final of a cup competition, their opponents in a lucrative two-legged tie being Don Revie's talented Leeds United side from the First Division.

Arthur Stewart - Rams midfielder signed from Glentoran.

In an attempt to revitalise his side, Clough signed midfielder Arthur Stewart from Glentoran in time for the home match with Middlesbrough on December 2nd. Replacing Bobby Saxton in the line up, the newcomer made an impressive debut, understandably tiring a little late on as the effects of an overnight land and sea journey from Ireland on the eve of the game took its toll. Although the Rams were again beaten, their 4-2 reverse was followed by a much improved performance at Blackpool, a well taken O'Hare strike giving them a share of the points. Significantly, Clough moved Ron Webster to right back for the game against the Seasiders, a position the Belper born player would occupy for the remainder of his career. Unfortunately, County seemed unable to find any real consistency in their performances and, despite a good 2-1 win in the return game with Charlton Athletic, they went into the League Cup clash against Leeds United on the back of a sequence of another four league games without a victory.

The semi final draw certainly captured the public's imagination, and 31,904 flocked to the Baseball Ground to see the first leg on January 17th, 1968. County put on a magnificent performance against their quality opponents, literally matching the First Division side in every aspect of the game. The only goal of the night came in the 64th minute when Bobby Saxton conceded a penalty for handball, John Giles converting the spot kick with ease. At the time, Saxton did not realise the consequences of his actions. Although he appeared in the Rams 2-0 3rd Round FA Cup defeat, coincidentally also against Leeds, he was off-loaded to Plymouth Argyle for £12,000 soon afterwards. Following the earlier sale of Buxton, it was another demonstration of the ruthless streak that Clough the manager possessed. Before the second leg of the semi-final, the Rams played out seven-goal thrillers with both Plymouth and Cardiff City. At Home Park on January 20th, they trailed 3-1 with half an hour to play, but their substitute Barker capped a wonderful fightback with an 88th minute winner. Against Cardiff, the Rams never recovered from a poor first half and, despite the scoreline, were a well beaten side. Clough's side battled hard in the return game with Leeds but they were beaten 3-2 at Elland Road and exited the competition on a 4-2 aggregate - a more than creditable effort against one of the country's best teams who had, to name but three, Billy Bremner, Jack Charlton and Peter Lorimer in their line up.

**Kevin Hector scores from the spot
against Bristol City, 6th April 1965.**

Against Queens Park Rangers on February 17th, County showed another frustratingly brief glimpse of their true potential. The table-topping Londoners arrived at the Baseball Ground on the back of a nine game unbeaten run, but returned South after being thrashed 4-0 by a Hector-inspired Rams side who scored twice in the first fourteen minutes. Despite the defeat, Rangers stayed at the top of the table, whilst Derby's first home win in six starts moved them up to 14th. Sadly Clough then saw his team slump yet again, just one win in five games resulted in ending the month of March as a mid table side whose season was effectively over. With the future in mind, defender Phil Waller was sold to Mansfield Town for £6,000 while forward Gordon Hughes moved to Lincoln City in a £5,000 deal. Taylor's contacts with the non-league game did however produce another addition to the squad, twenty year old Jim Walker being signed from Cheshire semi-professional side Northwich Victoria.

In front of decreasing home crowds, the campaign petered out with a series of mediocre displays to the extent that after beating Bristol City 3-1 on April 6th, a game in which Hector netted his nineteenth league goal from the penalty spot, Clough's side failed to win any of their final six fixtures. Their worst performance was a 2-1 home reversal at the hands of a poor Hull City side on April 20th, Malcolm Lord and Ian Butler netting the visitors' markers. The final game of the campaign saw the Rams defeated 3-1 at home by Blackpool, a contest in which Walker made his debut. Given all the excitement that had surrounded Clough's appointment and his early signings, the Rams final finishing position of 18th in the table was a major disappointment. Just as had been the case in so many seasons before, the defence had struggled throughout; this time keeping a clean sheet on just four occasions.

It was not however all doom and gloom. McFarland played exceptionally well, despite the fact that the sale of both Saxton and Waller had left him, to all intents and purposes, without a natural partner in the heart of the back four. Both full back positions had also caused concern, with Webster, Daniel, Richardson, Wright, Robson and Mick Hopkinson all having appeared in one or other of the roles over the season. At least towards the end of the campaign Webster looked comfortable in the number two shirt, whilst the emergence of Robson on the left side was clearly a positive sign for the future.

Of the midfield players, although Durban adapted well to his new role and weighed in with his fair share of goals, Stewart appeared to be struggling in the latter part of the season after a promising start. Hector was undoubtedly the pick of the forwards, though Barker's ten league strikes were far more than might have been expected from a £2,000 signing having his first taste of league football. With County winning only eight of their twenty-one home league games, the contributions of O'Hare and Hinton were not fully appreciated by certain sections of the crowd. Hinton in particular was regularly baited for his dislike of the physical game, the tall winger having picked up the unfortunate nickname "Gladys" early in his Baseball Ground career. The goalkeeping position was also undecided. While Matthews, as the senior professional, remained popular, at the age of thirty-four he was understandably looking towards a future in management rather than another campaign between the posts. In the final analysis, despite their lowly finishing position, County were a side that had the potential to do much better. With the ultra confident Clough at the helm, the light at the end of their seemingly endless Second Division tunnel certainly shone a little brighter than it had in previous years.

APPEARANCES 1967/68

PLAYER	LEAGUE		FA CUP		LGE CUP		OTHERS		TOTAL	
MATTHEWS	37		1		7		0		45	
DANIEL	15		1		6		0		22	
HOPKINSON	21	(1)	0		4		0		25	(1)
WEBSTER	39		1		7		0		47	
SAXTON	20	(1)	1		6		0		27	(1)
WALLER	6	(1)	0		5		0		11	(1)
HUGHES	27		1		7		0		35	
DURBAN	39		0		7		0		46	
O'HARE	42		1		7		0		50	
HECTOR	41		1		7		0		49	
HODGSON	8		0		1		0		9	
THOMAS	0	(1)	0		0		0		0	(1)
RICHARDSON	30		1		5		0		36	
McFARLAND	40		1		0		0		41	
BUXTON	1		0		1		0		2	
HINTON	25	(1)	1		0		0		26	(1)
WRIGHT	12	(1)	0		0		0		12	(1)
BARKER	23	(4)	0		4		0		27	(4)
BUTLIN	2		0		1		0		3	
BOULTON	5		0		0		0		5	
STEWART	24		1		2		0		27	
ROBSON	4		0		0		0		4	
WALKER	1		0		0		0		1	
RHODES	0		0		0	(1)	0		0	(1)
TOTAL	**42**		**1**		**7**		**0**		**50**	

N.B. Substitute appearances in brackets.

SCORERS 1967/68

HECTOR	21	0	3	0	24
O'HARE	12	0	6	0	18
BARKER	10	0	2	0	12
DURBAN	9	0	2	0	11
HINTON	6	0	0	0	6
HUGHES	2	0	1	0	3
McFARLAND	2	0	0	0	2
STEWART	1	0	1	0	2
ROBSON	1	0	0	0	1
RICHARDSON	1	0	0	0	1
BUXTON	1	0	0	0	1
WALLER	1	0	0	0	1
HOPKINSON	0	0	1	0	1
HODGSON	0	0	1	0	1
OWN GOALS	4	0	1	0	5
TOTAL	**71**	**0**	**18**	**0**	**89**

KEY MATCHES OF 1967/68

Hector, O'Hare are much too smart for sorry Cardiff...

23rd September 1967, Football League Division Two

CARDIFF CITY 1 DERBY COUNTY 5

The Rams achieved their first ever victory at Ninian Park, easily overcoming a poor Cardiff City side that had not lost at home since Boxing Day 1966. Alan Durban captained the team against his former club, and although he had a great game, it was again the irrepressible Kevin Hector who stole the show with a brilliantly executed hat trick.

After an even opening, County decisively took control and struck two goals within the space of thirteen minutes. In the twentieth minute Hector netted the opener, and then, with the home defence appealing in vain for offside, John O'Hare extended the advantage with a well taken thirty-third minute strike. The second half was particularly one sided, with perhaps the only surprising feature of the entire game being that it took the Rams a full quarter of an hour to add to their tally. After Hector had made it 3-0, the Welsh side netted their consolation, Ron Bird getting up and scoring from the penalty spot after he had been fouled by Peter Daniel. With Roy McFarland in commanding form, the chances of a Cardiff fightback looked remote. They were ruthlessly extinguished in the last ten minutes - Hector notching his third on eighty-one minutes, and O'Hare his second, from close in, just three minutes later.

The 5-1 mauling represented the Rams' biggest away win since the 1959/60 season. Then a Peter Thompson brace inspired Harry Storer's team to a 5-0 success against Plymouth Argyle. It was Clough's side's third consecutive league victory, a performance which lifted them to 5th in the Second Division standings.

CARDIFF CITY: WILSON, COLDRICK, FERGUSON, WILLIAMS, MURRAY, HARRIS, JONES, ALLEN, TOSHACK, KING, BIRD. SUBSTITUTE: CLARKE.

DERBY COUNTY: MATTHEWS, DANIEL, RICHARDSON, WEBSTER, McFARLAND, WALLER, HUGHES, DURBAN, O'HARE, HECTOR, HODGSON. SUBSTITUTE: BARKER.

ATTENDANCE: 15,375
REFEREE: MR NEW

County rely on early goals...

27th September 1967, Football League Division Two

DERBY COUNTY 4 ROTHERHAM UNITED 1

Encouraged by the Rams' impressive 5-1 victory at Cardiff City four days earlier, a crowd of 28,251 turned up to witness the defeat of the Yorkshire side, with Kevin Hector's double strike giving him a tally of five in two games. Unfortunately, the task of admitting such a large midweek attendance on time was beyond the age-old Baseball Ground turnstiles. As a consequence, some spectators missed a brilliant opening fifteen minutes, during which time County netted three quick goals.

The triple blast was triggered when Gordon Hughes rounded the United goalkeeper Alan Hill to score in the sixth minute. The second seven minutes later reaffirmed Hector's position as one of the Second Division's most deadliest of marksmen. After picking up a pass, he beat a defender for pace before lashing in a superbly taken strike from the edge of the penalty area. On the quarter hour, Hector the scorer became Hector the provider; his lightning speed again exposing the defence and allowing him to tee up an easy marker for John O'Hare. The visitors quickly replied, with Laurie Sheffield reducing the deficit just four minutes later.

With Rotherham surprisingly looking the better side for long periods, County did not wrap up the points until five minutes from time. Then O'Hare returned his strike partner's earlier favour, a neat pass allowing Hector to rifle a shot into the net. The quartet of goals confirmed the Rams, along with Birmingham City, as the division's joint top scorers with twenty-two in nine league games.

DERBY COUNTY: MATTHEWS, DANIEL, RICHARDSON, WEBSTER, McFARLAND, WALLER, HUGHES, DURBAN, O'HARE, HECTOR, HINTON. SUBSTITUTE: HODGSON.

ROTHERHAM UNITED: HILL, WILCOCKSON, HARRITY, HASELDEN, THOMPSON, TILER, CHAMBERS, GALLEY, SHEFFIELD, CHAPPELL, PRING. SUBSTITUTE: BURGIN FOR TILER (65).

ATTENDANCE: 28,161
REFEREE: MR JONES

Derby misery as Bolton hit five...

28th October 1967, Football League Division Two

BOLTON WANDERERS 5 DERBY COUNTY 3

The Rams lost this game after their shocking defending allowed the home side chance after chance. The defeat at Ipswich had warned Brian Clough that his side was not yet the finished article, but this performance merely emphasised just how far away they were from being genuine promotion contenders. Their frustration at getting beat was also increased by the fact that Bolton themselves played no better than any other middle of the table team might have done.

Things had looked much brighter early on; Alan Durban spotted Wanderers goalkeeper Alan Hopkinson off his line and chipped the Rams ahead after eleven minutes. With the County defenders then opting to don their Keystone Kops uniforms, the Bolton striker John Byrom swept his side level, and then ahead, within the space of just four minutes. On sixteen minutes, he netted from eight yards after a poor clearance had gifted him the easiest of chances. Four minutes later it was 2-1, the former Blackburn Rovers man heading in a needlessly conceded corner.

In the second half, although John O'Hare headed a great goal from Ron Webster's fifty-fifth minute cross, within five minutes the Trotters were again in front. Gareth Williams, easily the best player on the pitch, took advantage of another piece of ball-watching to restore the lead. Further strikes from Roy Greaves after sixty--seven minutes, and Williams' second five minutes later, left County trailing by three and looking a well beaten side. Indeed, even when Kevin Hector reduced the arrears eleven minutes from the end, it was little more than a consolation effort.

BOLTON WANDERERS: HOPKINSON, HATTON, FARRIMOND, WILLIAMS, HULME, RIMMER, BROMLEY, GREAVES, BYROM, HILL, TAYLOR. SUBSTITUTE: BUTLER.

DERBY COUNTY: MATTHEWS, WRIGHT, DANIEL, WEBSTER, McFARLAND, SAXTON, HUGHES, DURBAN, O'HARE, HECTOR, HINTON. SUBSTITUTE: BARKER.

ATTENDANCE: 12,631
REFEREE: MR PARTRIDGE

O'Rourke hat-trick stuns Rams...

2nd December 1967, Football League Division Two

DERBY COUNTY 2 MIDDLESBROUGH 4

Although the Rams played better than in recent games, they never really recovered from going two goals behind within the opening twelve minutes. Clough gave a debut to Arthur Stewart, signed from Glentoran and having travelled overnight from Ireland to finalise his transfer. With Roy McFarland and Middlesbrough's John O'Rourke having both received a succession of rave reviews, the England manager Sir Alf Ramsey was amongst the crowd of 20,381.

The visitors opened the scoring in the seventh minute, centre forward O'Rourke netting an easy chance after firstly McFarland and then Pat Wright had failed to clear a shot from John Hickton. Before County had a chance to recover, they gave up another sloppy goal: Colin Boulton failed to gather a long pass from John Crossan and Hickton nipped in to increase Middlesbrough's advantage. To their credit, Derby battled back strongly and Kevin Hector reduced the arrears when he headed home a twenty-third minute free kick from Gordon Hughes.

The Rams continued to improve in the second half with Stewart having an impressive first game. However with the visitors strike force of Hickton and O'Rourke always looking more dangerous than Hector and John O'Hare, they wrapped up the game with another quick double strike salvo. On sixty-seven minutes, Hickton took the ball past a struggling McFarland and crossed for O'Rourke to make it 3-1. Six minutes later it was all over, Hickton again breaking past the defence to set up O'Rourke's hat trick goal. County notched a late consolation with two minutes remaining, Stewart chipping the ball in the penalty box for O'Hare to squeeze it into the net. It was unfortunately a case of too little too late as the Rams fell to their fourth consecutive league defeat.

DERBY COUNTY: BOULTON, WRIGHT, RICHARDSON, WEBSTER, McFARLAND, STEWART, HUGHES, DURBAN, O'HARE, HECTOR, HINTON. SUBSTITUTE:BARKER.

MIDDLESBROUGH: WHIGHAM, HICKTON, JONES, HORNER, ROOKS, SPRAGGON, KEAR, McMORDIE, O'ROURKE, CROSSAN, CHADWICK. SUBSTITUTE: MASSON.

ATTENDANCE: 20,381
REFEREE: MR COWAN

Battling Rams make Leeds work hard...

17th January 1968, Football League Cup Semi-Final 1st Leg

DERBY COUNTY 0 LEEDS UNITED 1

Although the Rams were beaten, they gave First Division Leeds United a far tougher contest than the Yorkshire side might have been anticipating. In a splendid display, Clough's team matched their opponents for skill as well as effort, and had it not been for a needlessly conceded penalty they would have gone into the second leg on equal terms.

County almost grabbed an early lead. After five minutes a neat move between John O'Hare and Ritchie Barker resulted in a cross which Kevin Hector headed just wide. The Rams top scorer again went close soon afterwards, his diving header from a corner being kicked off the line by Terry Cooper. Still the probing continued, the Rams' inventive moves bringing out the best of Jack Charlton and the superb Norman Hunter at the heart of the visitors' defence.

When Leeds did attack, their normally deadly strikers found both Ron Webster and Bobby Saxton in commanding form. Sadly however it was Saxton who literally handed United their one goal advantage; Jimmy Greenhoff centred a sixty-fourth minute corner and the Rams defender, under no pressure at all, handled the ball to concede an obvious penalty. Teams with the quality of Leeds United rarely waste such gift-wrapped opportunities and John Giles duly blasted his shot into the back of the net.

At the end the Rams trooped off to a magnificent reception, their efforts having made a complete nonsense of their 15th place standing in the Second Division. They had certainly given their supporters a glimpse of what their side, boosted by the return of Roy McFarland and Alan Hinton and perhaps a couple of new faces, might just achieve.

DERBY COUNTY: MATTHEWS, DANIEL, RICHARDSON, WEBSTER, SAXTON, STEWART, HUGHES, BARKER, O'HARE, HECTOR, DURBAN. SUBSTITUTE: HOPKINSON.

LEEDS UNITED: SPRAKE, REANEY, COOPER, BREMNER, CHARLTON, HUNTER, GREENHOFF, LORIMER, MADELEY, GILES, GRAY. SUBSTITUTE: BELFITT.

ATTENDANCE: 31,904
REFEREE: MR RICHARDS

Leeds just too good for second division Derby...

7th February 1968, Football League Cup Semi-Final 2nd Leg

LEEDS UNITED 3 DERBY COUNTY 2 (AGGREGATE 4-2)

Just as they had done at the Baseball Ground, the Rams gave their all against Leeds United, but the class of their opponents shone throughout and in the end the scoreline flattered the Second Division side. The home team, having relied on a penalty to beat Clough's bravehearts in the first leg, needed no such luck second time around, the Rams defence often looking bewildered by United's flowing football.

And yet it was Kevin Hector who stole the early accolades, when his header from a John O'Hare centre silenced the Elland Road crowd as it zoomed past Gary Sprake and into the net. The goal

Reg Matthews was constantly in action at Elland Road, above seen turning aside a shot and below, collecting under a challenge from Jack Charlton.

stunned Leeds into action and they were quickly level when Rod Belfitt forced the ball home after a scramble in the Rams goalmouth. In honesty, after that the Yorkshire club took over and played some great football. A minute before half time, Eddie Gray shrugged off two weak tackles and rolled an equally weak shot past Reg Matthews to make the aggregate score 3-1.

After the interval Belfitt's second goal ended the Rams' lingering resistance, and doing as they pleased United on another night might have scored six or seven. However in the eighty-ninth minute the Rams gained a deserved consolation, Alan Durban slipping the ball into the path of Arthur Stewart - the midfielder firing a fine shot past Sprake. It was Leeds then who progressed to the League Cup Final to face Arsenal. For the Rams it was back to their Second Division campaign, the impressive surroundings of Elland Road being replaced by the rather more familiar sights of forthcoming away trips to Portsmouth, Millwall and Huddersfield Town.

LEEDS UNITED: SPRAKE, REANEY, COOPER, BREMNER, MADELEY, HUNTER, GREENHOFF, LORIMER, BELFITT, GILES, GRAY. SUBSTITUTE: BATES FOR COOPER (85).

DERBY COUNTY: MATTHEWS, DANIEL, RICHARDSON, WEBSTER, WALLER, STEWART, HUGHES, BARKER, O'HARE, HECTOR, DURBAN. SUBSTITUTE: ROBSON.

ATTENDANCE: 29,367
REFEREE: MR HOWLEY

Hector and Hinton embarrass leaders...

17th February 1968 Football League Division Two

DERBY COUNTY 4 QUEENS PARK RANGERS 0

After their encouraging League Cup displays against Leeds United, the Rams dominated this encounter and never looked in any danger after taking an early lead. Top of the table Rangers were a major disappointment, with only their star striker Rodney Marsh appearing capable of causing the home defence any significant problems.

County sizzled into action and, inspired by Alan Hinton, netted the opener after ten minutes, Kevin Hector scoring his 20th goal of the season from the wingers' low centre. Just four more minutes had elapsed before it was 2-0: the visitors' goalkeeper Ron Springett failed to hold on to a corner, and Hinton smashed a volley high into the net. The Rams continued to swarm forward and Hector's speed over the surface constantly threw the Rangers back line into a state of panic. The hour mark had passed before the third goal arrived when Arthur Stewart carried the ball unchallenged into the penalty area and lofted a shot beyond the startled Springett. Hinton, who tormented Dave Clement for the entire game, set up the final strike. He beat the full back for the umpteenth time and crossed for Hector to tee up an easy eighty-second minute chance for Roy McFarland - his first goal as a Rams player.

It was a tremendous all round performance from Clough's side, even Reg Matthews getting in on the action with a save from a dubiously awarded Mike Keen penalty. The result marked a double for the Rams over the Londoners, a marker from Hector having given them a deserved 1-0 success at Loftus Road earlier in the season. The supporters went home in a happy mood, their only frustration being that it was the first Baseball Ground victory they had seen witnessed since Huddersfield Town had been beaten 1-0 on October 21st.

DERBY COUNTY: MATTHEWS, RICHARDSON, HOPKINSON, WEBSTER, McFARLAND, STEWART, DURBAN, BARKER, O'HARE, HECTOR, HINTON. SUBSTITUTE: WALLER FOR RICHARDSON (64).

QUEENS PARK RANGERS: SPRINGETT, CLEMENT, HARRIS, KEEN, KEETCH, HAZELL, MORGAN (IAN), SANDERSON, LEACH, MARSH, MORGAN (RON). SUBSTITUTE: WATSON.

ATTENDANCE: 22,854
REFEREE: MR FINNEY

Rams beaten again - season ends in a whimper...

4th May 1968, Football League Division Two

DERBY COUNTY 1 BLACKPOOL 3

The Rams ended their campaign with a third consecutive home defeat, a modest Seasiders team proving far too good for them. As a consequence, they slipped a further two places down the table to 18th - one worse than under the management of Tim Ward. Indeed the only bright spot for Brian Clough was the mature performance of teenager John Robson who, as well as defending superbly netted his first goal for the club.

Things had looked so different in the opening minutes. Robson rattled in a twenty-five yard shot after good approach work by Kevin Hector. After that it was a case of the visitors taking control, the Rams all too infrequent attacks being ended by a mixture of no nonsense defending and their own inability to exert any real control in midfield. The equaliser came in the sixteenth minute, a cross from Henry Mowbray being headed past Reg Matthews by the unchallenged Tom White, the visitors all action bustling centre forward. With eight minutes left in the first half County fell behind, Tony Green setting up Alan Skirton who scored with ease. With sections of the 20,635 crowd already starting to slip away, a third goal sealed the victory. In the eighty-second minute, Alan Suddick netted the

John Robson, scorer against Blackpool, developed into a very reliable left back.

best goal of the contest, the midfielder beating two half-challenges before cutting in and curling a neat shot past Matthews.

It was a desperate way to finish a campaign that had promised so much. Although County had scored an impressive seventy-one goals, the fact that they had conceded seven more summed up their problems. It was clear that Clough's rebuilding work still had a distance to go before the Rams could contemplate ending their long exile from the First Division.

DERBY COUNTY: MATTHEWS, WRIGHT, HOPKINSON, ROBSON, McFARLAND, STEWART, HINTON, BARKER, O'HARE, HECTOR, WALKER. SUBSTITUTE: DURBAN.

BLACKPOOL: TAYLOR, ARMFIELD, MOWBRAY, CRAVEN, JAMES, McPHEE, SKIRTON, GREEN, WHITE, SUDDICK, HUTCHINSON. SUBSTITUTE: MILNE.

ATTENDANCE: 20,635
REFEREE: MR ROPER

3.

The Arrival of a Legend
(1968/69)

WHEN CLOUGH AND TAYLOR sat down to reflect on their first year in charge, two positions in the line up dominated their thoughts. Firstly, there was a requirement to replace the ageing last line of defence Reg Matthews and, once that had been achieved, find an experienced campaigner to play alongside Roy McFarland. The goalkeeping problem was resolved within a couple of weeks, Les Green joined the Rams from Rochdale for a fee of £7,000, the twenty-six year old having impressed Taylor during an earlier stint at Burton Albion. The partner for McFarland appeared to be a more difficult proposition. Whilst there were plenty of central defenders around with a wealth of games behind them, County needed a leader, a player who could take the team back to the First Division and once there play on for a couple of seasons as well.

**Dave Mackay,
a Football Legend.**

The events that followed were initially greeted with a reaction of outright disbelief. When the July 1968 Derby Evening Telegraph billboards proclaimed "Rams Sign Mackay", even the most loyal of the clubs supporters thought it was merely a clever ploy by Clough to drum up support for the campaign ahead. And who could blame them?. Dave Mackay had gained fame in the Hearts side that dominated Scottish football in the 1950s. After moving South, he had helped Tottenham

Hotspur win both the 1960/61 Championship and FA Cup. Twice more, in 1962 and 1967, the iron man of a midfielder had climbed the Wembley stairs as an FA Cup winner with the London side, the second time after recovering from breaking his left leg on two occasions. For good measure, he also had a European Cup Winners' Cup medal and twenty-two Scotland caps to his name. Without question Dave Mackay was one of the very few players around who was recognised as a "Footballing Legend" by both the press and his fellow professionals alike.

Remarkably, the Rams had landed the best purchase of the close season. Prompted by his partner, Clough had audaciously travelled to the Spurs training ground and asked Mackay to join his side. The thirty-three year old Scot was however all set to return to Hearts as their player-manager. Only one thing was delaying the deal being completed. Mackay was an immensely proud man who, realising his salad days were well behind him, did not want the Hearts faithful to make comparisons about his ability with what they remembered from a decade before. Clough though was exceptionally persuasive. Mackay received a signing on fee of £14,000 spread over a three year contract whilst Tottenham, in recognition of his services, allowed him to move for a nominal £5,000 fee. One thing was for certain, second time around County would have a central defensive pairing that most strikers would, on paper, find hard to penetrate.

Mackay also had business interests to consider. He had a thriving club tie shop in the capital and so it further was agreed that his Derby base would be the Midland Hotel, the town's premier accommodation establishment. In another shrewd move, Clough recalled McFarland from his existing digs and placed him in the hotel as well. The thinking was clear; under the veteran's guidance the young defender's education would continue socially as well as professionally.

The only other transfer activity over the close season was the sale of popular locally born full back Mick Hopkinson to Mansfield Town for £5,000. The deal, which ended Hopkinson's nine year association with the club, meant Clough's summer spending, even given Mackay's £14,000, amounted to just £21,000.

The season opened with a trip to Ewood Park to face Blackburn Rovers. McFarland earned the Rams their first point of the season, his header in the 7th minute coming after the home side had taken the lead with an early penalty. Chesterfield Town were then beaten 3-0 at the Baseball Ground in the 1st Round of the

League Cup, all of the goals coming in a seventeen minute spell in the second half. Mackay led out the team for the first time at home in the league on August 17th against Blackpool. The Seasiders, who had been tipped by many as likely promotion candidates, included England capped full back Jimmy Armfield in their line up as well as a twenty year old Tommy Hutchinson on the left wing. In front of a crowd of 24,760 that included Sir Alf Ramsey, County led 1-0 at the interval but conceded an equaliser five minutes after the restart when a Tony Green strike completed the scoring. Four days later County made the short journey to Bramall lane to play Sheffield United, who had been relegated to the Second Division four months earlier and were managed by Arthur Rowley, the scorer of an amazing 434 Football League goals. They returned empty handed, their 2-0 defeat stemming from an inability to gain any control whatsoever of the midfield area. After gaining two points from the first three fixtures, Clough's side were in 18th place in the table, well below the pace setters Middlesbrough and Crystal Palace.

Clough named an unchanged line up for the trip to Huddersfield Town. Again though, the problems in midfield were evident from early on and a goal in each half from Paul Aimson gave the home side their first victory of the season. It was clear that County were in urgent need of a combative presence in the middle of the park, a player who could regularly win the ball and provide a link between the defence and attack. Conscious of the fact that the next three league games were at home, Clough again moved characteristically quickly. By the following Wednesday he had agreed a £65,000 deal with Sheffield United for Willie Carlin, the diminutive midfielder who had controlled proceedings in the one-sided defeat in South Yorkshire just eight days earlier. Not that the drubbing against the Steel City side had been Clough and Taylor's first experience of twenty-seven year old Carlin. They had tried to sign him at the start of the 1967/1968 season when he was at Carlisle, a member of the Brunton Park side that had won promotion from the third division in 1964/65. The Liverpool-born schemer, already with 225 league games under his belt, made his debut against Hull City and replaced Arthur Stewart who had struggled in the early games. Although the contest ended in a 2-2 draw, the Rams side had a distinctly better balance to it. A few eyebrows had been raised at the size of the fee paid for the midfielder, but his tenacity and wholehearted attitude served Derby superbly well over the months that followed.

The Rams won their first league game of the campaign at the fifth attempt. Goals from McFarland and John O'Hare secured a 2-0 success against Oxford United on the last day of August. The visitors had been promoted from the Third Division the previous season and included both Graham and Ron Atkinson in their side, the latter of course later going on to achieve fame as a manager and more recently television commentator and pundit.

The first game of September 1968 was the 2nd Round League Cup tie at home to Stockport County. In front of an impressive midweek crowd of 21,549, the mid-table Third Division side found themselves outclassed and slumped to a 5-1 defeat. Alan Hinton netted a quartet of goals, including two from the penalty spot, and in doing so became the first Rams player to score four in a game since Alf Ackermam achieved a similar feat against Accrington Stanley in 1956. Hinton was again on the mark three days later, his 84th minute strike alongside a brace from Kevin Hector cemented a 3-1 Baseball Ground win over Aston Villa. Thanks to a Mackay inspired draw at Bristol City and consecutive victories against Fulham, Millwall and Bolton Wanderers, Clough's side ended the month in 5th place in the table. The press were also starting to take more of an interest in the side, and after five undefeated league performances during the month Mackay received the London Evening Standard's "Footballer of the Month" award.

County's increasingly healthy looking position on the pitch was matched by their supporters mounting enthusiasm and commitment. Season ticket sales had passed the £40,000 level in August, and attendances at the first six league matches at home had averaged 24,440 - a noticeable 17% increase on the overall average for the previous year. Additionally, the club shop on Osmaston Road was stocking a varied range of souvenir items. As well as the more traditional scarves at 15/6d (£0.78), hats at 8/6d (£0.43) and rattles at 7/4d (£0.37), visitors could also, if they so desired, purchase Rammybanks at 9/6 (£0.48) and Derby County Trolls at 5/6d (£0.28).

In between the games against Millwall and Bolton came the 3rd Round League Cup encounter against First Division Chelsea at Stamford Bridge. The London club, managed by Dave Sexton had made an impressive start to their campaign and, after losing just one of their opening ten matches, stood in 4th place in the standings. Although the home side started the game as understandably strong favourites, a determined performance from the Rams saw them fully deserve the chance of a replay after

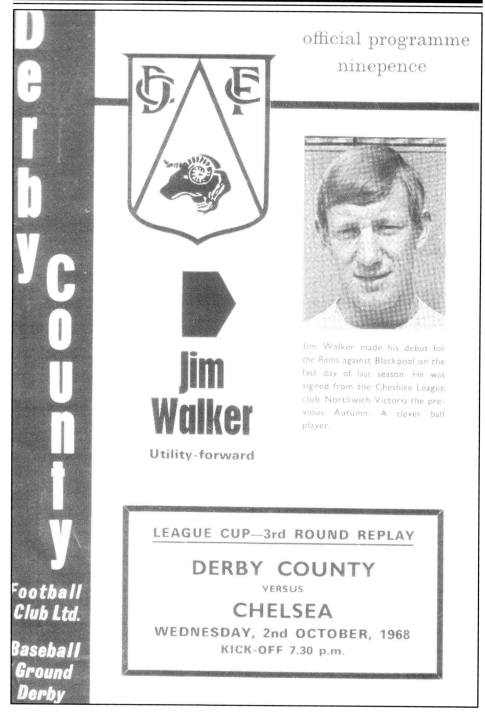

Cover of programme for the Chelsea game.

limiting the Peter Osgood-led Chelsea front line to few chances in a 0-0 draw. The return game seven nights later at the Baseball Ground has long been an integral part of Derby County folklore. Inspired by a bumper crowd of 34,346, Clough's side put on a marvellous display. Despite going a goal behind within the half hour they responded magnificently and, in a thrilling climax to a second half of non-stop attacking, scored three times in the final thirteen minutes to triumph 3-1. It was a result which thrust the Rams into the following morning's sports page headlines, although on a remarkable night of action featuring British clubs they shared the column inches with news of Liverpool's exit from the Fairs Cup on the toss of a disc against Athletico Bilbao, and Cardiff City's stormy departure fom the Cup Winners' Cup in Oporto, Portugal.

After such an effort, the players were both physically and emotionally drained. After a days rest, they travelled North for the visit to Middlesbrough. The Teesiders, who boasted John Hickton, the division's top scorer from 1968, in their line up were unbeaten at home and with fifteen points from their opening eleven games were 2nd in the standings. Again though, another resilient display from a back four which included Ron Webster in his 200th league game, saw Clough's side return home with a 0-0 draw. It was a scoreline that meant the Rams had conceded just one goal in their previous five league matches. Although the results over the previous weeks had gone so well, Clough knew the effects of playing so many games in such a short space of time had left several of his team nursing injuries, with McFarland in particular struggling with a bad groin strain. The time seemed ripe to bolster the squad. Accordingly, John McGovern, a nineteen year old winger cum midfielder, was signed from Hartlepools for a fee of £7,500, the young Scot having originally joined Clough at the North East club three years earlier as a sixteen year old schoolboy. After an unbeaten run of eleven games, County were defeated on October 9th against a much improved Hull City side at Boothferry Park. A solitary goal from Tigers' Ian Butler secured the points, the first match the Rams had lost since the signing of Carlin. It proved however to be the briefest of lapses in form. By the 26th of the month 1-0 victories had been recorded over Preston North End, Portsmouth and Birmingham City, with the crowd at the Baseball Ground for the visit of the Midlands side being 34,218 - the first time in league play the Rams had exceeded the 28,000 barrier.

The reward for the defeat of Chelsea was a visit to Everton on October 16th. The Rams again held their nerve against a First Division side, that despite the Toffees including amongst others both Alan Ball and Joe Royle in their line up. At the final whistle, County fully deserved another away 0-0 draw, achieved in front of an attendance of 44,795. The size of the crowd was swelled by the remarkable number of County supporters who made the journey to Merseyside, around 10,000 in total. Such was the interest in the game that, as well as the thousands who travelled by car, bus and rail, a number of fans took advantage of a £5/10s (£5.50) fare arranged by the supporters association to fly to Liverpool airport from Castle Donington on a British Midland Vickers Viscount flight. Another crowd in excess of 34,000 watched the replay at the Baseball Ground. Although the Rams could not, quite understandably, reach the level of play they had achieved against Chelsea, a stunning well taken goal from Hector in the 30th minute was enough to ensure their progression to the last eight of the competition.

**HEADS! Roy McFarland (5) clashes with Joe Royle (9)
against Everton, 23rd October 1968.**

After their performances over the four games against opposition from the top flight, County went into their quarter-final game at home to Third Division Swindon Town full of confidence. However, without the injured Hinton they struggled throughout the entire ninety minutes and were held to a scoreless draw. With Hinton joined on the sidelines by the flu-ridden O'Hare, the Rams re-organised forward line again found the going tough against a rugged defence in the Bonfire Night replay. The only goal of the contest came in the first half when a cross from Don Rogers took a wicked deflection into the net. It was enough to ensure that Swindon would face Burnley in the two-legged semi-final.

Just as had been the case after the defeat at Hull City, the Rams bounced back immediately and their 2-1 home success against Charlton Athletic on November 9th moved them into 2nd place in the table. It was a position they maintained the following week when an Alan Durban goal gave them a hard fought draw in Cardiff, the defence coping well with the threat posed by John Toshack, the Welsh striker who two years later moved to Liverpool for a fee of £110,000.

The programme for the home game against Carlisle United on November 23rd featured the first of a series of articles written by Mackay. Although the club had requested permission from the Football League to pay Mackay £2,000 for the articles, the League secretary had requested that none were included until the Management Committee had fully considered the request. Although County were subsequently informed that the payment was a breach of the League regulations, the articles continued to appear in subsequent programmes. At the time, nobody really recognised the seriousness of the offence, the ramifications not coming back to haunt the club until eighteen months later... As for the game itself, the 23,395 crowd saw six goals on a mudbath of a pitch, with the final 3-3 scoreline certainly suiting the visitors much more so than it did the Rams.

Free from the distraction of a midweek fixture, Clough used the week leading up to the game at Crystal Palace on November 30th as a time for rest and recuperation. The team travelled South early and enjoyed a three night stay at a top hotel. After a leisurely Saturday morning breakfast in bed for those who wanted it, the players arrived at Selhurst Park in a relaxed frame of mind. Once the game started the Rams midfield were in fine form, and the London side were beaten 2-1 thanks to goals from McFarland and Carlin. With top of the table Millwall slumping 3-0 on their visit to Portsmouth, the Second Division table read as follows:

	GP	W	D	L	GF	GA	PTS
DERBY COUNTY	**20**	**10**	**7**	**3**	**24**	**17**	**27**
MILLWALL	21	11	4	6	36	23	26
CRYSTAL PALACE	21	11	4	6	37	27	26

County had risen from 19th in the table to 1st place within the space of three months. The fact that they remained unbeaten in the league during the month of November also brought a further recognition for Clough, the Rams boss being voted "Manager of the Month" for the Second Division.

County stuttered to a 1-1 draw against Norwich City on December 7th, and followed that with an away point against Preston North End on a frozen Deepdale surface. A second half brace from Hector was the highlight of a 2-1 Baseball Ground win over Portsmouth on December 21st, a result that was achieved with reserve team full back John Richardson deputising for the injured Mackay. The crowd for the Boxing Day home clash against second placed Middlesbrough again exceeded 34,000, the Rams edging the points thanks to a fine two goal haul from Hinton which set up an exciting 3-2 victory.

Having seen off their nearest rivals, County travelled to Lancashire for an FA Cup 3rd Round tie against First Division Burnley on January 4th 1969. With Mackay again absent and McGovern replacing Jim Walker, they found themselves pitted against a home side who seemed intent on winning at all costs. Despite producing the more creative football, the Rams lost 3-1, and additionally had John Robson unfortunately dismissed in the 38th minute following a clash with the Clarets midfielder Ralph Coates. On their return to league action, a Bury side which included Bobby Collins were beaten 2-0 at the Baseball Ground, the two Rams teenagers Robson and McGovern both having outstanding matches, the latter on just his fourth senior appearance.

On January 14 the Rams faced a Birmingham City team that, despite being in the bottom half of the table, had netted an impressive thirty-two goals in twelve games at St Andrews, the highest tally in the division. Although County again dominated their opponents, they dropped a vital point, Hector's goal in the 44th minute equalising the home side's opener that had come just four minutes earlier. It was a result that extended County's unbeaten run to thirteen games and left them four points ahead of the chasing pack, which was led by the much improved, Toshack-inspired Cardiff City. It was however to be unlucky thirteen for the Rams, as four days later they lost 2-0 against a Charlton Athletic team managed by South African Eddie Firmani, goals from Matt Tees and Ray Treacey giving the Addicks their victory in front of a crowd of 30,115.

County's ascent to the top of the Second Division table, allied to the crowds of around 34,000 who had squeezed into the Baseball Ground for the more attractive fixtures, also presented the Directors with an interesting dilemma. They were obviously keen to increase the overall capacity for the prospect of a long-awaited return to First Division football. However, their draft plans for a new cantilever stand above the Popular Side terracing had to go on hold until promotion had hopefully been achieved and the last home game played. That meant that the extensive building work required would need to be completed in just four months - in

OUCH! John O'Hare in the thick of the action against Charlton, 18th January 1969.

**Willie Carlin hits the post, but O'Hare netted the rebound.
Bury, 25th January 1969.**

readiness for the start of the 1969/70 campaign. That said, given the lean times the club had faced in its more recent history, discussions regarding the new structure probably made a welcome change from their normal boardroom deliberations.

After the disappointment of the defeat at Charlton, consecutive victories were achieved against Bury at Gigg Lane, where O'Hare netted the only goal after Carlin's shot had hit the post, and Cardiff City at the Baseball Ground. The 2-0 success over the Welsh side on February 1st carried added significance as it put County four points ahead of their nearest rivals Middlesbrough, who themselves drew 0-0 at Bolton Wanderers on the same day. The winter weather then intervened and, especially given the size of the Rams squad, provided an unexpected opportunity to rest an assortment of aching limbs. Their scheduled games against Carlisle United, Crystal Palace and Norwich City were postponed as arctic weather fronts swept across the country, Clough's side not returning to competitive action until March 1st. When the postponements extended into a third week, Clough even arranged a friendly fixture against Leicester City in Cork, that game though like the league matches falling victim to the extremes of the weather.

Kevin Hector turns away in celebration of a goal against Bolton, 5th April 1969.

The enforced break left the Rams with thirteen games to play in the space of fifty days, six matches at home and seven on the road. Blackburn Rovers were the first side to visit the Baseball Ground; goals from Hector, O'Hare, Carlin (in his 250th league game), and debutant Frank Wignall ensuring a 4-2 victory. Clough had paid Wolverhampton Wanderers £20,000 for the powerfully built twenty-nine year old Wignall, signed to provide attacking cover for the final third of the season. Four days later, also at home, County's form deserted them and a goal from Rob Woodruff earned Crystal Palace a 1-0 victory. The result ended the Rams' run of twenty-one unbeaten games at home in league and cup competitions, a sequence that had started with the 1-1 draw with Blackpool on August 17th. Again though, the Rams returned to form in style. A penalty from Hinton secured a 3-2 win at Blackpool and by the end of March they had recorded wins against Huddersfield Town, Oxford United and Aston Villa, as well as securing a point from their rearranged visit to Carlisle United.

County therefore went into their three game Easter programme still four points ahead of Crystal Palace and Middlesbrough, all of the trio having played thirty-six matches. After a 1-0 victory at Fulham on April 2nd, the Rams thrashed Bolton Wanderers 5-1 on Easter Saturday with five players finding the net in an excellent display of attacking football. The victory confirmed that the Rams would be promoted and four games remained to ensure that their return to the top flight would be as Second Division champions. Two days later, 34,976 packed in to the Baseball Ground to see Sheffield United defeated by an 85th minute goal from Durban; just his third of the season, but

**Job well done.
Dave Mackay, Roy McFarland
and John Robson,
Millwall, 12th April 1969.**

one that opened up a seven point gap at the top of the table. The task ahead seemed simple, County needed just two points from their final three games whilst Palace, by now their sole challengers, needed to win all of their four remaining fixtures.

The Rams confirmed their position as champions at Millwall on April 12th, bizarrely after confusion over team colours by wearing the London side's second strip of red shirts. A close range goal from Carlin in the 22nd minute secured the vital two points and additionally gave Mackay's troops their ninth away victory of the campaign. Two more from Carlin set up a 4-1 against Norwich City before County took to the field as champions, fittingly enough at the Baseball Ground, for their final game of the season. Bristol City were left with the unfortunate task of attempting to spoil the party celebrations, but a hat trick from Durban plus strikes from Hector and Hinton confirmed a comfortable 5-0 victory. Derby County had finally ended their sixteen-season exile from the First Division with a playing record which read as follows:

GP 42   W 26   D 11   L 5   GF 65   GA 32   PTS 63

Miss Derby County celebrates with the players.

Statistically, it had been a remarkable season. The total of twenty six victories broke the club record for a forty-two game campaign, the 1925/26 Harry Bedford-inspired side having recorded twenty-five, coincidentally also in a Second Division promotion season. Only one other Rams side had conceded less than thirty-three goals in a season, although the twenty-eight conceded by the 1911/12 team came from a thirty-eight match schedule. County's sixty-three points also set a Club record for a forty-two game season, that 1925/26 team having lost ten matches in eventually accumulating fifty-seven.

The entire side had played a part in the success. Robson and McGovern, still both teenagers, had demonstrated a maturity well beyond their years, whilst right back Webster had been a model of consistency in his first full season in the position. The addition of Carlin had a marked effect on the midfield, his resilience complementing perfectly the vision and attacking flair of Durban. Whilst Hector had been the side's top goalscorer for the third successive season, his tally owed a lot to the work rate of O'Hare and the courage of Hinton in avoiding the challenges of desperate defenders. In goal, Green, despite a few early mistakes, had handled well, continually defying those who had been critical of his size. Finally the pairing of McFarland and Mackay had been outstanding from the first game; McFarland simply dominating his opponents both in the air and on the ground, and Mackay, with his barked instructions and touches of pure class, inspiring everyone around him. The Scot was the heartbeat of the side, a figure who gained instant respect from colleagues and opponents alike. It was fitting that in a further acknowledgement of the Rams' achievements he was, along with Tony Book of Manchester City, elected to receive the "Footballer of the Year" award, another accolade to add to his long list of honours in the game.

**1968/69 Squad with the Second Division
Championship Trophy.**

APPEARANCES 1968-69

PLAYER	LEAGUE		FA CUP	LGE CUP	OTHERS	TOTAL	
GREEN	42		1	8	0	51	
RICHARDSON	4		1	1	0	6	
ROBSON	42		1	8	0	51	
STEWART	4		0	2	0	6	
McFARLAND	42		1	8	0	51	
MACKAY	41		0	8	0	49	
WALKER	23	(3)	0	8	0	31	(3)
BARKER	7	(4)	0	3	0	10	
O'HARE	41		1	7	0	49	
HECTOR	41		1	8	0	50	
HINTON	41		1	6	0	48	
WEBSTER	38		1	7	0	46	
CARLIN	36		1	6	0	43	
DURBAN	36		1	7	0	44	
McGOVERN	18		1	0	0	19	
DANIEL	2		0	0	0	2	
WIGNALL	4	(2)	0	0	0	4	(2)
BUTLIN	0		0	1	0	1	
TOTAL	**42**		**1**	**8**	**0**	**51**	

N.B. Substitute appearances in brackets

SCORERS 1968-69

HECTOR	16	0	4	0	20	
HINTON	7	0	5	0	12	
O'HARE	10	0	0	0	10	
McFARLAND	9	0	0	0	9	
CARLIN	8	0	0	0	8	
DURBAN	6	1	1	0	8	
WIGNALL	4	0	0	0	4	
BARKER	2	0	0	0	2	
MACKAY	1	0	1	0	2	
WALKER	1	0	0	0	1	
OWN GOALS	1	0	1	0	2	
TOTAL	**65**	**1**	**12**	**0**	**78**	

KEY MATCHES OF 1968/69

County improve, but still seek first win...

28th August 1968, Football League Division Two

DERBY COUNTY 2 HULL CITY 2

After four league games without a win, the Rams included new signing Willie Carlin in their line up, the former Sheffield United man replacing the previously disappointing Arthur Stewart. Hull arrived at the Baseball Ground with an identical record to County, the Yorkshire club being one of the pundits "fancied" sides before the campaign started.

Any latecomers missed the only booking of the game, Les Green being cautioned before the kick off for marking out the goal area with his boot. The Rams had the best of the early play, their best chance falling to John O'Hare who forced the City goalkeeper Ian McKechnie to make a fine save. Then, in the thirty-fourth minute Kevin Hector opened the scoring, the Rams striker rising like a salmon at the falls to head in Alan Hinton's cross.

The final minutes of the half saw the game burst into a goal scoring frenzy. On forty-one minutes a Roy McFarland mistake allowed centre forward Chris Chilton to set up Alan Jarvis, who scored from close range. Just three minutes later the visitors were ahead, a ridiculous mix up between Green and John Robson allowing Ken Wagstaff the easiest of strikes. It seemed that the interval would arrive with County trailing, but within twenty-seven seconds it was 2-2. Hinton floated over a free kick and McFarland headed the ball across for Ritchie Barker to score from close range.

With Carlin more of an influence in the second period, the Rams pushed on for the winning goal but could not breach the visitors' resolute defence. It was a much improved showing from Clough's team, one which suggested that better results were not too far away.

DERBY COUNTY: GREEN, WEBSTER, ROBSON, CARLIN, McFARLAND, MACKAY, WALKER, BARKER, O'HARE, HECTOR, HINTON. SUBSTITUTE: DURBAN.

HULL CITY: McKECHNIIE, BANKS, BEARDSLEY, PETIT, WILSON, GREENWOOD, JARVIS, WAGSTAFF, CHILTON, SIMPKIN, BUTLER (IAN) SUBSTITUTE: BUTLER (DENNIS).

ATTENDANCE: 24,650
REFEREE: MR SPITTLE

Durban shines as Rams win again...

21st September 1968, Football League Division Two

DERBY COUNTY 1 MILLWALL 0

The Rams extended their unbeaten league run to six games with a single goal victory over fellow promotion chasers Millwall. The visitors included the unsettled Eamon Dunphy in their side, the Eire international who subsequently moved into journalism and most recently worked with Roy Keane in ghost-writing his controversial autobiography.

The Londoners revealed their intentions from the kick off, a packed defence and lone striker suggesting that they would be perfectly satisfied with a scoreless draw. As a consequence, with the County back four coming under minimal threat, the midfield trio of Alan Durban, Willie Carlin and Jim Walker dominated the first half. The only goal came after twenty minutes, an Alan Hinton cross was headed clear to the edge of the penalty area and Durban capped a great individual performance by netting a left foot volley. Although the visitors pressed forward a little more after the interval, they created little until Derek Possee got clear - only for Roy McFarland to slide across and force the right winger to fire well wide. Unfortunately, as the Rams also found the tidy Millwall defence increasingly hard to break down, the contest developed into a middle of the park stalemate.

With nine minutes left, Ritchie Barker came on to replace Walker, the substitute going closest to extending the lead. The two points lifted Clough's side up three places in the table to 6th, whilst the Lions manager Bennie Fenton saw his team drop to 5th. Significantly for the Rams, it was also their third consecutive clean sheet, with the unerring Dave Mackay marshalling the side superbly.

DERBY COUNTY: GREEN, WEBSTER, ROBSON, DURBAN, McFARLAND, MACKAY, WALKER, CARLIN, O'HARE, HECTOR, HINTON. SUBSTITUTE: BARKER FOR WALKER (81).

MILLWALL: KING, GILCHRIST, CRIPPS, JONES, KITCHENER, BURNETT, POSSEE, WELLER, CONLON, JACKS, DUNPHY. SUBSTITUTE: NEIL.

ATTENDANCE: 25,000
REFEREE: MR KEW

Derby destroy mighty Chelsea...

2nd October 1968, Football League Cup 3rd Round Replay

DERBY COUNTY 3 CHELSEA 1

Without a shadow of doubt, this was the finest display by a Derby County team for many a long season. Trailing First Division Chelsea 1-0 at half time, they poured forward and laid siege to their opponent's net, inspired by a seemingly endless chant of "Derby, Derby, Derby" which echoed around the rafters of an overflowing Baseball Ground.

The Rams opened at an incredible pace. Alan Hinton won the ball in his own half, surged seventy yards and crossed for Alan Durban, the Welsh international's shot being excellently turned aside by Peter Bonetti. Kevin Hector then had an effort kicked off the line, and moments later Willie Carlin again forced the overworked goalkeeper into action. It seemed to be only a matter of time until the first goal arrived. Unfortunately for County, when the strike came it was a brilliant individual effort from Chelsea's Alan Birchenall. On twenty-six minutes, he picked up a pass from Peter Houseman and lashed in an unstoppable shot from thirty yards out. Although County went straight back onto the attack, they could not find a first half equaliser, despite their pressure producing a series of corner kicks.

**THEY SHALL NOT PASS... Roy McFarland and Dave Mackay
keep out Chelsea.**

After the interval, Clough's side again created chance after chance. Bonetti however was magnificent and defied them until the seventy-seventh minute. Carlin then carried the ball towards the visitors' penalty area, before backheeling it for Dave Mackay to blast a dipping drive into the corner of the net. Six minutes later it was 2-1. Jim Walker, in marvellous form, crossed perfectly for Durban to head the Rams ahead. With the noise at a crescendo, Hector wrapped up the memorable victory, beating Bonetti to the ball after John O'Hare had gone close. The London side were well beaten, their only consolation being that they had faced a team who at times had played to the absolute maximum of its ability.

DERBY COUNTY: GREEN, WEBSTER, ROBSON, DURBAN, McFARLAND, MACKAY, WALKER, CARLIN, O'HARE, HECTOR, HINTON (ALAN). SUBSTITUTE: BARKER.

CHELSEA: BONETTI, HINTON (MARVIN), McCREADIE, HOLLINS, WEBB, HARRIS, BIRCHENALL, TAMBLING, OSGOOD, HUTCHINSON, HOUSEMAN. SUBSTITUTE: LLOYD.

ATTENDANCE: 34,346
REFEREE: MR JAMES

Ten man County outplay Clarets and lose...

4th January 1969, Football Association Cup 3rd Round

BURNLEY 3 DERBY COUNTY 1

Despite playing very well, the Rams were defeated by First Division Burnley in a physical encounter at Turf Moor. It was a result which extended their dismal recent record in the FA Cup, County having last reached the fourth round of the competition in the 1962/63 season. Additionally their frustrations at being beaten were deepened by the thirty-eighth minute sending off of John Robson, the left back having clashed with the Burnley midfielder Ralph Coates.

Clough's side started well, but the site of Kevin Hector being ruthlessly challenged twice within the opening moments was an indication of the tactics Burnley intended to apply from the outset. The first goal was a poor one for the Rams to give away; Dave Thomas hit a speculative free kick into the Rams penalty area and, as everyone waited for someone else to react, the ball crept into the net at the near post. Two minutes before the interval the home side scored again when Frank Casper turned and beat Les Green easily, a shot the Rams goalkeeper would have on any other occasion expected to save with ease.

Even when reduced to ten men, County still looked dangerous. However another "giveaway" goal after fifty-one minutes sealed their fate; Green failed to collect a long cross and Coates turned the ball back for Casper to score his second from close in. The visitors finally got a reward for their efforts nine minutes from time, Alan Durban directing home a superb volley from an Alan Hinton free kick.

The worst foul of the entire contest came immediately after the Rams goal, a crude challenge from Colin Blant leaving Roy McFarland writhing in agony - a melee ensued, and although the Clarets player was booked, several others from either side were lucky not to have their names taken as well.

BURNLEY: THOMSON, SMITH, LATCHAM, MERRINGTON, WALDRON, BLANT, THOMAS, COATES, CASPER, BELLAMY, COLLINS. SUBSTITUTE: O'NEIL.

DERBY COUNTY: GREEN, WEBSTER, RICHARDSON, DURBAN, McFARLAND, ROBSON, McGOVERN, CARLIN, O'HARE, HECTOR, HINTON. SUBSTITUTE: WALKER.

ATTENDANCE: 22,842
REFEREE: MR HOWLEY

Hector brace extends Rams lead at the top...

1st February 1969, Football League Division Two

DERBY COUNTY 2 CARDIFF CITY O

County gained two more points in their quest for promotion, although on this occasion they met an organised Cardiff side who controlled the midfield area but created little against a defence within which Roy McFarland was outstanding. The Rams centre half, facing the highly rated John Toshack, dominated his opponent to the extent that the visitors created just two real chances in the entire ninety minutes.

The rain had reduced the Baseball Ground surface to a quagmire, but Kevin Hector shone in the conditions, the Rams top scorer emerging as the man of the match after two well taken goals. His first strike summarised everything good about the Derby striker; a long free kick from Dave Mackay into the Cardiff penalty area ran loose and Hector whipped it into the net in an instant - despite having to angle in his shot from the narrowest of angles. The second was much simpler and yet equally well taken, Hector timing his run perfectly to head an Alan Hinton corner kick past Fred Davies in the visitors' net.

Cardiff's best spell came at the start of the second half. Toshack had a volley and a header well saved by Les Green who, apart from a couple of suspect punches under challenge, handled the ball confidently and again defied those who say that his chances of becoming a top class goalkeeper are minimal given his lack of inches. The victory carried Clough's side four points clear at the top of the Second Division table with twenty-nine games played, although the rain which accompanied this contest proved merely to be a prelude to a spell of wintry weather which sidelined them, and most others, for the next three weekends.

DERBY COUNTY: GREEN, WEBSTER, ROBSON, DURBAN, McFARLAND, MACKAY , McGOVERN, CARLIN, O'HARE, HECTOR, HINTON. SUBSTITUTE: WALKER.

CARDIFF CITY: DAVIES, CARVER, BELL, SUTTON, MURRAY, DERRETT, JONES, CLARK, LEA, TOSHACK, KING. SUBSTITUTE: HARRIS.

ATTENDANCE: 34,589
REFEREE: MR BARKER

Les Green gathers, almost to Dave Mackay's amusement, against Cardiff.

Late spot kick gives Rams full points...

8th March 1969, Football League Division Two

BLACKPOOL 2 DERBY COUNTY 3

After their shock defeat against Crystal Palace in midweek, the Rams recovered well from conceding an early goal and eventually fully deserved the two points which maintained their position at the top of the table. Additionally, to gain a victory against the Tangerines away from home was particularly satisfying, Blackpool having been, just as they were in this contest, one of the teams County had struggled to beat in recent times.

On this occasion it was the midfield trio who provided the basis for the success, with Alan Durban having one of his best games of the season. And yet it was the home side who went ahead in the twelfth minute, Alan Suddick hit a free kick towards the Rams net and Ron Brown nipped in to head past a stationary Les Green. It was a strike which shook Clough's side into action, and they fully deserved their thirty-fifth minute equaliser. A hard working John O'Hare won a corner kick and was in place to nod in Alan Hinton's perfect centre to the near post. County could then have gone ahead twice before the interval, but Alan Taylor did superbly well to save efforts from both O'Hare and Durban.

With the play almost entirely in the Blackpool half after the interval it came as no surprise when Roy McFarland put the Rams ahead seventeen minutes after the restart. Dave Mackay chipped a free kick beyond the defensive wall and the centre half demonstrated his skills by turning well and stabbing the ball into the net. To their credit, the Tangerines hit back almost immediately and John Craven hooked home a sixty-sixth minute equaliser. Not content with just a point, the visitors continued to press forward and were rewarded four minutes from the end. McFarland was barged over after a corner and Hinton sealed the win with a well taken penalty kick.

**Roy McFarland puts the Rams ahead
2-1 against Blackpool.**

BLACKPOOL: TAYLOR, ARMFIELD, BENTLEY, CRAVEN, JAMES,
ALCOCK, BROWN, GREEN, SUDDICK, JOHNSTON, HUTCHINSON.
SUBSTITUTE: McPHEE FOR JOHNSTON (63).

DERBY COUNTY: GREEN, WEBSTER, ROBSON, DURBAN, McFARLAND,
MACKAY, McGOVERN, CARLIN, O'HARE, HECTOR,
HINTON. SUBSTITUTE: WIGNALL.

ATTENDANCE: 18,853
REFEREE: MR KEW

Clough's Derby confirmed as Champions...

12th April 1969, Football League Division Two

MILLWALL 0 DERBY COUNTY 1

Although the Rams won this contest by a single goal, the scoreline was deceptive. For long periods they completely outplayed their hosts and, had it not been for a tremendous display of goalkeeping from Brian King, they would have scored four or five in the first half alone.

From the kick off, Clough's side constantly attacked their opponents' net and King was soon called into action, the burly shot stopper doing particularly well to save a trademark Alan Hinton

RESPECT- Millwall applaud the Rams onto the pitch.

thirty yarder. Such was the Rams pressure however, it seemed only a matter of time before the opening goal came. When it arrived in the twenty-second minute, it rounded off a very neat move. Ron Webster hit a perfect cross towards Roy McFarland at the far post, and his header across the front of goal was gleefully nodded home by Willie Carlin. With Les Green a virtual spectator, the visitors continued to stroke the ball around in style, particularly so given the dry dusty surface, caused largely by the strong wind which was circling around the appropriately named Coldblow Lane SE14.

The Lions changed their tactics after the interval and proceeded to punt long balls deep into the Rams half. It was a ploy which McFarland appreciated more than anyone, his aerial dominance alongside the poise of John Robson dictating that the home side created just one chance, a shot from Derek Possee which Green came out quickly to block.

It was a victory which confirmed Derby as the champions, their form away from home having been superb with just one game lost in the last thirteen - and remarkably nine wins recorded. It all meant that their last game of the campaign against Bristol City could be played out with a party atmosphere encompassing the Baseball Ground terraces.

MILLWALL:KING, BROWN, BURNETT, JACKS, KITCHENER, DORLEY, POSSEE, JONES, PETERSON, WELLER, DUNPHY. SUBSTITUTE: CRIPPS FOR DUNPHY (58).

DERBY COUNTY: GREEN, WEBSTER, ROBSON, DURBAN, McFARLAND, MACKAY, McGOVERN, CARLIN, O'HARE, HECTOR, HINTON. SUBSTITUTE: WIGNALL.

ATTENDANCE: 13,735
REFEREE: MR CORBETT

Celebration time at the Baseball Ground...

19th April 1969, Football League Division Two

DERBY COUNTY 5 BRISTOL CITY 0

Poor Bristol City. . . they were in the wrong place at the wrong time on Saturday. The visitors were cast as the unfortunate opponents to a Rams side who celebrated winning the Second Division championship by putting on a sumptuous display of attacking football. Although Alan Durban took the scoring honours with a hat trick, it would be inappropriate to single out one player; this was a team performance which was at times as good as anything produced all season - in any division.

The goal bonanza started in the sixteenth minute. Alan Hinton crossed from the left and after Gordon Parr had mistimed his clearance, Durban ran in to head the ball into the net. It was 2-0 just after the half hour, Durban again hitting the target after Kevin Hector had headed a Roy McFarland pass into his path. The Welsh international netted his third one minute before the interval, Willie Carlin stepped over another Hinton cross and Durban slotted his shot past Barry Watling.

The best strike of the five came in the sixty-fourth minute, Carlin carried the ball into the penalty area and then backheeled it for Hinton to smash a ferocious ground shot into the far corner. The rout was completed two minutes from the end when Hector headed in a corner as the City defence again succumbed to the Rams pressure. It could have been more; McFarland, roving forward at will, twice hit the bar with brilliant efforts, and Hinton also had a penalty saved.

Despite the goals, the sight of the day was Dave Mackay holding aloft the championship trophy to the acclaim of the delirious home supporters. The image, shown on the front cover, is fascinating for two reasons. Firstly, it shows Clough giving his captain a glance of total respect and admiration, whilst secondly Mackay's face, even given all of the honours he had won in the game, is a clear indication of just how much leading the Rams to the title meant to him.

DERBY COUNTY: GREEN, WEBSTER, ROBSON, DURBAN, McFARLAND, MACKAY, McGOVERN, CARLIN, O'HARE, HECTOR, HINTON. SUBSTITUTE: WIGNALL.

BRISTOL CITY: WATLING, JACOBS, BRIGGS, WIMSHIRST, CONNOR, PARR, SKIRTON, KELLARD, BARTLEY, GARLAND, SHARPE. SUBSTITUTE: TAINTON.

ATTENDANCE: 31,644
REFEREE: MR COWE

Champions - The Rams in front of the Normanton End.

4.

BACK WITH THE BIG BOYS
(1969/70)

THE RAMS PROMOTION SIDE received a major boost to their confidence when Clough decided against making any additions to his squad in readiness for the return to First Division football. Not that the Baseball Ground was a quiet place over the summer of 1969. As the days and weeks progressed, the Ley Stand took shape, the intention being that it would be ready for the first league game of the season on August 9th. Remarkably, thanks to many long hours work, the building contractors completed the task on time and the new structure gave the ground a revised theoretical capacity of 42,000.

County's rise from the depths of the Second Division had also significantly strengthened the relationship between Clough and Sam Longson. The Chairman treated his young manager like a surrogate son, although in reality their blossoming friendship served the intentions of both men very well. Early in his career, Clough had absorbed one particularly important lesson from Harry Storer; a good manager needed to involve himself in every aspect of the running of the club. Accordingly, he interpreted Longson's amicable and overly generous nature as a sign of weakness, a trait he could exploit to his advantage. For his part, Longson had ambitions of a place at the management table of the Football League. That, he calculated, would be easier to achieve if he were seen to be at the head of a successful side in the top flight of the game.

On the pitch, County's preparations were sealed with a 6-0 Baseball Ground thrashing of German side Werder Bremen on August 5th. Four days later Derby took their First Division bow against Burnley, the new look one shilling (£0.05) programme having an impression of a goalkeeper catching a ball against the backdrop of the new stand on its cover. Clough named the same eleven that had beaten Bristol City on the last day of the 1969 season. The Lancashire side had knocked County out of the FA Cup

Programme cover for the Rams first
game back in the First Division.

in a stormy 3rd Round tie eight months earlier, and Dave Mackay led out a team with revenge clearly in mind. However after opening well, the Rams forwards again found their visitors to be in an uncompromising mood. The final whistle sounded with the scoreline blank, although Les Green was required to save an 82nd minute penalty to keep his side in the game.

By the end of the month, County's performances were again beginning to generate more and more column inches in the national press. They had climbed to 3rd in the table behind the Merseyside giants Everton and Liverpool. County were undefeated after victories against West Bromwich Albion and Ipswich Town, the East Anglian side having been beaten both home and away, and draws against Coventry City, Stoke City and Wolverhampton Wanderers. It was form which set up a mouth watering clash with Everton on the first Saturday of September. In front of the "Match of the Day" cameras, at the Baseball Ground for the first time, Clough's side put on a magnificent performance and won 2-1 with markers from John O'Hare and Kevin Hector. Victories against Southampton and Newcastle United extended the unbeaten run to ten games, with significantly just four goals conceded. After the Rams 1-0 win at St James Park on September 11th, their supporters looked at the updated league table with a sense of amazement; not only were County still unbeaten, more importantly they sat at the very top of the First Division, an incredible achievement for a side just promoted. Of course, the critics said that balloon would burst, readily suggesting that the team that Clough and Taylor had built on low cost purchases would soon slip down the standings - just as quickly as it had climbed to the top.

For the players, their next game could not have been better timed. The Tottenham Hotspur home fixture had been penciled into their diaries with the notation "must win" ever since the schedules had been announced. It was the first time Dave Mackay would have the opportunity to face his former club, the London side he had served with such distinction for seven seasons. Although over the previous year the young Rams side had learned that their captain expected them to approach every game in a professional manner, irrespective of the opposition, - this undoubtedly was one encounter that carried an extra significance. There would be a requirement to raise their performance to give Mackay the victory he craved for, anything else would be unacceptable. In his book, 'The Legends of Derby County', Ian Hall likened the sight of Mackay leading out the Rams to that of an engine on a train with its smoke belching, steam flying and whistle blowing... At 2.57pm on October 20th, the Dave Mackay Express undoubtedly arrived onto the Baseball Ground pitch with a little more pace than usual. In his analogy Hall additionally advised that anyone who got in the way of the engine would suffer. At around 4.45pm, the Spurs side which included household names such as Jimmy Greaves and Alan Mullery trooped off after having well and truly suffered. They had been thrashed 5-0, a record attendance of 41,826 having witnessed a scintillating display of attacking football as good as anything Derby had produced for many seasons, even surpassing their second half performance against Chelsea in the previous year's League Cup competition.

A routine 3-1 League Cup victory against Hull City followed, but then football's perpetual habit of bringing people down to earth intervened. It was certainly a case of after the Lord Mayor's Show when County visited Hillsborough on September 27th. Despite having plenty of the ball, they slipped to a single goal defeat against a mediocre Sheffield Wednesday team which had won just two of its first eleven matches. More worryingly McFarland, who had been substituted against Hull, played the entire game with a nagging groin injury which greatly reduced his effectiveness.

For supporters of any team, one of the beauties of a first season in a higher division is that the next quality opponents are always just around the corner. Accordingly, no sooner had the Rams fans

Fans outside the Baseball Ground in the week of the United game.

**Kevin Hector puts the Rams ahead against
Chelsea, 11th October 1969.**

digested the humiliation of Tottenham, than they had the visit of
Manchester United to look forward to. Fans queued for hours in the
week before the game to get a ticket, and another 40,000 plus
crowd packed into the Baseball Ground on October 4th to see
George Best, Bobby Charlton and Denis Law et al beaten 2-0
thanks to an own goal from John Fitzpatrick and a near post
header from Hector. County's form then stuttered. They fell to a 3-
1 home defeat against Coventry City, and followed that with a draw
at Chelsea and a 1-0 defeat at home to Manchester City. When they
were defeated for the third time in four games, a 2-0 reversal at
Leeds United on October 25th, the earlier expressions about the
Rams' inability to maintain their early form seemed to be coming
horribly true.

It was then, as if almost to confound their critics, that Clough's
side conjured up a performance almost of breathtaking
proportions. On November 1st, Liverpool were systematically taken
apart by the Rams' flowing play which produced four goals, and
saw a fifth disallowed for offside. It was the first time since the
1964/65 season that the Merseyside club had conceded four goals

in a league game and, long before the final whistle, they looked a well beaten side. Seven days later however, County found themselves as the recipients of a four goal thrashing; Arsenal, inspired by John Radford, netted all of their markers in a twenty minute second half spell during which the Rams defence was for once non-existent. Although Sunderland were then defeated 3-0 at the Baseball Ground, Clough's side then suffered further defeats at the hands of West Ham United and their East Midlands rivals Nottingham Forest. The overall effect was that, by the end of the month, the Rams had slipped down to 7th place in the league - ten points behind the leaders Everton. The League Cup campaign also came to an end in November. After defeating Hull City the Rams beat Crystal Palace 3-0 in a home 4th Round replay before exiting the competition 1-0 to Manchester United at Old Trafford, again in a second game, with the sides having earlier played out a scoreless ninety minutes at the Baseball Ground.

If there was one criticism that could have been levelled at Clough over the autumn months, it was that he did not move to strengthen his team. As early as September, he had publicly indicated that funds, thought to be around £100,000, were available for new players. Although there had been the routine tentative enquiries, nothing had been finalised and a number of the squad had continued to play for weeks with niggling injuries. McFarland in particular with his ongoing groin and hamstring problems would have, had a quality replacement been available, benefited greatly from a period of extended rest. In his defence, Clough was in reality merely following the policy adopted by his contemporaries at the time. Injured players were routinely patched up and pushed back out to play as quickly as possible. Many of the treatments available to players were primitive, a situation compounded by the emergence of cortisone injections to mask pain for the duration of a game. The unfortunate legacy of such practices is that far too many of the performers from the era are today literally crippled with arthritis and other long term muscle and joint problems.

The Rams' form improved during December, with victories being achieved against Crystal Palace, Newcastle United and West Bromwich Albion - all without a goal being conceded. Although they additionally fell to single goal defeats at Everton and Stoke City there was enough in both of those performances to suggest that the corner had been turned. Perhaps significantly, although only Palace and Sunderland had scored fewer away goals than the Rams, the results of November had seen Clough, in the privacy of the dressing room, be critical more of his defenders rather than the often seemingly goal shy forwards.

The FA Cup journey began with a 4-1 replay win against Preston North End, that result coming after a 1-1 draw at Deepdale. It put the Rams into the hat for the 4th Round for the first time since the 1962/63 season. On January 24th 1970, County also disposed of Sheffield United to progress to the 5th Round, an away game at Queens Park Rangers. In the league, although the Rams gained revenge over Sheffield Wednesday, they slumped to defeat at both Tottenham Hotspur on Mackay's first return to his beloved White Hart Lane, and Manchester United, so ending the month in 9th place with fourteen wins and thirty-three points from thirty games.

In order to cover a variety of injury and illnesses, Clough utilised his limited reserve strengths in the month either side of the New Year. Unfortunately, none of the trio of Frank Wignall,

" So Dave, what's Derby like?" Jimmy Greaves and Dave Mackay at White Hart Lane, 10th January 1970.

Jim Walker or Arthur Stewart did enough to suggest that they were ready to command a first team place on a regular basis. Indeed, of the cover players, only long serving defender Peter Daniel seemed capable of reliably stepping up into the first team as and when required. With that in mind, and the fact that a solid sequence of results could produce a finishing place high enough to qualify for Europe, the management duo finally made their first purchase of the season. In February 1970, the £100,000 was spent on Terry Hennessey from Nottingham Forest, the twenty-nine year old centre back-cum-midfielder having been outstanding in Rams 2-0 defeat by the Lace City side four months earlier. The fee was a record for

Terry Hennessey, the Rams first £100,000 player.

Derby County and demonstrated that rather than having to continue to rely on lower cost buys, they now intended to compete with the bigger clubs for the better international quality players, Hennessey prior to his arrival at the Baseball Ground having already made thirty-one appearances for Wales.

With Hennessey on board, Clough also gave notice that Pat Wright's Baseball Ground career was effectively over. The former Shrewsbury Town full back had been a major disappointment and had in fact worn the Rams shirt on just thirteen occasions. He was allowed to move to Southend United on loan until the end of the season, his fate being sealed in September 1970 when he was off loaded, as Billy Hodgson had been before him, to Rotherham United. Jim Walker also went on loan during the month of March 1970, the midfielder cum winger travelling North to Clough's former club Hartlepool United. Walker did though return from loan and stayed with the Rams until early in the 1974/75 season, his periodic appearances coming as and when others were injured.

The new look midfield of Alan Durban, Willie Carlin and Hennessey performed excellently and the Rams immediately started to look a much better side. Although they only drew with Chelsea and Burnley, they got a massive boost from a sweet 3-2 revenge victory over Arsenal, two goals in a minute after half time securing the points. The confidence gained from that display prompted a run of four straight wins that swept them back into a top four position, and opened up the possibility of qualification for the 1970/71 Inter Cities Fairs Cup, the predecessor of the modern day UEFA Cup competition. Liverpool were beaten 2-0 at Anfield with Hennessey netting his first goal for the club. County then tallied three against West Ham United, Nottingham Forest and Crystal Palace with only the Midlands team finding the net in reply. The 3-1 victory at the Trent Ground also saw O'Hare score for the fifth game in succession, and so record his tenth goal in eleven matches. It was certainly a rich vein of form for the player who, despite his marvellous close control, still had his Baseball Ground critics - fans largely who preferred their centre forwards to be more in the aggressive mould of players like Jackie Stamps.

County went into their three game Easter schedule still in 4th place in the table, unbeaten in seven games but still a massive twelve points behind the leaders Everton. On Good Friday, they beat Manchester City 1-0 at Maine Road thanks to a goal from McFarland. Twenty-four hours later, a superb John McGovern effort was enough to gain a hard fought point at Sunderland, the Rams team returning to Derby immediately after the game to spend two nights in the Midland Hotel in readiness for the Bank Holiday Monday visit of Leeds United. Sadly for the 41,011 who attended

Peter Grotier saves in the 3-0 defeat of the Hammers at the Baseball Ground, 7th March 1970.

the Leeds game, the outcome was determined when teams were announced before the kick off. Faced with a European Cup semi-final clash with Celtic on the Wednesday, the United manager Don Revie opted to send an entire reserve team to the Baseball Ground. It was a decision that represented his conceding of the Championship to the Howard Kendall, Alan Ball and Colin Harvey inspired Merseyside club. Although Leeds were subsequently fined £5,000 for fielding under strength teams, they were in fairness midway through a fixture schedule that required them to play six games in fourteen days in three different competitions. For the record, Clough's side coasted to a 4-1 victory, but found even the slightest of their mistakes booed by the disappointed onlookers who had expected to see top class encounter. The supporters' frustration at seeing such an inferior quality Leeds side was however tempered by the fact that the win guaranteed their side a place in the Fairs Cup competition. Although a 2-0 defeat of Wolverhampton Wanderers on April 4th merely added to the air of celebration around the Baseball Ground, everything went horribly sour just four days later.

As part of an ongoing purge into the financial affairs of Football League clubs, County's books had been the subject of an inspection carried out by representatives of the League's management team. It was subsequently announced that there had been "gross negligence" in the administration of the club. Accordingly, County were found guilty of eight offences, the major items being a failure to lodge new contracts in respect of Wignall, John Richardson and Green, and the payment for, and continued appearance of, the Mackay programme articles. Despite the inspectors acknowledging that the Directors were in the process of amending their procedures, the Rams were fined a record £10,000, and stingingly additionally banned from all European games, friendly or competitive, for one season. It was a terrible blow, especially after such a tremendous season. However, as was noted by many, as Derby over their history had paid more in fines than any other club, there was a lingering suspicion that the severity of the punishment was intended to serve as a warning to everyone else.

To the players credit, they gained a 1-1 draw at Southampton on the last day of the season to extend the unbeaten run to twelve games, a result which confirmed a final finishing position of 4th behind Everton, Leeds United and Chelsea. It was a magnificent achievement for a club just promoted. The upturn in the Rams fortunes had been incredible, Clough had taken on a team in decline and within the space of three seasons had shaped it into one capable of competing with the best in the country. More remarkably, it had been done with largely lower transfer fee signings who had been moulded into an effective unit, the individual parts of which at times complemented each other to perfection. In financial terms what had been achieved was staggering; for net cost of less than £250,000 Clough had rebuilt the team, to an extent that of the Tim Ward side only Hector, Durban and Webster were now first team regulars. The quarter of a million pound figure takes on an added significance when it is compared with the British record transfer fee at the start of the 1969/70 season - the £165,000 Leeds United had paid Leicester City for Alan Clarke. The defence, so praised in the Second Division after nineteen clean sheets, had responded by keeping just one less against forwards of far greater ability and experience - a performance of night and day proportions in comparison with the 1967/68 team which kept out their opponents on just four occasions. It was a hallmark for Clough's future teams, any success being firmly based on a solid back four which did the simple things very well and as a consequence gave away few goals. Indeed, only Everton had conceded fewer during the campaign, with Clough's side giving up a meagre fourteen in their twenty-one Baseball Ground league fixtures. The public had responded to the new look side with unwaning enthusiasm. The Rams' average home League attendance in the promotion year had been 27,659 - this time around, on average, almost 36,000 had watched each game with the matches against Tottenham Hotspur, Manchester United, Manchester City, Liverpool and Leeds United all attracting crowds in excess of 40,000. Given the Baseball Ground's infamous one yard gap between the touchline and the crowd, the atmosphere at those five games in particular was electrifying.

Statistically, O'Hare finished as the top scorer in league play, his tally of thirteen pipping Hector by one. It was the first time in four seasons that the "King" had not been the club's top marksman. Hinton as the wide man had again provided the ammunition for the pair; his brave running and crosses, often from remarkably tight angles, had left some of the division's hard men reeling in his wake. Although Hennessey had rejuvenated the Rams midfield, the trio of Durban, Carlin and McGovern had also played above expectation at the higher level. At the back, the Mackay and McFarland pairing had performed with a better understanding than ever before - the young centre half emerging as a very rare talent indeed, a defender who was as comfortable creating attacks as he was preventing them. The full backs had also made notable contributions, with Webster settling well on the right side of defence. Robson meanwhile seemed unfazed by even the most dangerous of opponents, belying his nineteen years almost in every game.

And so in the summer of 1970, the nation's thoughts turned to England's World Cup campaign in Mexico. Closer to home, memories of the defeats of Tottenham and Liverpool were relived by supporters across the county - the Rams were back in the top flight and were determined to stay there. For Clough and Taylor, their thoughts soon turned to the preparations for the 1970/71 campaign. It would be the last year of Mackay's three year contract, and finding a suitable replacement for the ageing war horse would not be an easy task.

APPEARANCES 1969-70

PLAYER	LEAGUE		FA CUP	LEAGUE CUP		OTHERS	TOTAL	
GREEN	42		4	6		0	52	
WEBSTER	38		3	6		0	47	
ROBSON	39		4	5		0	48	
DURBAN	41		4	6		0	51	
McFARLAND	38		4	6		0	48	
MACKAY	39		4	6		0	49	
McGOVERN	32	(1)	4	6		0	42	(1)
CARLIN	40		4	6		0	50	
O'HARE	41		2	6		0	49	
HECTOR	41		4	6		0	51	
HINTON	42		4	6		0	52	
WIGNALL	5	(6)	2	0	(2)	0	7	(8)
RHODES	1		0	0		0	1	
DANIEL	8		1	1		0	10	
STEWART	1	(1)	0	0		0	1	(1)
WALKER	2		0	0		0	2	
HENNESSEY	12		0	0		0	12	
TOTAL	**42**		**4**	**6**		**0**	**52**	

N.B. Substitute appearances in brackets

SCORERS 1969-70

O'HARE	13	2	1	0	16
HECTOR	12	2	2	0	16
DURBAN	9	4	0	0	13
HINTON	6	0	4	0	10
CARLIN	6	0	2	0	8
McFARLAND	5	0	1	0	6
McGOVERN	4	0	0	0	4
MACKAY	2	0	0	0	2
WIGNALL	2	0	0	0	2
HENNESSEY	2	0	0	0	2
OWN GOALS	3	0	0	0	3
TOTAL	**64**	**8**	**10**	**0**	**82**

KEY MATCHES OF 1969/70

Penalty save ensures Rams gain point...

9th August 1969, Football League Division One

DERBY COUNTY 0 BURNLEY 0

The Rams commenced their First Division campaign with the visit of Burnley, the Lancashire side having knocked them out of the FA Cup in a rough Third Round tie at Turf Moor eight months earlier. Whilst Clough chose to field the same eleven that had won promotion, the Clarets manager Harry Potts gave a debut to goalkeeper Peter Mellor, a small fee signing from Cheshire non-league team Witton Albion.

County pressed forward from the start and had the majority of the play in the first twenty minutes. Mellor was soon called into action, the 6' 2" twenty-one year old being forced to save well from both Alan Hinton and Willie Carlin. Having absorbed the initial spell of pressure, the visitors settled down and their defence broke down several further attacks with ease. On the few occasions after that when the Rams threatened to break clear, they were frustrated by the aggressive tackling of Mike Docherty and Brian O'Neil. Indeed, as the contest wore on, the visitors began to look the slightly better side.

Although they failed to create any real chances of their own, the Clarets had an opportunity to steal the game in the eighty-second minute. Roy McFarland handled a shot from O'Neil and the referee Mr Fussey pointed to the penalty spot. Frank Casper took the kick, but Les Green dived to his left and blocked the shot which was then cleared.

With two minutes left, Mellor collided with John O'Hare and departed with a dislocated finger. Full back Les Latcham took over between the posts, but was not required to make a save. The points were thus shared, which on reflection of the whole ninety minutes was a fair result.

DERBY COUNTY: GREEN, WEBSTER, ROBSON, DURBAN, McFARLAND, MACKAY, McGOVERN, CARLIN, O'HARE, HECTOR, HINTON. SUBSTITUTE: WIGNALL.

BURNLEY: MELLOR, ANGUS, LATCHAM, O'NEIL, WALDRON, TODD, THOMAS, COATES, CASPER, DOCHERTY, KINDON. SUBSTITUTE: PROBERT FOR MELLOR (88).

ATTENDANCE: 29,451
REFEREE: Mr FUSSEY

Peter Mellor saves as John O'Hare closes in against Burnley.

Spurs humiliated by rampant Rams...

20th September 1969, Football League Division One

DERBY COUNTY 5 TOTTENHAM HOTSPUR 0

Tottenham arrived at the Baseball Ground having won their previous four away games and occupying 4th place in the table. It was an opportunity for Dave Mackay to line up against his former club for the first time, that fact plus the added attraction of Jimmy Greaves in the Spurs side drew a crowd of 41,826 - a figure that established a record for the Rams' new look ground.

Although the visitors opened up with some neat passing, once Clough's players gathered their poise, they took control of every aspect of the game. After fifteen minutes, Durban intercepted a poor pass from Mike England and placed a fine shot wide of Pat Jennings. Just five minutes later, John O'Hare again turned past the lumbering England, his quick pass allowing Kevin Hector to net the second in style. Tottenham had a chance to get back into the game when Greaves cracked a fierce volley towards the net, but Les Green reacted well and dived across his goal to make a fabulous save. It was as if the Spurs players knew it was not going to be their day, and when Carlin headed home an Alan Hinton corner after twenty-three minutes, the match was effectively over as a contest.

In the second half, the Rams midfield trio of Durban, Carlin and John McGovern again dominated the play and as a consequence County created chance after chance. On sixty-two minutes it was 4-0, Carlin beat three men before finding Durban who in turn set up O'Hare to score with ease. The inspired Durban headed his second six minutes later, but a groin injury then saw him replaced by Frank Wignall with twenty minutes remaining.

The result represented Tottenham's worst defeat since 1964 when Burnley had thrashed them 7-2. It was also a scoreline that sent out a stark warning to the rest of the First Division: Derby County were ready to take on the very best.

DERBY COUNTY: GREEN, WEBSTER, ROBSON, DURBAN, McFARLAND, MACKAY, McGOVERN, CARLIN, O'HARE, HECTOR, HINTON. SUBSTITUTE: WIGNALL FOR DURBAN (70).

TOTTENHAM HOTSPUR: JENNINGS, BEAL, KNOWLES, MULLERY, ENGLAND, COLLINS, PEARCE, GREAVES, GILZEAN, PRATT, MORGAN. SUBSTITUTE: WANT FOR MORGAN (45).

ATTENDANCE: 41,826
REFEREE: MR CALLAGHAN

United shocked by County flair...

4th October 1969, Football League Division One

DERBY COUNTY 2 MANCHESTER UNITED 0

The press speculation before this fixture was that United, with ten unbeaten games behind them, would be too good for the Rams, especially after their surprise defeat against Sheffield Wednesday. The visitors opted to start off with George Best in the centre forward position, a tactic intended to give Roy McFarland a difficult ninety minutes. It was a ploy which failed miserably, County after an even opening going on to dominate their illustrious opponents.

After the referee had disallowed a Brian Kidd header after twenty-seven minutes, the Rams - with Hector looking a constant threat - pressed forward and took the lead a minute before half time. Alan Hinton dropped a corner kick to the near post and Hector, jumping with Alex Stepney, claimed the goal after the United goalkeeper punched the ball against his head. Derby were much improved in the second period and could have increased their advantage when Alan Durban's shot hit a post. The second goal came however after sixty-two minutes when Hector's centre was diverted in off John Fitzpatrick's knee.

The United supporters were incensed with sixteen minutes to play when their side had another effort disallowed, Best being adjudged to have handled the ball before John Aston hit the net. It was a decision which finally ended any hopes the visitors had of getting anything out of the game. Indeed, as the contest reached its conclusion, it was County who looked the more likely to add to their tally. With Everton winning by the odd goal in five at Wolverhampton Wanderers, United maintained their position at the top of the table, three points ahead of the Rams with both teams having played thirteen matches.

DERBY COUNTY: GREEN, DANIEL, ROBSON, DURBAN, McFARLAND, MACKAY, McGOVERN, CARLIN, O'HARE, HECTOR, HINTON. SUBSTITUTE: WIGNALL.

MANCHESTER UNITED: STEPNEY, FITZPATRICK, DUNNE, BURNS, URE, SADLER, MORGAN, KIDD, CHARLTON, ASTON, BEST. SUBSTITUTE: SARTORI FOR MORGAN (70).

ATTENDANCE: 40,724
REFEREE: MR PARTRIDGE

Brilliant Rams over-run Shankly's Reds...

1st November 1969, Football League Division One

DERBY COUNTY 4 LIVERPOOL 0

Liverpool conceded four goals in a league match for the first time since the 1964/1965 season. Just as Tottenham had been on September 20th, they were totally outclassed by the Rams' flowing football. Clough's side were inspired by the close control of John O'Hare who ensured that Ron Yeats, the visitors' centre half, spent the entire game chasing his shadow.

The match was won within the first quarter of an hour. In the thirteenth minute, following a flurry of action in front of the Liverpool net, John McGovern scored his first goal for the Rams, a swerving shot from the edge of the penalty area. Just forty or so seconds later it was 2-0; Kevin Hector dispossessed Geoff Strong and ran in on goal before confidently lifting his shot beyond Tommy Lawrence. Although the visitors had their fair share of the ball in the first half, they created little and, in the final third of the pitch, found Roy McFarland in majestic form.

The third goal after fifty-three minutes was a magnificent effort. Alan Durban's pass inside Chris Lawler sent Alan Hinton away down the wing and Hector met the winger's teasing far post cross with a diving header. In the sixty-ninth minute O'Hare cheekily backheeled Durban's cross over the line, but the referee disallowed the effort for offside. It mattered little. . . in the next minute Hector and O'Hare broke clear with Lawrence ahead of them. Hector, on a hat trick, unselfishly set up his striking partner for a well deserved goal.

After the defeats against Manchester City and Leeds United, it was a welcome return to form for the Rams, the result giving them a 4th place standing in the table. Their defensive record, with a meagre thirteen goals given away, was the best in the division.

DERBY COUNTY: GREEN, WEBSTER, DANIEL, DURBAN, McFARLAND, MACKAY, McGOVERN, CARLIN, O'HARE, HECTOR, HINTON. SUBSTITUTE: WIGNALL.

LIVERPOOL: LAWRENCE, LAWLER, STRONG, SMITH, YEATS, HUGHES, CALLAGHAN, HUNT, GRAHAM, ST JOHN, THOMPSON. SUBSTITUTE: EVANS.

ATTENDANCE: 40,953
REFEREE: MR BALDWIN

Toffees grab late win thanks to Ball...

20th December 1969, Football League Division One

EVERTON 1 DERBY COUNTY 0

This was certainly a Christmas cracker that arrived early, both teams putting on a superb display in the rain and snow of Goodison Park. Not that it was a contest of end to end football; Everton were in the ascendancy throughout the second half, but the Rams rearguard action stood firm until three minutes from the end.

Derby relied heavily on the determined attitude of the battle-worn Dave Mackay, and the sheer brilliance of Les Green to keep the Toffees at bay. Just before the interval, although Mackay handled in the penalty area, his goalkeeper spared his blushes with a marvellous save from Joe Royle's spot kick which seemed destined to find the corner of the net. The second forty-five minutes belonged to Everton, who created chance after chance, but their efforts were cleared off the line and Green made another unbelievable save from Howard Kendall. Although Kevin Hector had the Rams only two real chances, he failed to hit the target with either, and so Gordon West left the pitch without having had to make a save.

To the relief of the Goodison faithful, the winner came in the eighty-seventh minute. Just when it looked as though County would earn a point, Alan Ball collected a header from Tommy Jackson and his low shot eluded even the mighty Green. It was a victory that the home side deserved simply on the number of scoring opportunities they created, but the Rams' contribution to a splendid game, given the conditions, was immense. The two points reinforced Everton's position at the top of the table, whilst County slipped a place to 6th, ten points behind their Merseyside hosts.

EVERTON: WEST, WRIGHT, NEWTON, KENDALL, LABONE, JACKSON, HUSBAND, BALL, ROYLE, HURST, MORRISSEY. SUBSTITUTE: BROWN FOR HUSBAND (87).

DERBY COUNTY: GREEN, WEBSTER, ROBSON, DURBAN, McFARLAND, MACKAY, WALKER, CARLIN, O'HARE, HECTOR, HINTON. SUBSTITUTE: WIGNALL.

ATTENDANCE: 44,914
REFEREE: MR NEW

Inspired Mackay defies old rivals...

21st February 1970, Football League Division One

DERBY COUNTY 3 ARSENAL 2

County went into this fixture refreshed by a midweek break in Guernsey, and determined to end a sequence of three league games without a win. Arsenal included Peter Marinello in their line up, the former Hibernian player having joined them in a £100,000 deal a few weeks earlier.

It was the visitors who initially looked the better side, John Radford giving them the lead after thirteen minutes when he hooked a volley past the stationary Les Green. The Rams' equaliser came against the run of play when Kevin Hector intercepted a weak John Roberts back pass and whipped the ball past Bob Wilson from a narrow angle. It was then County's turn to give up a sloppy goal: an Arsenal corner was headed across the front of the net by Bob McNab, and Roberts scrambled it home to make the score 2-1 after thirty-five minutes.

Derby were a changed side in the second half. Just after the restart, Alan Hinton crossed from the left and Hector set up John O'Hare, who rolled the ball in to square the game. The winner came almost immediately afterwards. Dave Mackay lofted the ball towards the Arsenal goal and Wilson, under pressure from Willie Carlin, allowed it to curl beyond him and into the net. With Mackay now sensing that his Rams could claim the victory against his former club's keenest rivals, County pressed forward and both O'Hare and Hector could have increased their lead. O'Hare was in fact magnificent in the latter stages of the game, his close control and vision often leaving the Arsenal defence, Roberts in particular, looking embarrassingly poor.

DERBY COUNTY: GREEN, WEBSTER, ROBSON, HENNESSEY, McFARLAND, MACKAY, DURBAN, CARLIN, O'HARE, HECTOR, HINTON. SUBSTITUTE: WIGNALL.

ARSENAL: WILSON, STOREY, McNAB, McCLINTOCK, ROBERTS, KELLY, MARINELLO, GEORGE, RADFORD, SAMMELS, GRAHAM. SUBSTITUTE: COURT.

ATTENDANCE: 35,284
REFEREE: MR WALTERS

Rams complete easy double...

28th February 1970, Football League Division One

LIVERPOOL 0 DERBY COUNTY 2

The crowd at Anfield witnessed the start of a new Liverpool era. Having seen his side unceremoniously dumped out of the FA Cup by Second Division Watford, Bill Shankly decided it was time to ring the changes. Accordingly, Tom Lawrence, Ron Yeats and Ian St John, players who had become familiar names on Merseyside and beyond were omitted - a move which heralded the arrival of Ray Clemence and Doug Livermore into the Reds senior team.

Ray Clemence punches the ball clear at Anfield, watched by Roy McFarland and Emlyn Hughes.

Liverpool posed only an infrequent attacking threat to the Rams defence that was superbly marshalled by Dave Mackay, and boosted by Terry Hennessey's ability to easily switch between midfield and the back four as and when required. Indeed, it was Hennessey who opened the scoring after fourteen minutes, the Welsh international gliding a header into the net from a right side Alan Hinton free kick. When the home side did press forward it was again Hennessey, this time on his own line, who cleared the danger, with Bob Graham's header at the far post being hooked to safety.

Willie Carlin, another of the Rams' best performers, worked tirelessly, the tough midfielder being in his element against the club that had sold him to Halifax Town for £1,500 after just one appearance. With Derby controlling the middle of the field, it seemed only a matter of time before they scored again. The second goal when it came was a brilliant effort. After seventy-four minutes, Kevin Hector broke clear and crossed well for John O'Hare to steer a volley inside a post.

The result gave County the double over their opponents with six goals scored and none conceded. They moved up one position to 4th in the table, whilst Liverpool, without a home league victory since November 15th, occupied 9th place.

LIVERPOOL: CLEMENCE, LAWLER, WALL, SMITH, STRONG, HUGHES, CALLAGHAN, LIVERMORE, EVANS, THOMPSON, GRAHAM. SUBSTITUTE: LINDSAY.

DERBY COUNTY: GREEN, WEBSTER, ROBSON, HENNESSEY, McFARLAND, MACKAY, DURBAN, CARLIN, O'HARE, HECTOR, HINTON. SUBSTITUTE: McGOVERN FOR CARLIN (83).

ATTENDANCE: 43,594
REFEREE :MR JAMES

Derby net four against reserves...

30th March 1970, Football League Division One

DERBY COUNTY 4 LEEDS UNITED 1

This was the game that was decided before the first whistle. Although the Rams claimed the points which confirmed their place in the 1970/1971 Fairs Cup competition, it was a facile victory, achieved against the Yorkshire club's reserve side. The Leeds manager Don Revie, his troops facing a European Cup semi-final tie with Celtic forty-eight hours later, opted to rest all of his star performers - effectively handing the Championship to Everton. For those in the crowd of 41,011 who were intent on recording all of the team changes, it was an experience of nightmare proportions, United lining up with a full team of programme alterations.

Left winger Alan Hinton was the creator of all four of the Rams goals. In the twenty-third minute, he crossed to John O'Hare who neatly set up Frank Wignall, the twice-capped England international finishing the move in style. Two minutes later, an

A team full of changes. Leeds, 30th March 1970.

unmarked Roy McFarland headed home Hinton's corner to extend the home side's advantage. County added to their tally in the fifty-third minute, O'Hare taking another pass from his wide man before turning easily past David Kennedy and firing in off a post. The Leeds defender partially redeemed himself four minutes later however when he netted the United consolation strike.

Eight minutes from time Willie Carlin completed the rout when he prodded the ball home from close range, the goal coming after yet another perfect centre from the irrepressible Hinton. It was a strange experience for Clough's side. They had won 4-1 but such was the anger of their supporters at seeing such poor quality opposition, only a double figure goal tally would have prevented the booing that greeted any mistake.

DERBY COUNTY: GREEN, WEBSTER, ROBSON, DURBAN, McFARLAND, HENNESSEY, WIGNALL, CARLIN, O'HARE, HECTOR, HINTON. SUBSTITUTE: McGOVERN.

LEEDS UNITED: HARVEY, DAVEY, PETERSON, LUMSDEN, KENNEDY, YORATH, GALVIN, BATES, BELFITT, HIBITT, JOHANNESON. SUBSTITUTE: O'NEIL.

ATTENDANCE: 41,011
REFEREE: MR WALKER

5.

OF TRANSFERS
AND TELEGRAMS
(1970/71)

WITH THE PROSPECT OF European football so cruelly removed, Clough turned his immediate attention to the Watney Cup, a new eight-team pre-season competition. The two top scoring sides from each of the four divisions were invited to participate in the

WE WON THE CUP! Derby celebrate with victory over Manchester United in the Watney Cup, 8th August 1970.

**The Rams squad enter Osmaston Park
on a pre-season training run.**

tournament, excluding those involved in Europe and newly promoted clubs. Accordingly, over the first two weeks of August 1970, the Rams joined Manchester United, Fulham, Sheffield United, Reading, Peterborough United, Hull City, Aldershot and Reading in the knockout format event, all of the matches being covered by the BBC. For the Rams, what followed proved to be ideal preparation for the league season ahead. After defeating Fulham 5-3 after extra time, they overcame Sheffield United 1-0, and so faced Manchester United in an August 8th Baseball Ground final. With the visitors always struggling against Clough's fit, eager side who treated the game as seriously as they would any other Cup final, it was a one-sided contest. Goals from Roy McFarland, Alan Hinton, Alan Durban and Dave Mackay ensured an easy 4-1 victory, with Mackay stepping up to receive the winners trophy from Sir Stanley Rous. In addition to the silverware County, by way of prize money and television fees, received a healthy five figure sum. Although the amount was small in comparison to what might have been gleaned from a successful Fairs Cup campaign, it guaranteed a last minute rush for season tickets, and again thrust the Rams into the media spotlight.

The league schedule opened with a 2-1 defeat against Chelsea at Stamford Bridge on August 15th, the London side taking the points with a controversial winning goal by Derby-born forward Ian

Chelsea goalkeeper Peter Bonetti gathers unchallenged, 15th August 1970.

Hutchinson. In the 74th minute, Les Green made a reflex save from Peter Osgood which was, later in the year, hailed as the "Save of the Season" by no less a judge than Gordon Banks. Two markers from John McGovern were the basis for an impressive 4-2 win at Wolverhampton Wanderers, before Stoke City were the visitors to the Baseball Ground on August 22nd. Although the Rams won a mediocre contest 2-0, more worrying for Clough was the sight of Terry Hennessey hobbling off with a twisted knee after just fourteen minutes. With Durban also struggling after the Wolverhampton game, the Rams by-now notoriously small squad was again already starting to look over-stretched. Despite their problems, County remained unbeaten until the end of the month, and after five games were in 4th place in the table - behind Leeds United, Manchester City and Liverpool, Don Revie's side having yet again made a strong start to their campaign.

The Rams then lost two home league games within the space of four days; being defeated by the odd goal in seven in a thriller against Coventry City, and 2-1 by Newcastle United. If that was not depressing enough, worse soon followed. Although Third Division Halifax Town were routinely disposed of in the 2nd Round of the League Cup, McFarland limped out of that game after just thirty minutes with another hamstring strain. It was an injury that sidelined him for five of the next six matches. With his potential replacement Hennessey also a distance from fitness, County travelled to Southampton on September 12th with reserve team centre half Tony Rhodes in the league side for just the third time in his career. It proved to be a particularly daunting experience for the twenty-three year old as the Saints, with Ron Davies in superb form, netted four goals without reply to march off as easy winners. Despite the thrashing, Rhodes kept his place for the 1-0 home win over Burnley and the 2-1 defeat against West Bromwich Albion at the Hawthorns. Clough however was clearly unimpressed and several weeks later, without re-appearing, the former Baseball Ground junior was allowed to move to Halifax for just £4,000.

With Ron Webster having also spent a spell out of the side, the Rams list of serious injuries seemed never ending. It was certainly a contrast to the previous couple of seasons, Clough's team then having largely managed to keep playing despite an assortment of niggling problems. With their resources looking so limited, the management duo decided the time was right to again bolster the squad.

Taylor, with his unending list of contacts, had been closely monitoring the progress of Archie Gemmill at Third Division Preston North End, the tough hard-tackling midfielder being a player in the image of Willie Carlin. When Clough heard that Everton were close to signing the twenty-three year old, he moved quickly and in his own inimitable style. Having put the fundamentals of a deal in place, he arrived, transfer form in hand, at Gemmill's house - determined to persuade him that his future lay at the Baseball Ground rather than Goodison Park. Initially, neither the young Scot or his wife were in the mood for Clough's sweet talk. It was probably only after the Rams manager had helped with the washing up, and then settled down for the night in the spare room, did the couple realise that "no" was not going to be a viable option. The following morning, manager and quarry enjoyed a cooked breakfast together, and at around nine-thirty Archie Gemmill committed himself to Derby County. . . It was not the first time Clough had used such a personalised tactic. Three years earlier, in another of his nocturnal manouverings, McFarland's parents had been convinced that their son should sign for the

Rams. Convincing complete, a pyjama-clad Roy was summoned from his bed to complete the paperwork. His dream had been to play alongside his heroes at Anfield; instead, as he later admitted, he signed for Derby County at midnight without really knowing a great deal about them.

Gemmill's arrival led to the surprise departure of Carlin. When Leicester City offered a sizeable £40,000 for the thirty year old, Clough decided it was time to let one of the side's most popular players move on. Carlin himself was devastated. Apparently his first knowledge of the transfer had come via the Sunday papers. Although he had needed just as many pain killing treatments as anyone else, his performances in the First Division were still of a consistently high level. Certainly he had never seemed overawed at the prospect of facing the best players in the country; indeed for a man who had spent the majority of his career in the lower divisions he had done remarkably well, thriving on the challenge of top flight football. Two factors were central to Clough's thinking. Firstly, the Gemmill signing had cost the Rams £66,000, a figure which looked very shrewd indeed for a promising twenty-three year old if, after Carlin's departure, the net cost was reduced to around £26,000. Secondly, Dave Mackay would be leaving at the end of the season, and an adequate replacement would most certainly cost more than those currently available in the £60,000 - £70,000 price bracket, so any money Clough saved in September 1970 was undoubtedly earmarked to be spent later on in the campaign. Although Carlin was left feeling bitter at his treatment, he did at least have his share of two transfers, totalling over £100,000 in as many years to console him.

With Gemmill in the side, County posted 1-1 draws with both Tottenham and Everton, those results coming either side of their 4-2 League Cup success against Millwall at the Baseball Ground. It did not however mark the start of a revival. The next four games - Chelsea, Leeds United and Arsenal in the league, and Coventry City in the League Cup - were all lost, with the effect that after the defeat at Highbury on October 31st the Rams had slipped to 20th place in the table. Clough had already decided however that his team needed a change of scenery and routine, and within hours of the game against the Gunners the squad were aboard a flight from Luton to Majorca. It was a chance for them to enjoy a four day winter sunshine break, refresh themselves and generally put the problems of the past three months behind them.

**Eddie Kelly scores for Arsenal after a mix up
between Les Green and Dave Mackay, October 31st 1970.**

On their return they faced Liverpool on November 7th at the Baseball Ground, a game which was dominated by both defences and ended in a stalemate 0-0 draw. It was not a great performance from the Rams, but at least it was the first time since their defeat of Burnley on September 19th that they had prevented the opposition from scoring. The trip to the Mediterranean sunshine certainly seemed to have benefited County, as by the end of the month they had additionally drawn at Manchester City and defeated both Blackpool and Nottingham Forest. Unfortunately however, the 2-0 win over the Seasiders was marred by the subsequent loss of Hinton for eight games due to injury.

Without their influential left winger the Rams' league form either side of Christmas was again mediocre. After a surprise 4-2 home reversal against West Ham United, for whom Jimmy Greaves scored on his 500th league game, they again failed to find the net in their scoreless draw at Crystal Palace, and in a 1-0 defeat at Stoke City, a sixtieth minute goal from Harry Burrows giving the Potteries side their victory. Although the Boxing Day visit of Manchester United proved to be a pulsating affair, for two of the individuals involved it was a contest that had devastating repercussions. With the Rams leading 2-0 at half time, Les Green's judgement temporarily deserted him and, after he had gifted the visitors a trio of goals, the game ended as a 4-4 draw. The unfortunate goalkeeper was immediately dropped from the side after 129 consecutive league and cup appearances. His replacement, twenty-five year old Colin Boulton, seized his opportunity to the extent that Green never again played for the first team. Disillusioned, he returned to his native South Africa eight months later and resumed his career with Durban City. For the United boss Wilf McGuinness, it was a result which, on the back of a shock League Cup exit against Third Division Aston Villa, also cost him his job. Within days, the legendary Sir Matt Busby had been reinstated as United's temporary first team manager, a move which, not surprisingly given his respected status quickly jolted the Reds into a series of improved performances. County's brace of January 1971 league games resulted in a 2-1 home defeat by Wolverhampton Wanderers and a single goal success against Ipswich Town. The game at Portman Road proved to be Hennessey's last of the season, his appearances being curtailed by Clough's decision to leave his injury-prone record signing on the sidelines in an attempt to get properly fit.

At least Clough's side enjoyed slightly better fortunes in the FA Cup competition. After overcoming Fourth Division Chester City, thanks to markers from Frank Wignall and Gemmill, they gained revenge for the defeat by Wolves, beating the Midlands club 2-1 in a tremendous 4th Round tie on an almost unplayable Baseball Ground surface. The attendance of 40,567 produced gate receipts of £18,246, the first time in their history that the Rams had exceeded the £15,000 mark. Although they then exited the competition on a 1-0 scoreline against a David Johnson-inspired Everton at Goodison Park, it was the second season in succession that they had reached the 5th Round. By way of emphasising just how deep the decline had been prior to Clough's arrival, it was the first time that feat had been achieved since the competitions of 1949 and 1950.

When Gemmill joined the Rams, he had become the second person in a relatively short time to make the journey from Deepdale to the Baseball Ground. A few months earlier Stuart Webb, an articulate and ambitious man, had been appointed as the company secretary. From the outset, Taylor in particular had been suspicious of the motives of the immaculately dressed newcomer. Webb had business aspirations of his own within the travel industry, and in his early days at the club took the opportunity of fully ingratiating himself with the Directors. His logic was undoubtedly sound, the stock value of a company secretary with direct access to a travel business would surely rise in an organisation on the threshold of European football for the first time. By February 1971, Webb's style of all-encompassing administration was emerging as a potentially dangerous cloud on Clough's immediate horizon, the manager viewing the secretary's involvement in the running of the club as more of a hindrance to him than a help. The signing of Colin Todd presented Clough with the chance to demonstrate exactly who was in charge of Derby County, an opportunity that was seized with an amazing degree of audacity. With Mackay coming to the end of his contract, the Sunderland defender had been selected as his replacement. In this particular case there was no need for Taylor to go and make an assessment of the twenty-two year old's abilities, Clough having already coached him, alongside O'Hare, in the same Roker Park youth team. Todd's future at the North East club had been a topic of speculation for several months, with a number of top teams vying for the signature of the £150,000-plus rated player. Again Clough moved without hesitation - just twenty four hours after informing the press that the Rams could not afford the highly rated Geordie, Todd became a County player in a massive £175,000 deal. It was an amount which dwarfed the £100,000 paid for Hennessey. And yet Clough did not even flinch at the size of the fee, he firmly believed that the achievements of the McFarland and Mackay combination would be eclipsed by the pairing of McFarland with Todd. Once the deal had been finalised, Clough was left with just one more task; he simply had to inform his Chairman that he had spent £175,000. Longson was at the time enjoying a holiday in the Caribbean, and whilst he was obviously aware of the need to replace Mackay, the first inkling he had of the deal was a "Love Brian" telegram informing him of the fee paid for the new signing.

Clough's view was that he could do no wrong. It was a case of him doing what, in his opinion, was right for Derby County and, with the sole exception of Taylor, the thoughts of anyone else mattered little. In reality few managers, then or indeed now, would have been able to survive the consequences of adopting such an authoritarian stance. In the case of Clough however, things were decidedly different. Whilst it was unheard of for a manager to conclude such a large transaction without the knowledge of the Directors, his previous transfer market activities had already been characterised by more than a fair share of individuality. Additionally, Clough boasted a very successful track record in relation to all of his major signings, and the prospect of Todd proving to be an exception to that record never even entered into

Archie Gemmill heads against the bar versus Manchester City, 13th March 1971.

his mind. His relationship with Longson also gave him a remarkable level of protection. As well as a healthy salary, the list of other benefits Clough and his family received was, by the early Seventies, almost unending. Expensive gifts, clothes even the use of a Mercedes had been showered on them by a Chairman whose generosity knew no bounds. Longson's business interests and power base was in Chapel-en-le-Frith in the North of Derbyshire. Although he was a very well respected individual locally, the signing of Todd certainly lifted the eyebrows of his immediate business and social peers. Privately and then publicly they started to contemplate if the Chairman of Derby County had as much control of affairs at the Baseball Ground as he had led them to believe. It was an episode which, for the first time, left Longson feeling a sense of betrayal. It was not the amount of money that concerned him, it was more the way the deal had been concluded that led to him beginning to question his managers increasing sense of power. He was also having to continually placate his fellow Directors, one or two of whom felt that their own financial input gave them an absolute right, irrespective of any footballing knowledge, to decide how such contributions were spent.

Todd made his debut in a 2-0 defeat of Arsenal at the Baseball Ground on February 27th. That victory lifted the Rams to 13th place and came after the return of Hinton had prompted wins against West Ham United, Crystal Palace and Blackpool. Again though, and so frustratingly, County then seemed to lose their way just when a revival was in the offing. Given that Leeds United had, with the exception of the Easter 1970 "reserve team" farce, beaten the Rams six times in as many meetings under Clough's management, a 1-0 defeat, courtesy of a Peter Lorimer goal on March 6th was probably not unexpected. However after that, a desperately poor scoreless draw with Manchester City, with Gemmill who hit the bar being one of the few Rams to emerge with any credit, only proved to be the prelude for consecutive defeats against Liverpool, Newcastle United and Nottingham Forest. The last month of the season produced yet another turnaround in the quality of the Rams' performances, their results improving after Todd had switched to right back to cover for Webster who was injured in a 2-1 defeat by Tottenham Hotspur, his 300th league game for the club. The former Sunderland defender had not looked overly comfortable in a midfield berth and clearly relished a return to a position within the back four. County remained unbeaten in

**Liverpool's Ray Clemence dives at the feet of
Kevin Hector, 20th March 1971.**

their last six fixtures and recorded very impressive wins against Manchester United and Everton, those victories coming alongside more routine successes over Burnley and West Bromwich Albion, and scoreless draws with a defence-minded Southampton and a struggling Coventry City.

The game against the Baggies on the last day of the season allowed a Baseball Ground crowd of 33,661 to bid farewell to Mackay. Although the Rams coasted to a 2-0 victory which secured 9th place, the sight of the departing hero urging his players on deep into injury time was a fitting memory of a player whose passion for the game, even at the age of thirty-six, was as great as that of even the most enthusiastic of teenagers. Remarkably, and for the first time in his career, Mackay had also been an ever-present in the league side during what was at times a traumatic season.

In reality it had been a period of re-building. The acquisition of Gemmill and then Todd clearly indicated the management's view that a very good Derby County team could be made even better. Although two top ten finishing positions was credible enough for a side promoted from the Second Division, Clough had his sights set on the Championship itself and the lure of challenging the best Continental teams in the European Cup. The changes made to the side had also been a testimony to two of Clough's fundamental beliefs. Firstly the demise of both Carlin and Green had shown, yet again after the departure of Saxton, that Clough, the manager, was

**NO WAY THROUGH! Kevin Hector against
Southampton, 12th April 1971.**

**THAT HURT! John O'Hare is the victim of
a wild kick against Sheffield United.**

equally as ruthless as Clough the player had been a decade earlier. Here was a individual who in respect of footballing matters had scant regard for sentimentality. Secondly, it seemed to be imperative to him that the players along the spine of his side were both physically and mentally strong. Whilst the 1968/69 team had been based on a central line of Green, McFarland/Mackay, Carlin and O'Hare, the 1971/72 Rams would likely line up with Boulton, McFarland/Todd, Gemmill and O'Hare providing the backbone of their line up.

O'Hare again finished as the top scorer, netting thirteen league goals for the second season in succession. Given his style, it was significant that the barrel-chested target man, like Durban, seemed to find his better form on the drier pitches of autumn and spring. Additionally, O'Hare displayed a remarkable level of resilience, as he missed just two league games in his first four seasons at the Baseball Ground, that despite his ankles more often than not being the target for many a frustrated defender's boot. Also, and for the first time since the 1967/1968 campaign, three County strikers recorded a goal tally in double figures, in addition to O'Hare, Hector having netted eleven and Hinton ten. With the Rams having won just eight of their twenty-one home league fixtures, there was little surprise that the average attendance fell from almost 36,000 to 31,358, although the continuing employment worries for many regular supporters was certainly another factor in the decrease. It had been a difficult campaign, beset by injuries, though in the final analysis the 9th place finish was a credible performance, especially after the Rams had been 20th after the first three months.

APPEARANCES 1970-71

PLAYER	LEAGUE		FA CUP		LGE CUP	OTHERS	TOTAL	
GREEN	23		0		3	0	26	
WEBSTER	34	(1)	3		3	0	40	(1)
ROBSON	34	(1)	2		3	0	39	(1)
DURBAN	26	(2)	2		2	0	30	(2)
McFARLAND	35		3		3	0	41	
MACKAY	42		3		2	0	47	
McGOVERN	32	(2)	3		2	0	37	(2)
CARLIN	13		0		2	0	15	
O'HARE	42		3		3	0	48	
HECTOR	42		3		3	0	48	
HINTON	34		2		3	0	39	
WIGNALL	10	(7)	1		2	0	13	(7)
HENNESSEY	12		1		1	0	14	
RHODES	3		0		1	0	4	
RICHARDSON	8		0		0	0	8	
WALKER	1		0		0	0	1	
GEMMILL	31		3		0	0	34	
DANIEL	4	(1)	0	(1)	0	0	5	(2)
BUTLIN	1		0		0	0	1	
BOULTON	19		3		0	0	22	
TODD	14		0		0	0	14	
BOURNE	2		0		0	0	2	
TOTAL	**42**		**3**		**3**	**0**	**48**	

N.B. Substitute appearances in brackets.

SCORERS 1970-71

PLAYER	LEAGUE	FA CUP	LGE CUP	OTHERS	TOTAL
O'HARE	13	1	1	0	15
HECTOR	11	0	1	0	12
HINTON	10	1	1	0	12
McGOVERN	6	0	1	0	7
DURBAN	4	0	2	0	6
WIGNALL	4	1	0	0	5
GEMMILL	3	1	0	0	4
MACKAY	2	0	1	0	3
McFARLAND	2	0	0	0	2
OWN GOALS	1	0	0	0	1
TOTAL	**56**	**4**	**7**	**0**	**67**

KEY MATCHES OF 1970/71

Coventry sneak points in seven goal thriller...

2nd September 1970, Football League Division One

DERBY COUNTY 3 COVENTRY CITY 4

After three league games without surrendering a goal, a sloppy defensive display saw the Rams concede four against the Sky Blues, the Midlands side winning at the Baseball Ground for the second consecutive season. Coventry gave a debut to new defender Wilf Smith, although the £100,000 signing from Chelsea lasted just five minutes before limping off after a collision with Ron Webster.

Before the visitors introduced their substitute, County went ahead with a fine seventh minute goal from Kevin Hector, the Rams striker converting a cross to the far post from Alan Hinton. Whilst City were still re-organising themselves, they went 2-0 behind after fourteen minutes. A firm header from Willie Carlin was brilliantly parried away by Bill Glazier, but Hinton following up volleyed the ball into the net. The home side continued to push forward and it seemed to be only a matter of time before they increased their lead. Amazingly however, Coventry hit back and levelled the game with two goals in as many minutes. Just before the half hour, Ernie Machin got past Dave Mackay and his near post cross was swept in by Neil Martin. Although Hector went close from the restart, the visitors again raced away and equalised when left winger Dave Clements hit a low shot past Les Green.

Eight minutes into the second half Coventry went ahead when Martin notched his second, the centre forward heading in a far post cross from Clements. In what was turning out to be a marvellous contest, the Rams hit back and John McGovern made it 3-3 after fifty-nine minutes, the midfielder, under pressure from Willie Carr, getting on the end of a Hector centre. The equaliser seemed to inspire Clough's side - a superb flowing move ended with Frank Wignall being knocked off the ball in the penalty area, but Hinton's spot kick was brilliantly turned away by Glazier. Hector then hit the bar and McGovern had a marker disallowed for offside. Just when it seemed as though the points would be deservedly shared, Coventry grabbed a winner, Carr hitting an eighty-eighth minute shot past Green through a crowd of players.

DERBY COUNTY: GREEN, WEBSTER, ROBSON, WIGNALL, McFARLAND, MACKAY, McGOVERN, CARLIN, O'HARE, HECTOR, HINTON. SUBSTITUTE: DURBAN.

COVENTRY CITY: GLAZIER, COOP, CATTLIN, SMITH, BLOCKLEY, STRONG, JOICEY, CARR, MARTIN, MACHIN, CLEMENTS. SUBSTITUTE: HUNT FOR SMITH (10).

ATTENDANCE: 31,621
REFEREE: MR CAPEY

Rams defence no match for Davies and Channon...

12th September 1970, Football League Division One

SOUTHAMPTON 4 DERBY COUNTY 0

The Rams went into this game without both Terry Hennessey and Roy McFarland, the latter having limped out of the 3-1 midweek League Cup defeat of Halifax Town after thirty minutes. Without his experienced duo, Clough was forced to give Tony Rhodes just his third league start in seven seasons, the inexperienced twenty-three year old significantly having to mark Ron Davies - one of the division's best centre forwards. After the first half hour, it proved to be an uneven contest, the aerial threat from the Welsh international being such that the Saints eventually romped to an easy victory.

The opening goal came in the thirty-fourth minute. Les Green saved brilliantly from a Mike Channon header, but from the resulting corner Davies headed his side ahead, his header flying past Ron Webster who was standing on the line. Although County had plenty of possession in midfield, with both Kevin Hector and John O'Hare looking well held by the home defence, it seemed likely the Saints would add to their tally. And so it proved - within ten minutes of the second half starting, they had eased into a 3-0 lead. After fifty-two minutes Davies nodded in his second, and three minutes later Channon crept in at the near post to head home a cross from the veteran right winger Terry Paine. The thrashing was completed in the last minute, Channon netting his second after Davies and Paine had again left the Rams defence floundering.

With three of the Saints goals coming from headers from centres, the heart of the Rams defence had been ripped apart. Although Rhodes obviously struggled, he could take consolation from the fact that several far more experienced defenders had also found the heading abilities of Davies to be beyond them. The defeat saw County plunge five places in the table to 13th, whilst the home side moved up to 6th place.

SOUTHAMPTON: MARTIN, KIRKUP, HOLLYWOOD, FISHER, McGRATH, GABRIEL, PAINE, CHANNON, DAVIES, O'NEIL, JENKINS. SUBSTITUTE: WALKER.

DERBY COUNTY: GREEN, WEBSTER, ROBSON, DURBAN, RHODES, MACKAY, McGOVERN, CARLIN, O'HARE, HECTOR, HINTON. SUBSTITUTE: WIGNALL FOR DURBAN (65).

ATTENDANCE: 19,429
REFEREE: MR JONES

Rams struggle against "confident" Leeds...

24th October 1970, Football League Division One

DERBY COUNTY 0 LEEDS UNITED 2

County's run of games without a league victory was extended to five matches, their goal-shy forwards finding the Leeds defence, superbly marshalled by Norman Hunter, far too clever for them.

Gary Sprake gathers under pressure from Terry Hennessey.

Indeed, Gary Sprake in the visitors' goal had only one save to make, a tip around the post from a smart John McGovern effort, the young Scot being the Rams' best player.

Although the first half was scoreless, the visitors controlled the midfield area well, albeit against a far from match-fit Terry Hennessey and newcomer Archie Gemmill, who was playing just his fifth First Division game. The opening goal came seven minutes after the interval, a well worked Leeds free kick saw Terry Cooper slip the ball to Alan "Sniffer" Clarke who beat Les Green with a neat low shot. Before Clough's team could think about staging any sort of fightback, they fell further behind to a marvellous strike from Peter Lorimer. A cross into the heart of the home defence was headed clear by Roy McFarland, his clearance falling to the United winger who volleyed home a trademark cannonball from fully twenty-five yards out.

After the final whistle, Clough said that the difference between the two teams was confidence, a fair comment as Leeds moved two points clear of Arsenal at the top of the table, having lost just one of fourteen games. Conversely, the Rams slipped nearer to the relegation zone, their only comfort being that both McFarland and Hennessey managed to play a full ninety minutes to ease the club's injury crisis.

DERBY COUNTY: GREEN, WEBSTER, ROBSON, HENNESSEY, McFARLAND, MACKAY, GEMMILL, McGOVERN, O'HARE, HECTOR, HINTON. SUBSTITUTE: DANIEL.

LEEDS UNITED: SPRAKE, DAVEY, COOPER, BREMNER, CHARLTON, HUNTER, LORIMER, CLARKE, JONES, BELFITT, MADELEY. SUBSTITUTE: KENNEDY.

ATTENDANCE: 32,797
REFEREE: MR OLIVER

Tenacious Gemmill is County hero...

28th November 1970, Football League Division One

NOTTINGHAM FOREST 2 DERBY COUNTY 4

County won away from home in the league for the first time in over three months, and much to their supporters' delight it was a victory achieved against their close East Midlands neighbours. More importantly for Clough, his side took the points after twice coming from behind and with a line up that lacked both Roy McFarland and Alan Hinton.

Forest took an early lead when Bob Chapman blasted home an eighth minute corner from Ron Rees. Almost immediately however, the Rams came more into the game and equalised in the twenty-sixth minute, Archie Gemmill forcing the ball over the line after efforts from both Frank Wignall and John O'Hare had been blocked. Although the visitors then controlled proceedings, Forest restored their lead seven minutes later when, against the run of play, Ian Storey Moore headed home a volleyed centre from right winger Barry Lyons. Although the River Trent side led at half

Archie Gemmill at his best in a full-blooded local derby.

time, their hopes of recording a fourth win of the season were shattered by a devastating spell of Rams pressure. With Gemmill having a superb match, the game was level after fifty-six minutes when the County midfielder eased past two tackles and set up O'Hare to score. County soon took a lead for the first time, Wignall smashing a shot past Jim Barron after Kevin Hector's effort had been blocked by the now cruelly overworked goalkeeper. John McGovern made it 4-2 in the seventy-third minute, and Forest's hopes of salvaging the game nose dived when Moore fired a seventy-eighth minute penalty wide.

It was a marvellous ninety minutes of action, played in a real "local derby" atmosphere. Clough's decision to take his side away to Majorca after the October 31st defeat at Highbury seemed to have produced the desired effect, as following their defeat of Blackpool, it was the Rams' fourth game without defeat and a scoreline which lifted them to 14th place in the table.

NOTTINGHAM FOREST: BARRON, HINDLEY, WINFIELD , CHAPMAN, O'KANE, JACKSON, LYONS, RICHARDSON, CORMACK, REES, MOORE. SUBSTITUTE: COLLIER.

DERBY COUNTY: GREEN, WEBSTER, ROBSON, DURBAN, HENNESSEY, MACKAY, McGOVERN, WIGNALL, O'HARE, HECTOR, GEMMILL. SUBSTITUTE: DANIEL.

ATTENDANCE: 30,529
REFEREE: MR TAYLOR

Rams and Reds in eight goal thriller...

26th December 1970, Football League Division One

DERBY COUNTY 4 MANCHESTER UNITED 4

Manchester United staged a remarkable second half comeback at the Baseball Ground. However, their gaining of a point had more to do with the home side's lacklustre defending rather any flashes of individual brilliance by any of the Reds famed forward line. That said, for the holiday crowd of 34,068 it was an afternoon of marvellous entertainment, certainly not what might have been expected from two teams battling for points at the wrong end of the First Division table.

County swept up the field from the first whistle and went ahead in the third minute. They were awarded a free kick just outside of the penalty area, and Dave Mackay stepped up to hit a shot just inside Jim Rimmer's right hand post. With United creating little in attack, it was no surprise when Clough's side increased their advantage twenty minutes later: another Mackay free kick was only half cleared by Denis Law and although Roy McFarland's effort was blocked, Frank Wignall netted the close range rebound with ease.

At the start of the second half, the contest was transformed by three United goals within the space of four minutes. Their first, ten minutes after the restart, came when Law headed a cross from Willie Morgan beyond Les Green, the Rams goalkeeper being hopelessly positioned well off his line. Almost from the kick off the visitors were level, George Best prodding the ball over the line after Green had fumbled a Bobby Charlton corner. After fifty-nine minutes another corner from Charlton went beyond both McFarland and Mackay, and Law stooped to head his side ahead for the first time.

With Archie Gemmill reveling in the atrocious conditions, the Scottish midfielder then inspired the Rams to hit back twice themselves. After sixty-six minutes he raced clear, and after his shot was blocked, he recovered the ball before setting up an easy strike for Kevin Hector. Four minutes later the roles were reversed - Hector pushed the ball into the path of his colleague, and the firm shot that followed went in off Rimmer's leg and the post. To cap a magnificent contest, United equalised with yet another goal from a corner kick when Brian Kidd headed past Green who, after conceding a quartet of soft goals, was left to look for the proverbial hole in the ground. . .

DERBY COUNTY: GREEN, WEBSTER, DANIEL, HENNESSEY, McFARLAND, MACKAY, DURBAN, WIGNALL, O'HARE, HECTOR, GEMMILL. SUBSTITUTE: McGOVERN.

MANCHESTER UNITED: RIMMER, FITZPATRICK, DUNNE, CRERAND, URE, SADLER, MORGAN, BEST, CHARLTON, KIDD, LAW. SUBSTITUTE: GOWLING.

ATTENDANCE: 34,068
REFEREE: MR WILLIAMS

Last gasp O'Hare ensures Derby progress...

23rd January 1971, Football Association Cup 4th Round

DERBY COUNTY 2 WOLVERHAMPTON WANDERERS 1

After disposing of Chester City in the previous round, the Rams defeated Wolverhampton in a controversial game on a mud heap of a Baseball Ground pitch. Although it was a marginal decision that the game even started, the conditions made for a thrilling cup tie with the home side reversing the scoreline in the league match between the pair two weeks earlier.

John O'Hare and Kenny Hibbert, mud-splattered, tussle for the ball.

The outcome hinged largely on two crucial pieces of refereeing. With County on top and attacking, Mr Howley awarded them a twenty-seventh minute penalty, Scottish defender Frank Munroe being adjudged to have fouled Kevin Hector. The returning Alan Hinton blasted the spot kick firmly past the Wanderers goalkeeper Phil Parkes. With Archie Gemmill reveling in the mud and leaving opponents reeling in his wake, the home team continued to look by far the better side, although their attempts at continual possession were far too frequently halted by the referee's whistle, the Billingham-based official in all awarding forty-three free kicks.

The second discussion point came in the five minutes after half time. With the Rams again going forward, behind the play Dave Mackay appeared to strike Bobby Gould in the face, the Wolves striker remaining prostrate in the penalty area. Although Mr Howley duly consulted his linesman and booked Mackay, he awarded the visitors an indirect free kick rather than the expected penalty. Clough's side cleared any danger and hung on to their advantage until ten minutes from time. Then, Colin Boulton did well to palm away a Jim McCalliog header, but John Richards nipped in to chest the ball into the net. Just when it seemed that a replay would be required, the Rams settled the game with a well taken last minute goal. Hector picked up Alan Durban's blocked centre, looked up and knocked in a cross which John O'Hare diverted past Parkes with his chest. On the balance of play, it was a fair result, a fact the visitors' manager Bill McGarry and his players found particularly difficult to accept.

DERBY COUNTY: BOULTON, WEBSTER, ROBSON, DURBAN, McFARLAND, MACKAY, McGOVERN, GEMMILL, O'HARE, HECTOR, HINTON. SUBSTITUTE: WIGNALL.

WOLVERHAMPTON WANDERERS: PARKES, SHAW, PARKIN, BAILEY, MUNROE, McALLE, McCALLIOG, HIBBITT, GOULD, DOUGAN, WAGSTAFFE. SUBSTITUTE: RICHARDS FOR GOULD (71).

ATTENDANCE: 40,567
REFEREE: MR HOWLEY

New boy Johnson the pick of the Toffees...

13th February 1971, Football Association Cup 5th Round

EVERTON 1 DERBY COUNTY 0

County exited the FA Cup in a contest of few real chances on a heavy Goodison Park surface. Both defences were on top throughout, and yet ironically, the tie was decided by nineteen year old David Johnson, the most inexperienced striker on show.

The midfield area was congested from the outset as both teams vied for control, the Rams again opting to use John McGovern as a "man marker" on Everton's Alan Ball. It was Johnson however, on his senior debut at home, who caught the eye. Although he missed a golden opportunity in the eighteenth minute when he fired over after a poor Colin Boulton throw out, he handsomely made up for the error two minutes before the interval. Howard Kendall angled a centre into the penalty area, the young marksman responding by planting a superb header into the net, this time giving Boulton no chance of making a save.

With Joe Royle failing to create any aerial threat against Roy McFarland, the home side only created a few other half chances. That said, neither Boulton or his counterpart Gordon West inspired any great confidence with their handling of the wet ball in the cold icy conditions. To his credit, West did however prevent both Kevin Hector and Alan Hinton from grabbing an equaliser late on. Apart from the outstanding McFarland, midfielder Archie Gemmill was in irrepressible form alongside McGovern and Alan Durban, but in the end it was all to no avail, the Rams' dismal record of not reaching the 6th Round since 1950 being extended for another season.

Clough's disappointment at going out was undoubtedly eased when he discovered that his arch rival Don Revie had also seen his side defeated, Leeds United crashing to a 3-2 defeat at Fourth Division Colchester United in the day's shock FA Cup result.

EVERTON: WEST, WRIGHT, NEWTON (HENRY), KENDALL, KENYON, HARVEY, HUSBAND, BALL, ROYLE, HURST, JOHNSON. SUBSTITUTE: NEWTON (KEITH).

DERBY COUNTY: BOULTON, WEBSTER, ROBSON, DURBAN, McFARLAND, MACKAY, McGOVERN, GEMMILL, O'HARE, HECTOR, HINTON. SUBSTITUTE: DANIEL.

ATTENDANCE: 53,490
REFEREE: MR NEW

County ease past sorry Arsenal...

27th February 1971, Football League Division One

DERBY COUNTY 2 ARSENAL 0

The Rams achieved their fifth straight league victory, their 2-0 success over the North London side moving them up two more places in the table to 13th. Colin Todd also made his County debut, the designated replacement for Dave Mackay on this occasion occupying a midfield role alongside Archie Gemmill and John McGovern. The visitors decided to employ an offside trap to try and restrict the Rams attackers, but they visibly wilted as the home side gradually took complete control of the contest.

With Roy McFarland in marvellous form, the not insignificant threat of Arsenal's John Radford was blotted out from the outset, and in honesty the Gunners had little else to offer. Clough's side took the lead in the thirty-first minute. Alan Hinton was fouled by Pat Rice, and after picking himself up, the winger delivered a perfect kick towards the far post, Kevin Hector's header across the face of the goal being prodded home by the onrushing McFarland. Although the remainder of the half passed without further goals, the Rams killed the game off within just six minutes of the restart. John O'Hare found Hector out on the left, and the "King" cut sharply inside before blasting a shot past Wilson, the despairing Arsenal goalkeeper beaten at his near post.

The Rams almost added a third when Hector's speed took him past the defence in a run from the half way line. Arsenal, in the end, seemed just glad to get back to the sanctity of their dressing room, so easily had they been defeated. It was hard to believe that County had been beaten at Highbury on the last day of October 1970, their form since that defeat resulting in eighteen out of a possible twenty-eight points being gained.

DERBY COUNTY: BOULTON, WEBSTER, RICHARDSON, TODD, McFARLAND, MACKAY, McGOVERN, GEMMILL, O'HARE, HECTOR, HINTON. SUBSTITUTE: DURBAN.

ARSENAL: WILSON, RICE, McNAB, STOREY, McLINTOCK, SIMPSON, ARMSTRONG, SAMMELS, RADFORD, KENNEDY, GEORGE. SUBSTITUTE: GRAHAM FOR RICE (73).

ATTENDANCE: 35,775
REFEREE: MR LAING

Colin Todd made his Rams debut against Arsenal.

6.

AND THE WINNERS ARE
(1971/72)

WITH THE RAMS HAVING again missed out on qualification for European football, Clough viewed the Texaco Cup, a sixteen team knockout tournament in its second season, as a credible alternative. He was a firm believer in the value of such competitions, arguing that whilst the financial rewards for taking part were limited, the opportunity for his players to possibly experience a Cup final was not to be missed. Whilst the Watney Cup triumph had been a prelude to the 1970/71 league season, the Texaco tournament was scheduled to run throughout the season with all games being contested on a two-legged basis, the eventual winners earning prize money in excess of £10,000. Although Clough obviously wanted to do as well as possible, he realised the additional games would also be an ideal chance to play several of the reserve side in senior fixtures: something, given the Rams limited resources, that would do no harm at all. The first round draw paired County with Dundee United, the opening home leg being set for September 15th, a little more than a month after the commencement of the league campaign.

The Rams first fixture was an attractive home league game against Manchester United, second half goals from Frank Wignall and Kevin Hector giving them a deserved 2-2 draw after the visitors, with markers from Denis Law and Alan Gowling, had established a two goal advantage in the opening half hour. Wignall was again in a goalscoring mood four days later, the experienced striker netting County's second in a poor quality 2-0 victory over West Ham United at the Baseball Ground. The solid enough start was maintained at Leicester on August 21st, two goals in four second half minutes easing Clough's side to the win which moved them up to 3rd in the table - and with the injured McFarland still to be added to the side. Perhaps surprisingly, when the England centre half did return, County conceded two goals in each of his first two games, drawing 2-2 with both Coventry City and Southampton. That said, a third consecutive draw, 0-0 at Ipswich, meant that August had seen the

Rams unbeaten, and occupying 2nd place behind the unexpected leaders Sheffield United.

The scoreless game at Portman Road started a sequence of matches in which the Rams defence was at its best. By October 2nd, five games later, they were still unbeaten and only Chelsea's Tommy Baldwin had scored against them, his strike coming in a 1-1 draw at Stamford Bridge. Although the home game against Tottenham Hotspur ended in yet another 2-2 draw, the Rams had cause to feel hard done by, the referee allowing both of the visitors' dubious goals. It was however a result which extended the unbeaten run to twelve games and left Clough's side in 4th place in the standings. It was also Wignall's penultimate appearance in a County shirt, the former England striker moved on to Mansfield Town a few weeks later having been, for a £20,000 purchase, a very productive cover striker indeed.

Tottenham's Alan Gilzean heads against the bar but Martin Chivers netted the rebound, 9th October 1971.

**George Best scores the only goal for
Manchester United, 16th October 1971.**

County experienced mixed fortunes in their early season Texaco and League Cup encounters. Dundee found themselves outplayed at the Baseball Ground, six players hitting the target in the Rams convincing 6-2 success, a performance which formed the basis of an eventual 8-5 aggregate progression to the second round of the sponsored competition. In the League Cup however, Leeds United again got the better of Clough's side, a 0-0 draw in Derby being followed by a 2-0 replay win for Don Revie's side in a tremendous game at Elland Road. The defeat meant the Rams midweek efforts could be focussed on the Texaco games, and by December 8th they had beaten fellow First Division sides Stoke City (4-3 on aggregate)and Newcastle United (4-2 on aggregate) to reach the Final, thereby gaining the right to face another Scottish club, Airdrieonians.

Back in the league, the unbeaten run came to an end against the leaders Manchester United on October 16th. A goal from George Best in the 52nd minute gave the home side both points and although the Rams remained in 4th place, they were just four points behind the revitalised Old Trafford club. By the end of November, although Derby had fallen to 2-1 defeats at both Wolverhampton Wanderers and Huddersfield Town, they had also recorded impressive wins against Arsenal, Nottingham Forest, Crystal Palace and Sheffield United to maintain a healthy 3rd place. Significantly, in that quartet of victories only Arsenal's George

Ron Webster (seen in 1972) headed a brilliant goal against Manchester City, 4th December 1971.

Graham had managed to beat Colin Boulton, whilst going forward the Rams had accumulated another ten goals. As many seasoned observers had predicted, Clough's side were becoming very hard to score against, the clean sheet they achieved in the 3-0 win against the Blades being their tenth in eighteen matches.

When Manchester City visited the Baseball Ground on December 4th, the crowd of 35,384 witnessed a superb display from Alan Hinton who scored the Rams' first goal and created the other two. The game also marked a personal milestone for Hinton, as his twenty-third minute penalty was his 50th goal for the the club. After the spot kick, the irrepressible winger also set up headers for Ron Webster and Alan Durban, the marker from the right back being one of the best seen by the home supporters for a long time. Although Francis Lee pulled one back for the visitors in the second half, Clough's side were splendid value for their 3-1 victory.

After the New Year the Rams turned their attentions to the FA Cup competition. After beating a spirited Shrewsbury Town 2-0, they demolished Notts County 6-0. The Third Division promotion hopefuls, who included Willie Carlin in their line up, found a rampant Derby side just too good for them. Durban took the scoring honours with a hat trick to go alongside markers from Hector, Hinton and John Robson. It set up a fascinating February 26th 5th Round tie with Arsenal at the Baseball Ground, the London side gaining an early psychological edge when they defeated the Rams 2-0 at Highbury in a league match two weeks before the cup encounter.

**Alan Durban nets the 4th goal against
Notts County, 5th February 1972.**

The cup tie itself was a game of epic proportions, County fighting back twice to equalise goals from the Gunners striker Charlie George. The strike which gave the Rams a 2-2 draw came from Durban, the midfielder heading home Hector's cross just two minutes before the final whistle. When the replay in London three nights later ended scoreless after extra time, the teams were faced with the rare prospect of a third game on a neutral ground. And so on March 13th, Filbert Street, the home of Leicester City, became the venue for the next installment of the enthralling contest. With sides being apparently so closely matched, many thought a piece of individual brilliance or a mistake would eventually decide the outcome. Sadly for Derby County, and in particular John McGovern, the latter proved to be the case. After just four minutes, the Rams midfielder intercepted an Arsenal attack and, instead of playing the easy ball out to Hinton, decided to knock it back to Colin Boulton. It was a woefully hit pass which enabled Ray Kennedy to nip in and shoot past the stranded goalkeeper. Although any dreams of Wembley had been shattered for another year at least, the Rams could again concentrate on their attempt to win the Championship for the first time,

With the transfer deadline approaching, the two weeks before the second replay also saw County become embroiled in an elongated transfer dispute with Nottingham Forest and Manchester United. The player at the centre of the argument was Ian Storey Moore, Forest's highly regarded left winger. Clough was eager to increase his squad numbers in readiness for the run-in to the end of the season, and had targeted Storey Moore, despite already being aware that United were already deep in negotiations with Forest for the winger's signature. What happened next bordered on the ridiculous. At the game against Wolverhampton Wanderers on March 4th, a clearly confused player was introduced to the 33,456 Baseball Ground crowd as the latest addition to the playing staff signed, according to Clough, in a £200,000 deal. Unfortunately, as Forest were all too keen to point out, they had not yet completed the appropriate paper work for the deal to proceed. Four days later, much to Clough's immense displeasure, United announced that their discussions with Forest were complete and Storey Moore had indeed moved to Old Trafford. The Rams manager immediately fired off a stern letter of protest to Alan Hardaker, the secretary of the Football League, a man not known to take kindly to any sort of criticism, or more worryingly to allow even the slightest breach of regulations to go unpunished. It was certainly not the type of dealing Longson wanted to be connected with. His cherished seat on the League Management Committee was at stake, something he now realised more than ever was dependent upon his organisation having a sound record of inter-club diplomacy and a clear financial conscience.

However, even before the campaign reached its conclusion, Clough and Taylor again severely tested the Chairman's resolve. Within weeks of the embarrassing Storey Moore episode, the management duo resigned and announced that they were to take charge at Coventry City. In a calculated move, a proviso was added that salary increases might persuade them to reconsider. With the club on the verge of a potentially lucrative European expedition, and possibly even the Championship itself, Longson quickly assessed the situation. He realised, his own fires of ambition burning as brightly as ever, that if he let the pair depart, he would be widely castigated. Being known as the Chairman of the club who lost its management team within weeks of potentially its finest hour held little appeal. Accordingly, Clough was given a rise of £5,000, Taylor receiving a couple of thousand less. It was only after the increases had been agreed, that Longson found out that the Sky Blues interest had already waned. Although he did not say it publicly at the time, he again felt totally betrayed by Clough's actions. In private and in his more blunt Derbyshire terms, he admitted however to having been conned by his manager, who was by now intent on operating without any restriction being placed upon him.

The league defeat at Highbury had a galvanising effect on the Rams' efforts to capture the Championship crown. They won seven of their next eight league fixtures, a sequence that culminated in a magnificent display against Leeds United on April 1st. In front of an Easter Saturday Baseball Ground crowd of 38,611, they created chance after chance and eventually battered Don Revie's side into a 2-0 defeat. They were inspired by a vintage performance from John O'Hare, his control and turns being so neat that his minder Jack Charlton was, at times, reduced to the role of a lumbering giant. Fittingly it was O'Hare, in his 200th league appearance for the club, who opened the scoring in the 16th minute, and then secured the points in the 69th minute - his shot going in off Norman Hunter. The victory was County's first over Leeds since the Easter farce of two seasons earlier, but far more importantly it took them to the top of the table.

The Rams second goal; a John O'Hare shot hits the goalkeeper and goes in off Norman Hunter. Leeds, 1st April 1972.

The run-in to the title, already having witnessed more twists and turns than the very best Agatha Christie novel, produced another major surprise just forty-eight hours later. Clough's side, in a buoyant mood after their defeat of Leeds, crashed right back down to earth when they were beaten 1-0 at home by Newcastle United. To make matters worse, McFarland required stitches after a clash of heads with United's Tommy Gibb. To his credit, he returned to the field after the incident, bravely completing the ninety minutes and the next two games - a 0-0 draw against West Bromwich Albion and a 4-0 thrashing of Sheffield United - with the wound protected by a distinctively large white bandage. . . It was certainly a case of the captain leading his side by example.

An easy 3-0 win over Huddersfield Town kept the Rams in 1st place, but they again tested their supporters' nerves by slipping to defeat at Manchester City in front of a massive Maine Road crowd of 55,023. Goals from Rodney Marsh and Francis Lee gave the Mancunians a 2-0 success and, in their last fixture, enabled them to replace County at the top of the standings which, at the final whistle, read as follows:

	GP	W	D	L	GF	GA	PTS
Manchester City	42	23	11	8	77	45	57
Liverpool	40	24	8	8	64	29	56
Derby County	**41**	**23**	**8**	**8**	**68**	**33**	**56**
Leeds United	40	23	9	8	70	29	55

Before the Rams could turn their thoughts to their final league fixture, the second leg of the Texaco Cup final against Airdrieonians had to be played at the Baseball Ground, the teams having drawn 0-0 in Scotland back in January. In naming his side for the April 26th midweek game, Clough had both injury problems and international call ups to consider. With Webster already ruled out after the defeat in Manchester, the central pairing of McFarland and Todd were also both carrying injuries and deemed to be unfit. The duo, with one eye on the potentially title-deciding game with Liverpool, were also subsequently withdrawn from the England squad to face West Germany in the quarter-final of the European Championships - that contest taking place two days before the May 1st clash with the Merseyside club. Additionally, O'Hare and Gemmill were in the Scotland squad to face Peru in a friendly game. Clough, rather than withdraw all four of his players, decided to allow the pair to represent their country at Hampden Park. The Final itself turned out to be a physical encounter, the Scottish side deciding that an aggressive approach was the best way to deal with

**Roger Davies scored on his senior
debut versus Airdrieonians, 26th April 1972.**

the threat of the County attack. Hinton opened the scoring with a 40th minute penalty, and then after 51 minutes Roger Davies on his senior debut headed the Rams into a two goal lead. Although the visitors pulled one back late on, County were by far the more creative side and, after the Watney Cup triumph, added another piece of silverware to the club's trophy cabinet.

With Webster's injury still preventing him from returning to the line up against Liverpool, Clough sprang a major surprise by naming sixteen year old Steve Powell at right back, the former Bemrose pupil having joined the club on schoolboy terms two years earlier. Although the youngster had played in a couple of league matches earlier in the season, it was a remarkably brave decision to select such an inexperienced performer for such an important game. Powell, whose father Tommy had made 406 Rams appearances between 1948 and 1961, rose to the challenge magnificently and throughout displayed a maturity well beyond his tender years. With so much at sake for both sides, it was never going to be a contest that was full of goals. The outcome was decided in the 62nd minute when McGovern netted the only strike with a shot from the edge of the penalty box. Given that the young midfielder had gifted Arsenal their all-important goal in the FA Cup, it was fitting that he should make amends with such a vital strike in the championship run in. The two points gave Derby a total of fifty-eight and temporary 1st place. Their opponents and Leeds United each still had a game to play however and both could, dependent upon results, still emerge as the champions. The mathematics were such that Leeds needed only to draw their match at Wolverhampton Wanderers to take the title on goal average. Liverpool meanwhile, if they won their remaining game at Arsenal, could finish a point ahead of the field. Both contests were scheduled for Monday May 8th, with a further consideration being that they came just forty-

Steve Powell signs as a schoolboy.

eight hours after the FA Cup final between Leeds and Arsenal. The Rams management duo were in no mood to sit around and wait for their challengers to complete their campaigns. Although McFarland and Todd travelled to London to report for the next England fixture, the remainder of the squad flew with Taylor to enjoy the sunshine of Calla Millor in Majorca. It was certainly a well deserved reward after a season which, with the Texaco competition, had seen them play a massive total of fifty-seven games. Clough decided to enjoy a quieter family break with his wife, children and parents, and headed of to Tresco in the Scilly Isles.

Although Leeds, having beaten Arsenal 1-0 in the Cup Final, remained favourites to clinch the title, Revie decided to leave nothing to chance. His players became the first for many seasons not to enjoy a Saturday night Cup winners' banquet, the traditional chance to unwind after the Wembley game and the media-intrusive build-up of the week before. So instead of relaxing as a group, the United squad found themselves being whisked back to their hotel for an early night, a decision many later felt was detrimental to their performance against Wolverhampton.

As it transpired, the Yorkshire club's forty-second and final league game proved to be one too many. Their physically and mentally exhausted players were unable to gain the point they required to clinch the "Double", a controversial contest ending 2-1 in favour of the home side in front of a bumper Molineux crowd of 53,379. Meanwhile, two hours South at Highbury, the game between Arsenal and Liverpool kicked off with the Merseysiders needing both points to finish at the top of the table. Although they had a late "goal" disallowed for offside, they were in the end easily held by a Gunners team determined to make up for their Wembley defeat. It was therefore the Rams who emerged as Champions for the first time in their history. As the results filtered around the globe, the celebrations started in earnest. While Clough enjoyed drinks with his family in Tresco, the scenes in Spain were much more raucous; the players' champagne party undoubtedly being funded by Taylor's discovery on the Monday morning that County remained at 8/1 with the bookmakers to stay ahead of their two rivals.

Several Northern journalists suggested that it was a title won by default, the basis of their argument largely being made around the fact that Leeds had gone so close despite having had to play, following hooliganism, their first four "home" games away from Elland Road, and that they had been required to face Wolverhampton so soon after the Cup Final. That said, as Clough vociferously argued, the season was decided over forty-two games and in losing just eight in total, his side had lost one less than both Leeds and Liverpool.

Remarkably, the Championship was won using just sixteen players, six of whom played at least forty league games; Boulton, and Hector being ever-presents. To win the League with such a small squad was testament indeed to their resilience, as a number played for long periods with injuries that certainly would have benefited from rest. The basis for the triumph was the defensive prowess. The Rams kept twenty-three clean sheets and conceded thirty-three goals in all, with just ten being given up at the Baseball Ground. Attacking wise, the white-booted Hinton finished up as the top scorer, although his total of fifteen included eight penalties. In open play O'Hare had his best season in a Rams shirt and netted a thirteen for the third consecutive season, one of his best being his superb chip in the 3-0 defeat of Leicester City.

Superb strike from John O'Hare v Leicester, 18th March 1972.

All in all it was a magnificent season, witnessed by an average crowd of above thirty-three thousand, a remarkable figure considering the uncertainty that still surrounded the town's biggest employer Rolls Royce. As the celebrations engulfed the entire county, the reality of what was ahead sunk in. In a little more than four months, the Rams would be facing the best sides in Europe. It was a tantalising prospect. . .

The Directors celebrate with champagne whilst fans could enjoy their favourite tipple in a special edition tankard (below).

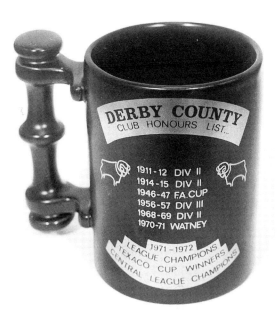

Above: The Championship-winning squad with their trophies, and below, celebrating later England call-ups with assistant manager Peter Taylor.

Above: A young fan is treated to a closer look at the championship trophy, and below, John McGovern, scorer of the vital goal against Liverpool.

APPEARANCES 1971-72

PLAYER	LEAGUE		FA CUP		LGE CUP	OTHERS *		TOTAL	
BOULTON	42		5		2	8		57	
WEBSTER	38		5		2	5		50	
ROBSON	41		5		2	6		54	
McGOVERN	39	(1)	5		1	6		51	(1)
HENNESSEY	17	(1)	0	(1)	0	8		25	(2)
TODD	40		5		2	6		53	
GEMMILL	40		5		2	3		50	
WIGNALL	10	(1)	0		2	3		15	(1)
O'HARE	40		5		2	5		52	
HECTOR	42		5		2	6		55	
HINTON	38		5		2	8		53	
McFARLAND	38		5		2	2		47	
DURBAN	31		5		1	4		41	
POWELL	2	(1)	0	(1)	0	2		4	(2)
WALKER	3	(3)	0		0	2	(2)	5	(5)
BAILEY	1		0		0	2	(1)	3	(1)
DANIEL	0		0		0	5		5	
BUTLIN	0		0		0	3		3	
BOURNE	0		0		0	1		1	
DAVIES	0		0		0	1		1	
LEWIS	0		0		0	1		1	
PARRY	0		0		0	1		1	
TOTAL	**42**		**5**		**2**	**8**		**57**	

* Texaco Cup
N.B. Substitute appearances in brackets

SCORERS 1971-72

HINTON	15	2	0	3	20
O'HARE	13	0	0	4	17
HECTOR	12	3	0	2	17
DURBAN	6	4	0	1	11
WIGNALL	5	0	0	1	6
McFARLAND	4	0	0	0	4
McGOVERN	3	0	0	1	4
ROBSON	2	1	0	1	4
GEMMILL	3	0	0	0	3
TODD	2	0	0	1	3
WALKER	1	0	0	2	3
WEBSTER	1	0	0	0	1
BUTLIN	0	0	0	1	1
DAVIES	0	0	0	1	1
OWN GOALS	2	0	0	0	2
TOTAL	**69**	**10**	**0**	**18**	**97**

KEY MATCHES OF 1971/72

Spoils shared in first day thriller...

14th August 1971, Football League DivisionOne

DERBY COUNTY 2 MANCHESTER UNITED 2

This was a magnificent opening to the new season. Both teams played some very attractive football with Clough's side coming back from two goals down to gain a point. The crowd of 35,386, many of whom were caught in the pre-game thunderstorm, had a great afternoon's entertainment, the contest continuing a superb sequence of matches between the pair at the Baseball Ground, the previous installment having been the 4-4 Boxing Day draw of eight months earlier.

And just like the December 1970 fixture, the Rams defence, which was lacking the injured Roy McFarland, found the corner kicks of Bobby Charlton too much for them. In the sixteenth minute, the veteran United star found Brian Kidd at the far post and his header across the front of the goal was bundled home by Denis Law. Ten minutes later, Charlton did it again; this time, although his right wing corner was missed by both Law and Terry Hennessey, it was steered in by Alan Gowling.

The second half was a complete turnaround, County attacked from the outset and reduced their deficit within the first five minutes. Alan Hinton floated over a 50th minute centre and after Frank Wignall had challenged Alex Stepney, the ball ran loose to Kevin Hector who gleefully stabbed it into the open net. In the immediate aftermath, although the United goalkeeper remained on the turf, the referee had no hesitation in awarding the goal. On the hour mark, the Rams equalised when John O'Hare headed a Hinton cross on to the bar, and Wignall nipped in to head the rebound past Stepney from close range. The home side continued to press forward, but United decided that a point was good enough and pulled most of their side back behind the ball. On reflection, a draw was just about the fairest result both teams having played an equal role in an enthralling game.

DERBY COUNTY: BOULTON, WEBSTER, ROBSON, McGOVERN, HENNESSEY, TODD, GEMMILL, WIGNALL, O'HARE, HECTOR, HINTON. SUBSTITUTE: DURBAN.

MANCHESTER UNITED: STEPNEY, O'NEIL, DUNNE, GOWLING, JAMES, SADLER, MORGAN, KIDD, CHARLTON, LAW, BEST. SUBSTITUTE: ASTON.

ATTENDANCE: 35,386
REFEREE: MR PUGH

County exit League Cup after Lorimer brace...

27th September 1971, Football League Cup 2nd Round Replay

LEEDS UNITED 2 DERBY COUNTY O

After eleven unbeaten games, the Rams were defeated at Elland Road in their League Cup replay, the teams having fought out a scoreless draw in Derby almost three weeks earlier. This proved to be a magnificent contest with both attacks creating numerous scoring opportunities. As it transpired though, it was the home side who progressed to face West Ham United, thanks largely to their Scottish winger Peter "Lash" Lorimer who netted a well taken goal in either half.

And yet it was the visitors who started the strongest: Kevin Hector twice went close to scoring early on, his seventh minute effort being saved by Gary Sprake and a later chance being blocked by a defender's dive. Leeds then lost Billy Bremner after twenty-three minutes, the combative midfielder coming out worse and requiring five stitches in his shin after a clash with fellow Scot Archie Gemmill. They reorganised themselves quickly however and took the lead just nine minutes after the substitution. Although a Lorimer's free kick was twice blocked by the Rams defensive wall, it was eventually crossed into the path of full back Paul Reaney who nodded it across the goal for the kick taker to score with a firm eight yard shot. The second and decisive strike came in the sixty-third minute. United won another free kick after Roy McFarland had been adjudged to have fouled Paul Madeley, and second time around Lorimer avoided the wall, his ferocious free kick going past Colin Boulton to seal the victory.

The Rams created good chances of their own though to get on the scoresheet. Sprake saved well from both Gemmill and Hector in the second half, and a fine shot from John Robson flew to safety after being deflected off Norman Hunter. Although it was the strikes of Lorimer which saw Leeds go through, their best player was undoubtedly midfielder John Giles who seemed to be at the heart of everything of note that his side produced.

LEEDS UNITED: SPRAKE, REANEY, COOPER, BREMNER, CHARLTON, HUNTER, LORIMER, YORATH, BELFITT, GILES, MADELEY. SUBSTITUTE: MANN FOR BREMNER (23).

DERBY COUNTY: BOULTON, WEBSTER, ROBSON, TODD, McFARLAND, GEMMILL, McGOVERN, WIGNALL, O'HARE, HECTOR, HINTON. SUBSTITUTE: DANIEL.

ATTENDANCE: 29,132
REFEREE: MR HOMEWOOD

Quick start sets up Rams victory...

23rd October 1971, Football League Division One

DERBY COUNTY 2 ARSENAL 1

After their first league defeat of the season at Old Trafford, the Rams bounced back in style at the Baseball Ground, their midfield dominating the contest from the outset, with Archie Gemmill in particular having a marvellous game. Strangely however, despite their obvious superiority, Clough's side found themselves almost hanging on in the final minutes, a consequence of their inability to convert more of the good chances that they created.

The game started at an incredible pace and County could have scored in the first minute, Kevin Hector having a neat header cleared off the line by Sammy Nelson. The first goal came nine minutes later when an exchange of passes between Gemmill and Roy McFarland allowed the Scottish international to hit a low cross into the penalty area; John O'Hare, despite the attention of Nelson, sweeping a sweet effort past Wilson and into the visitors' net. Despite their continued pressure on the Arsenal goal, the Rams conceded a soft equaliser. In a rare attack, the Gunners forced a corner and from George Armstrong's kick George Graham headed home after Colin Boulton had missed the winger's centre.

What turned out to be the winning goal came on the stroke of half time. Hector's pace took him into the eighteen yard area where he was fouled by Pat Rice, the referee giving a penalty which Alan Hinton easily struck past Wilson. After the interval Nelson again cleared the ball off the line, his second block preventing Alan Durban from extending the Rams advantage. Steve Powell came on for his league debut with twenty-two minutes to play, the sixteen year old replacing the injured Ron Webster. The change upset Derby's rhythm, but although the visitors finished strongly and forced a series of corners, they found McFarland in commanding form and as a result County maintained their lead until the final whistle.

DERBY COUNTY: BOULTON, WEBSTER, ROBSON, TODD, McFARLAND, McGOVERN, GEMMILL, DURBAN, O'HARE, HECTOR, HINTON. SUBSTITUTE: POWELL FOR WEBSTER (68).

ARSENAL: WILSON, RICE, NELSON, KELLY, McLINTOCK, ROBERTS, ARMSTRONG, GEORGE, RADFORD, KENNEDY, GRAHAM. SUBSTITUTE: SIMPSON FOR KELLY (75).

ATTENDANCE: 36,480
REFEREE: MR HALL

BRILLIANT! John O'Hare opens the scoring against Arsenal.

Brilliant County outclass City...

4th December 1971, Football League Division One

DERBY COUNTY 3 MANCHESTER CITY 1

The Rams hit back from their defeat at Huddersfield Town with a superb performance, a display which at times left the multi-talented City side simply chasing shadows. The Blues defence struggled all afternoon with the speed and accuracy of Alan Hinton, the County wide man scoring the first goal and brilliantly creating two more in as many minutes.

Clough's team attacked from the outset and netted their first marker in the twenty-third minute. Ian Mellor fouled John McGovern in the penalty area, and Hinton calmly slotted his tenth spot kick of the campaign into the corner of the net. It was a goal which signalled the start of a marvellous spell of attacking football, the Rams' approach play being so creative that it was a surprise that City kept them at bay for thirteen minutes. In the thirty-sixth minute, the crowd witnessed a strike of the rarest quality, scored by the unlikeliest of marksmen in Ron Webster. Midfielder Alan Durban sent Hinton scurrying down the wing with a great pass, the head-high centre which followed being perfectly headed past Joe Corrigan by the onrushing full back. For Webster, who had galloped the length of the pitch to get into a scoring position, it was just the sixth goal of his senior career, his last having been way back in the October 1966 5-1 demolition of Milwall.

Before the fans in the main stand had settled back in their seats, it was 3-0. Hinton again escaped the clutches of the visitors back four, this time he centred perfectly for Durban to score his first goal of the season. Still the Rams pressed forward and John O'Hare soon forced Corrigan into making a brilliant reflex save. The visitors lone consolation strike, in the sixty-fifth minute, also came from the penalty spot. John Robson's match-long tussle with Mike Summerbee saw the City winger go down, and the contest's other eighteen yard expert, Francis Lee, fired his effort past Colin Boulton. Although the referee cautioned five players, only the bookings of Lee and Summerbee were for dangerous tackles; such was the Rams domination, it was never an over-physical game.

DERBY COUNTY: BOULTON, WEBSTER, ROBSON, TODD, McFARLAND, McGOVERN, DURBAN, GEMMILL, O'HARE, HECTOR, HINTON. SUBSTITUTE: HENNESSEY.

MANCHESTER CITY: CORRIGAN, BOOK, DONACHIE, DOYLE, BOOTH, OAKES, SUMMERBEE, BELL, DAVIES, LEE, MELLOR. SUBSTITUTE: TOWERS.

ATTENDANCE: 35,384
REFEREE: MR JOHNSON

Derby thrash local rivals...

19th February 1972, Football League Division One

DERBY COUNTY 4 NOTTINGHAM FOREST 0

The Rams won this clash with their nearest rivals with ease, almost the entire game being played in the visitors' half of the pitch. From the kick off, County controlled every aspect of the proceedings with John McGovern and Archie Gemmill in particular making light of the very heavy playing surface.

Although the Rams opening goal did not come until the thirty-fourth minute, once ahead they never ever looked like surrendering their lead. Then, Kevin Hector hit a superbly weighted pass to Alan Hinton, who in turn chipped the ball beyond Jim Barron and into the net. Immediately afterwards, John Winfield was booked for a crude lunge on Ron Webster, with only the swift intervention of the referee preventing an ugly melee developing between several players. It was 2-0 seven minutes before half time, McGovern again parted the defence and John O'Hare slipped his effort past the Forest goalkeeper.

After the restart, Hinton netted his second when his sharp free kick was fumbled into the net by Barron - the visitors' shot stopper, by his own standards, having a very poor game indeed. Hinton missed the chance of a hat trick when he hit a post, but Hector completed the thrashing when he collected a wild clearance and aimed a well-hit shot into the corner of the net. It gave Clough's side the seasonal double over Forest, their frustration at being beaten at Highbury the previous week being well and truly eased in the best possible way.

Manchester City destroyer Alan Hinton.

DERBY COUNTY: BOULTON, WEBSTER, ROBSON, DURBAN, McFARLAND, TODD, McGOVERN, GEMMILL, O'HARE, HECTOR, HINTON. SUBSTITUTE: HENNESSEY.

NOTTINGHAM FOREST: BARRON, GEMMELL, WINFIELD, CHAPMAN, HINDLEY, COTTAM, LYONS, O'NEIL, CORMACK, RICHARDSON, MOORE. SUBSTITUTE: McINTOSH.

ATTENDANCE: 31,801
REFEREE: MR MATTHEWSON

Late goal gives Rams extra point...

11th March 1972, Football League Division One

TOTTENHAM HOTSPUR 0 DERBY COUNTY 1

The Rams maintained their challenge for the championship with a goal in the closing minutes. It was a result which marked their first victory at White Hart Lane since the 1933/34 season when George Jobey's side won 2-1 thanks to markers from Jack Bowers and Dally Duncan.

Throughout the contest it was clear that Clough's team would be perfectly happy to return home with a point; they created little and their goal came from the penalty spot after both defences had dominated the opposition attack. In the first half, although Martin Chivers looked dangerous when he ran at the Rams defence, Tottenham's best chance came when both Martin Peters and Roger Morgan both had shots blocked by defenders in the space of a few seconds. The Rams best forward was Kevin Hector who almost scored when he forced Pat Jennings to save well from an Alan Hinton cross. The deciding goal came in the eighty-seventh minute. A mix up between Jennings and defender Mike England gave Hector an opportunity, albeit from a narrow angle, and the Spurs goalkeeper pulled the Rams man down as was preparing to shoot. Hinton, successful with all his previous nine penalties of the campaign, maintained his record when his spot kick went just inside the right hand post.

With Roy McFarland and Colin Todd in superb form, the Rams ultimately benefited from allowing the home side so few chances. The victory put County in an ideal frame of mind for their FA Cup second replay against Arsenal which was scheduled for forty-eight hours later. For Tottenham meanwhile, it was their first defeat in six games, their defensive prowess having restricted their five opponents prior to the Rams to just one goal between them.

TOTTENHAM HOTSPUR: JENNINGS, EVANS, KNOWLES, HOLDER, ENGLAND, BEAL, GILZEAN, PERRYMAN, CHIVERS, PETERS, MORGAN. SUBSTITUTE: PEARCE.

DERBY COUNTY: BOULTON, WEBSTER, ROBSON, HENNESSEY, McFARLAND, TODD, McGOVERN, GEMMILL, O'HARE, HECTOR, HINTON. SUBSTITUTE: DANIEL.

ATTENDANCE: 36,310
REFEREE: MR MORRISSEY

Magical Marsh too good for frail Rams...

22nd April 1972, Football League Division One

MANCHESTER CITY 2 DERBY COUNTY 0

County's hopes of emerging as the First Division champions took a major jolt as they were swept aside by a rampant City side who were inspired by their recent £200,000 signing Rodney Marsh. The former Queens Park Rangers striker scored the first goal and played a major role in the second, no doubt leaving Brian Clough to wonder what might have been, Marsh having arrived in Manchester in the same week as the Rams manager had made his abortive attempt to sign Ian Storey Moore from Nottingham Forest.

Although County might argue that they were unlucky, particularly after losing right back Ron Webster with a knee injury in the thirty-fifth minute, their midfield trio of Alan Durban, John McGovern and Archie Gemmill were always in reality second best. As a consequence City could have scored quite a few more had their finishing been as sharp as their approach play. Colin Bell missed a couple of easy first half chances, and it was left to Marsh to open the scoring in the twenty-fifth minute, a superb run at the Rams defence left Roy McFarland and John Robson in his wake and his low cross shot went beyond Colin Boulton and into the corner of the net.

Derby's best two chances came soon after the interval. Firstly, Kevin Hector lost control with just Joe Corrigan to beat, and then John O'Hare, under pressure from Bell, hit a post after a great pass from Durban. It proved to be a brief resistence, and City sealed the contest in the sixty-seventh minute when Marsh was flattened by Terry Hennessey and Francis Lee blasted home the resulting penalty kick. It was the home side's last game of the season and the two points took them to the top of the table with fifty-seven points. As the 55,000-plus Maine Road crowd acknowledged their heroes, a bruised and battered looking Rams team were left to concentrate on their two remaining fixtures, the Texaco Cup final against Airdrieonians and a crucially important final game showdown with fellow title contenders Liverpool.

**John O'Hare, under pressure from Colin Bell,
hits the post at Maine Road.**

MANCHESTER CITY: CORRIGAN, BOOK, DONACHIE, DOYLE, BOOTH, JEFFERIES, LEE, BELL, SUMMERBEE, MARSH, TOWERS. SUBSTITUTE: HILL.

DERBY COUNTY: BOULTON, WEBSTER, ROBSON, DURBAN, McFARLAND, TODD, McGOVERN, GEMMILL, O'HARE, HECTOR, HINTON. SUBSTITUTE: HENNESSEY FOR WEBSTER (35).

ATTENDANCE: 55,023
REFEREE: MR BURTENSHAW

McGovern gives Rams chance of title...

1st May 1972, Football League Division One

DERBY COUNTY 1 LIVERPOOL 0

The Rams season came down to their last game, the league standings before the kick off confirming that a victory over the Merseyside club would give them a theoretical chance of winning the championship for the first time in their history. With Ron Webster still injured, Clough sprang a major surprise by naming sixteen year old Steve Powell at right back, a decision which produced gasps of astonishment from a Monday evening crowd of nearly 40,000 who had crammed into the sunswept Baseball Ground.

The visitors arrived with an impressive sequence of results behind them, they had taken twenty-eight points out of the previous thirty, and had not been beaten since Leicester City had recorded a 1-0 success against them on January 8th. The famous "Red Brick Wall" defence had also been almost impregnable, just three goals having been conceded since that reverse at Filbert Street. It was obvious then that this was never going to be a high scoring encounter, the likelihood being that one goal would decide the outcome.

What followed was a tense contest dominated by the central defensive pairings of Roy McFarland and Colin Todd for the Rams,

Liverpool's Tommy Smith outjumps John O'Hare.

and the equally impressive Larry Lloyd and Tommy Smith for the visitors. Kevin Hector went closest to scoring in the first half, his header from an Alan Durban flick being tipped to safety via the crossbar by Ray Clemence, who had earlier been booked for a foul on the Rams striker. The only strike came in the sixty-third minute, Archie Gemmill ran across the edge of the Liverpool penalty area and slipped the ball towards Durban, the Welsh international in turn leaving the ball for John McGovern to strike it past Clemence, falling backwards as he did so.

Although the Liverpool substitute John McLaughlin forced Colin Boulton into making a fine save, the Rams defence held on to secure the vital two points. With the results seven nights later going their way, Clough's side emerged as the First Division champions with a total of fifty-eight points. The celebrations which greeted the news were remarkable, supporters across the county taking to the streets to enjoy a marvellous moment in the history of their club.

DERBY COUNTY: BOULTON, POWELL, ROBSON, DURBAN, McFARLAND, TODD, McGOVERN, GEMMILL, O'HARE, HECTOR, HINTON. SUBSTITUTE: HENNESSEY.

LIVERPOOL: CLEMENCE, LAWLER, LINDSAY, SMITH, LLOYD, HUGHES, KEEGAN, HALL, HEIGHWAY, TOSHACK, CALLAGHAN. SUBSTITUTE: McLAUGHLIN FOR HEIGHWAY (72).

ATTENDANCE: 39,159
REFEREE: MR THOMAS

7.

FROM ANFIELD
TO ZELJEZNICAR
(1972/73)

IN PREPARATION FOR THE Rams' involvement in the European Cup, further improvements were made to the Baseball Ground over the summer of 1972. With games in the competition being televised in colour at home and abroad, over £50,000 was spent on erecting new, pylon-mounted floodlights. In addition, and following similar work at the Osmaston End of the ground, seats were installed in the middle tier of the Normanton Stand, a move which reduced the overall theoretical capacity to around 38,500. Unfortunately as the work continued, the club despite again not being involved in the transfer market, still managed to create more than its fair share of the pre-season headlines.

At the beginning of August, the Management Committee of the Football League levied a fine of £5,000 on the club for a breach of the transfer regulations. It was the outcome of the Ian Storey Moore affair, and significantly came shortly after Clough had excused his side from the annual pre-season Charity Shield contest in favour of a friendly game against AOD of The Hague. If that was not unsettling enough Clough, seemingly more determined than ever to air his views, then demanded the right to have freedom of speech on any topic. It was almost as though he saw the Championship success as an emboldenment of his managerial style. Coming so soon after his threatened move to Coventry City, it again put him at odds with the Board. The pressure on Longson had already been increased by a verbal instruction from the authorities to control his manager's actions, plus the fact that Jack Kirkland, a long term critic of Clough, was next in line to be given a seat on the Board. As a consequence, even the Chairman was now tiring of Clough's unpredictable actions and announcements. Their relationship, which a few years before had almost been akin to that of a father and son, became so strained that the pair were by now hardly on speaking terms. It seemed to be only a matter of time before a day of reckoning would arrive. In the meantime, whilst an uneasy truce existed, Clough continued to use his weekly column in the Sunday Express to voice his opinions on a wide range of issues, being particularly critical of the England national team and its preparations for major tournaments.

The league season commenced with a hard fought 1-1 draw at Southampton on August 12th, Alan Hinton netting the Rams goal with a piledriver free kick. Although another point was gleaned at Crystal Palace three days later, the Rams were then defeated 2-1 at home by Chelsea in a rough encounter on August 19th. The referee cautioned four players and several others; Roy McFarland and Colin Todd were lucky to escape with just a telling off for blatant fouls. It was only County's second league defeat at the Baseball Ground in seventeen games, the result of a confidence-lacking display which Clough saw as unacceptable. Both full backs, Ron Webster and John Robson, were dropped from the line up to face Manchester City, teenagers Steve Powell and Alan Lewis coming

**Alan Hinton, Rams scorer against Southampton,
12th August 1972.**

Chelsea,
15th August 1972.

Left: I'M IN CHARGE!
Mr Morrissey lectures
Roy McFarland.

Below: John O'Hare
challenges
Dave Webb.

into the side to replace them. A goal in the 58th minute from Jim Walker secured victory against the Mancunian club, the Rams climbing three places in the table to 12th. Despite that win, a position outside of the top ten was hardly the start expected from the team defending the Championship.Almost immediately however, Clough was presented with an unforeseen opportunity to again strengthen his squad. On the day he had demoted Webster and Robson, Leicester City signed the Orient full back Denis Rofe for £112,000. The deal put in doubt the future of David Nish, City's highly regarded, but unsettled, left back. As the Filbert Street side had also, just days earlier, secured the services of Frank Worthington for £150,000, they seemed certain to want to quickly recoup some of their outlay. Within twenty-four hours Nish was a Derby County player. The fee paid for the classy defender was £225,000, a new British transfer record. It was a reminder of the Rams' glory days of the late Forties, the signings then of Billy Steel and John Morris confirming them as the biggest spending club in the country.

With Nish going straight into the side at left back, it was Robson who found himself surplus to requirements. He realised, just as Willie Carlin had done before him, that sentiment formed only a very minor part of Clough's footballing psychology. Indeed, the player scooped from junior soccer in the North East made only seven more league appearances before being sold to Aston Villa for £90,000. However, with the new defender not eligible for the initial European Cup games, it was November before Robson finally left the Baseball Ground. By then, County had also received £50,000 from Luton Town for Barry Butlin, the reserve team striker having completed a long-term loan with the Second Division side. Not that the signing of Nish made an immediate impact. His debut came in a 1-0 defeat at Norwich City, that loss being followed by another single goal reversal against Everton at Goodison Park. With the Rams ending the first month of the season in a lowly 16th place, the media were quick to refer to Clough's side as the "Fallen Champions", a tag not readily removed by a fortunate win against Liverpool and a 2-1 defeat at bottom-placed West Bromwich Albion.

Four days after the defeat at the Hawthorns, County took their bow in the European Cup. At the time, the format of the competition provided for games to be contested on a home and away, aggregate score, knockout basis - the early rounds being played in the autumn and the quarter-finals onwards being decided the following spring. For a side experiencing competitive matches against overseas opposition for the first time, the Rams' overall performance was nothing short of remarkable. At the Baseball Ground on September 13th, the Yugoslavian champions Zeljeznicar were beaten 2-0, markers from McFarland and Archie Gemmill easing Clough's side to an easy victory. In the return fixture, early goals from Hinton and John O'Hare killed off the game as a contest, County eventually confirming a very comfortable 4-1 aggregate success. After disposing of the Balkan side, Derby were paired with Benfica, the Eusebio-led, Lisbon-based, Portuguese Champions. On the eve of the first leg of the tie at the Baseball Ground on October 25th, Clough decided it was time to give his side a helping hand. Aware that the visitors had a side loaded with skilful performers, he instructed the groundsman to prepare the pitch by watering it thoroughly. . . overnight. It was a ploy that worked perfectly. Twenty-four hours later, the Portuguese players found themselves totally overwhelmed by the heavy conditions and the incredible atmosphere created by a tightly packed crowd of 38,100. After a magnificent display, County were worthy 3-0 victors with McFarland, Kevin Hector and John McGovern all netting first half goals. Two weeks later in Benfica's Stadium of Light, Derby produced a defensive display of the highest possible proportions. With Terry Hennessey having his best ever game for the club, they repelled the home attack for the entire ninety minutes, a performance that produced a 0-0 draw and silenced a crowd of over 75,000. Having remained unbeaten in two games against a side with the pedigree of Benfica, County's quarter-final opponents Spartak Trnava proved to be harder to overcome than might initially have been expected. In Czechoslovakia on March 7th 1973, County slipped to a single goal defeat, and relied on a Baseball Ground brace from Hector two weeks later to overcome what was in essence a very capable side.

The result set up an enthralling semi-final clash with Juventus, the Italian champions and undoubtedly one of the strongest club sides in Europe. Although the Rams were beaten 3-1 in the first leg of the tie in Turin on April 11th, it was not the scoreline as much as the manner of the defeat which incensed Clough and Taylor. As the home side took to falling over at the slightest provocation, the game was reduced to a procession of dubious refereeing decisions. McFarland and Gemmill however went into the official's notebook before half time for innocuous looking challenges, bookings which, as both had been cautioned earlier in the competition, eliminated them from the return contest. Clough's anger erupted at the press

**Eusebio of Benfica, on the day before the
European Cup game at the Baseball Ground.**

conference after the game, his reference to his hosts as "F******
cheating b*******" doing little for Anglo-Italian relations. It was
therefore an understandably subdued Rams party which returned
to the Midlands, their only consolation being that Hector's away
goal meant that the task facing them at the Baseball Ground was
slightly less daunting than it might otherwise have been.

Although, so frustratingly, Clough was without two of his star
performers for the return contest in Derby on April 25th, he was at
least able to welcome back Hinton to the side, the winger returning
after an absence of over a month. With County needing to win by
at least 2-0, the Italians, with the understandable intention of
giving nothing away, packed their defence from the outset. After a
scoreless first half, the Rams had a golden opportunity to take the
lead after fifty-six minutes. After a foul on Hector they were
awarded a penalty, but the normally reliable Hinton, with his lack
of competitive games, put the spot kick well wide. Six minutes later
the Rams' hopes evaporated when Roger Davies was sent off for
head butting. After that, scoring twice against such a robust
defence proved impossible and the game ended scoreless, the Old
Lady of Italian football progressing to meet Ajax in the final

Clough's very public allegations that his side had been unfairly
outmanoeuvred, both on and off the pitch, did not go unchecked.
The Sunday Times newspaper carried out an investigation which
intimated that bribery of the officials had taken place, although a
subsequent UEFA inquiry proved inconclusive, a fact which riles
Clough thirty years after the event. Irrespective of investigations, to
reach the semi-final of Europe's premier club competition at the
first time of asking spoke volumes for the Rams' versatility. Their
home games against Benfica and Juventus were incredible
occasions, almost unimaginable nights of excitement given the
precarious state the club had been in just six years earlier.

Away from the European games, the Rams' domestic season
could at best be described as inconsistent. During the three
months up to December, although they recorded a magnificent,
Hinton-inspired, 5-0 defeat of Arsenal, and a creditable 2-1 success
against high flying Tottenham Hotspur, their defensive prowess
deserted them in other games. Away from the Baseball Ground,
Leeds United put five past them, Manchester City four, and
Manchester United three - all defeats without the sterile County
attack hitting the net. Clough decided to remedy the situation by
introducing reserve team centre forward Davies into the side. The
6' 4" beanpole striker had been signed from Southern League club

Worcester City for £14,000, yet another player purchased on Taylor's recommendation. Davies marked his league debut, against Arsenal, with a goal, and by the middle of December had gained a regular place in the line up, O'Hare dropping back into a midfield role to replace the again increasingly injury-prone Hennessey.

The new formation worked well and during the month of December the Rams were beaten just once in six matches. They ended the year in 6th place, a fair reflection of their improvement being the 3-1 win against Manchester United on Boxing Day, the Mancunian club having easily defeated them with ease at Old Trafford three months earlier. A potentially disastrous half-season situation had been turned around very well, especially as during the autumn months the players were clearly distracted by the deepening off-field crisis involving Clough and the Directors. In Lisbon, Kirkland, by now the main protagonist against the management duo, although still not a Director, announced that he was out to "bury" Clough, a statement amazingly made at the time the side were on the threshold of qualification for the quarter-finals of the game's major club tournament. Longson's subsequent attempt to appease his fellow businessman with a directorship, whilst seeming a credible action, merely gave Kirkland an official position from which to continue his tirade of criticism against both men.

The New Year saw the Rams open their FA Cup campaign with a potentially tricky 3rd Round contest at Fourth Division Peterborough United. In a scrappy game, Davies netted the only goal in the 36 minute. The victory set up a home tie with Tottenham Hotspur on February 3rd, Davies again scoring County's marker in an exciting 1-1 draw. The replay at White Hart Lane four days later was a remarkable affair. In one of the FA Cup's greatest ever fightbacks, Clough's side recovered from 3-1 behind, to win 5-3 after extra time. Davies was again the Rams' saviour, his hat trick inspiring the late rally which saw them net four goals in thirty minutes. The media heaped praise on the new striker, a justified reaction as the trio took his tally to seven in six games since the turn of the year - a fantastic return for a player still making his way in the professional ranks.

Queens Park Rangers were the Rams 5th Round opponents, the London side visiting the Baseball Ground on February 4th. After a four goal blast in the first thirty-two minutes, the outcome was beyond doubt, Derby eventually coasting into the quarter finals on a 4-2 scoreline with Hector this time emerging as the hat trick hero.

**Tottenham's Pat Jennings saves a Roger Davies
header, 3rd February 1973.**

**Terry Hennessey passes out instructions before extra
time in the Tottenham FA Cup replay, 7th February 1973.**

With their supporters again beginning to dream of the Twin Towers of Wembley, the Rams were then drawn against the one side they wanted to avoid - the current Cup holders, and Clough's perennial bogey team, Leeds United. Again, the almost inevitable happened. Two weeks after losing 3-2 to the Yorkshire side in a physical league encounter, County again came off second best in the Cup tie. With United's Norman "bite yer legs" Hunter in magnificent form, the game was decided when Peter Lorimer netted the only goal on the half hour. It ended another memorable run in the competition, something the club had not been able to boast for a long time prior to Clough's arrival. The Rams' league form during the month of February was poor. Although Southampton were easily beaten 4-0 at the Baseball Ground, defeats against Birmingham City, Stoke City and Newcastle United saw them end the month, partially due to other results going their way, still in 6th position. The 2-0 defeat at St Andrews also marked the league debut of twenty-seven year old Tony Parry, the £3,000 signing from Hartlepool United coming into the side to replace the injured Todd. The Burton upon Trent-born player had joined County in unusual circumstances, Clough having been persuaded to purchase him to help stave off a financial crisis at his former club.

Sadly however, as one County player experienced First Division football for the first time, another, Terry Hennessey, faced an uncertain future. The Welsh international suffered another reoccurrence of the knee and achilles tendon injuries that had plagued his entire Baseball Ground career, and after an extended spell on the treatment table, was forced to announce his retirement from the game a year later. Other injury concerns disrupted Clough's selections throughout March, and as a consequence County were beaten 3-1 at Sheffield United after gaining a point in a poor 0-0 draw at Leicester City. On a brighter note, on the last day of the month the Rams completed the "double" over title chasing Arsenal, a goal from Steve Powell giving them a well deserved 1-0 victory.

Despite the disappointment of their exit from the European Cup, Clough's side finished the domestic campaign very strongly. The extended FA Cup run, and subsequent fixture rescheduling, meant that all of the last four league fixtures were played at home. With the pressure of defending the championship now removed, County produced some of their most attractive football of the season. Although they dropped a point against West Ham United, the trio of Everton, Ipswich Town and Wolverhampton Wanderers were all dispatched on the back of three-goal Rams performances. The run-in also witnessed the appearance of another league debutant, nineteen year old Graham Moseley coming in against Tottenham and West Ham to replace the suspended Boulton. The youngster had been signed, on Taylor's recommendation, from Blackburn Rovers after a series of impressive displays in the Lancashire side's reserve team. The hat trick of late victories saw the Rams end the season in 7th spot; frustratingly, just outside of a UEFA Cup qualification place.

It had been another long season, the Rams in all playing fifty-eight competitive fixtures. Although they never looked like defending the Championship, eventually won by Liverpool, it was a campaign to be long remembered for their magnificent displays in the European Cup. The emergence of Davies had additionally been a major bonus, the lanky target man having netted a total of thirteen goals in just twenty-six full appearances, worthy enough for third place in the scoring charts; behind Hector with a total of twenty-three and Hinton with fifteen. Significantly however, when Davies was signed, the £14,000 fee had done little to repair the fragile relationship between the management duo and the Board. Taylor, who had spotted the potential of the Worcester City striker, was forced to justify the fee to the Directors, several of whom thought the amount was excessive. It was an incident which lingered in the assistant manager's mind, and eventually convinced him that, despite whatever the team achieved on the pitch, his and Clough's future ultimately lay far away from the Baseball Ground.

In the immediate close season another announcement, seemingly insignificant at the time it was made, was to ultimately disturb the very foundations of the empire that Clough had built. London Weekend Television revealed that Jimmy Hill was leaving their football programme to front the BBC's coverage of the game. Obviously, his departure left a job vacancy that needed to be filled, ideally by a good communicator who could express his views on a wide range of footballing issues.

APPEARANCES 1972-73

PLAYER	LEAGUE		FA CUP		LGE CUP		OTHERS*		TOTAL	
BOULTON	40		5		3		8		56	
WEBSTER	26		4		0		4		34	
ROBSON	10		0		1		3		14	
DURBAN	11	(7)	1		1	(1)	2		15	(9)
McFARLAND	38		5		3		7		53	
TODD	41		5		3		8		57	
McGOVERN	39		5		3		8		55	
GEMMILL	34		5		3		7		49	
O'HARE	34		5		3		8		50	
HECTOR	41		5		3		8		57	
HINTON	27		1		3		6		37	
HENNESSEY	21		2	(1)	1		4		28	(1)
WALKER	5		0		0		0		5	
POWELL	22		1		3		4		30	
LEWIS	2		0		0		0		2	
NISH	34		5		3		4		46	
DANIEL	9		1		0		4		14	
DAVIES	19	(1)	5		0		2		26	(1)
BUTLIN	1		0		0		0		1	
SIMS	2	(1)	0		0		0	(1)	2	(2)
PARRY	4	(2)	0		0		0		4	(2)
MOSELEY	2		0		0		0		2	
TOTAL	**42**		**5**		**3**		**8**		**58**	

*European Cup
N.B. Substitute appearances in brackets

SCORERS 1972-73

HECTOR	14	5	0	4	23
HINTON	13	0	1	1	15
DAVIES	7	6	0	0	13
McFARLAND	5	0	0	2	7
O'HARE	4	0	0	1	5
GEMMILL	3	0	0	1	4
HENNESSEY	2	0	1	0	3
McGOVERN	1	0	1	1	3
POWELL	2	0	0	0	2
NISH	1	0	0	0	1
WALKER	1	0	0	0	1
DURBAN	1	0	0	0	1
TODD	1	0	0	0	1
OWN GOALS	1	0	0	0	1
TOTAL	**56**	**11**	**3**	**10**	**80**

KEY MATCHES OF 1971/72

Rams benefit from Lane's error...

2nd September 1972, Football League Division One

DERBY COUNTY 2 LIVERPOOL 1

County took to the field with David Nish making his home debut and Alan Hinton returning after a four game injury absence. Liverpool, on Bill Shankly's fifty-eighth birthday, gave a league debut to Frankie Lane, the former Tranmere Rover's shot stopper coming in to replace Ray Clemence. With both sides looking to recover after midweek defeats, the outcome of this contest hinged on a crucial two minute spell in the second half.

The Reds had by far the better of the opening exchanges and opened the scoring after seventeen minutes. Kevin Keegan, who had looked impressive from the outset, pushed the ball into the penalty area and John Toshack, after easily slipping by Steve Powell, drove his effort past Colin Boulton. Although the interval arrived with no addition to the scoreline, Shankly's team opened the second half seemingly determined to quickly increase their advantage. They forced four successive corners before, in the fifty-second minute, Steve Heighway crossed perfectly for Toshack. The Welsh international's header looked goalbound, but Boulton dived across to make a brilliant reflex save. Almost immediately, Hinton arched over a swerving cross to the Liverpool far post, the unfortunate Lane stepping back over his line as he caught the ball under a minimal challenge from Kevin Hector. The Rams were therefore level instead of being 2-0 behind, a stroke of luck which inspired them to push forward in search of the winning goal.

Terry Hennessey and John McGovern began to control the midfield area, and Lane partially redeemed himself with a good save from Archie Gemmill. With just three minutes remaining Nish exchanged passes with Gemmill and steered the ball into the path of John O'Hare who rolled it in as the defence converged on him. The two points lifted County to 13th place, whilst a second consecutive defeat for the Merseysiders saw them drop to 6th.

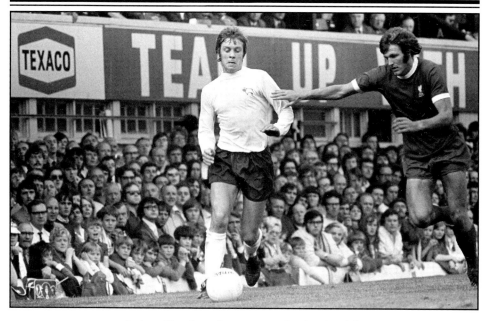

**John Toshack moves in to tackle
David Nish.**

**DERBY COUNTY: BOULTON, POWELL, NISH, HENNESSEY,
McFARLAND, TODD, McGOVERN, GEMMILL, O'HARE,
HECTOR, HINTON. SUBSTITUTE: DURBAN.**

**LIVERPOOL: LANE, LAWLER, HUGHES, SMITH, LLOYD,
CORMACK, KEEGAN, HALL, HEIGHWAY, TOSHACK,
CALLAGHAN. SUBSTITUTE: LINDSAY.**

ATTENDANCE: 32,524
REFEREE: MR GOW

"Magical" Rams stun Benfica...

25th October 1972, European Cup - 2nd Round First Leg

DERBY COUNTY 3 BENFICA 0

The mighty Benfica, five-time finalists and twice winners of the European Cup, were swept aside by a magnificent first half performance from an inspired Rams side. The Portuguese defence simply had no answer to the guile of the County attack, within which Kevin Hector was outstanding. At the other end, a subdued Eusebio, already the scorer of sixteen league goals in seven games, was easily contained by the unbreachable combination of Roy McFarland and Colin Todd.

In front of a capacity 38,100 crowd, Clough's side scored an all-important, confidence-boosting early goal. In the eighth minute, McFarland climbed above the Benfica defence to head home Alan Hinton's cross, the winger having worked a short corner routine with Hector. Twenty minutes later, Hinton was again the provider; his left side corner was nodded on by McFarland to Hector who lashed in a dipping left foot shot. The overworked Henriques was then required to save well from Hinton and Hector within the space of just a few seconds. Amazingly however, it was 3-0 before half time. In the thirty-ninth minute, a tentative Peter Daniel lob fell loose to John McGovern, the alert midfielder shooting past the visitors' goalkeeper from the edge of the penalty area.

It would have been grossly unfair to have expected the Rams to play as well after the interval. That said, although the visitors, in their sixty-sixth European contest, came more into the game, they created little until Colin Boulton was forced to make late stops from Graca and Toni. After the game, Clough summed up his team's efforts in just one word - "magical". It was a perfect description of a display to be forever etched in the memory of all those who witnessed it.

DERBY COUNTY: BOULTON, ROBSON, DANIEL, HENNESSEY, McFARLAND, TODD, McGOVERN, GEMMILL, O'HARE, HECTOR, HINTON. SUBSTITUTES: NONE USED.

BENFICA: HENRIQUES, MALTA DA SILVA, HUMBERTO, MESSIAS, ADOLFO, JALMA GRACA, NENE, TONI, BAPTISTA, EUSEBIO, SIMOES. SUBSTITUTES: JORDAO FOR BAPTISTA (55).

ATTENDANCE: 38,100
REFEREE: MR LOOW (SWEDEN)

Hinton outguns sorry Arsenal...

25th November 1972, Football League Division One

DERBY COUNTY 5 ARSENAL 0

Having achieved their first away win of the season at West Ham United, the Rams demolished the Gunners with a scintillating display of attacking football. Although it was a victory based on a team performance, Alan Hinton was magnificent, constantly tormenting the visitors' goalkeeper, Bob Wilson, who was returning after a seven month absence following a cartilage operation.

The best chances in the opening quarter of an hour both fell to Charlie George. The Arsenal striker shot wide when well placed, and then forced Colin Boulton to make the first save of the game. County hit back and took the lead on twenty-one minutes thanks to Wilson's uncertainty. The goalkeeper failed to hold Archie Gemmill's cross and John McGoven scored after Kevin Hector's effort had been blocked. Hinton then took over. After thirty-seven minutes he cut in from the left and planted an unstoppable shot in the far corner of the net. Three minutes later it was 3-0, Hinton curled in a perfect cross beyond Wilson and Roy McFarland headed home with ease. Immediately from the kick off Derby scored again. Peter Storey conceded a free kick, and the irrepressible winger curled the ball for Hector to head firmly past the despairing Wilson. A 4-0 lead with three goals in five minutes produced a deserved half time standing ovation. And yet within two minutes of the restart it was 5-0, Roger Davies heading his first league goal in just his third senior game..

After such a remarkable passage of play, the remainder of the game saw both sides create chances without there being any further addition to the scoreline. For County the result was their best in the league since the humiliation of Tottenham Hotspur in September 1969. It also took their unbeaten league run to three games, a sequence that was subsequently extended by victories against Wolverhampton Wanderers and Coventry City, and a draw at Newcastle United.

Arsenal goalkeeper Bob Wilson receives treatment during the Rams' easy victory.

DERBY COUNTY: BOULTON, WEBSTER, NISH, HENNESSEY, McFARLAND, TODD, McGOVERN, GEMMILL, DAVIES, HECTOR, HINTON. SUBSTITUTE: DURBAN.

ARSENAL: WILSON, RICE, McNAB, STOREY, McLINTOCK, SIMPSON, MARINELLO, BALL, RADFORD, GEORGE, KELLY. SUBSTITUTE: ARMSTRONG FOR MARINELLO (60).

ATTENDANCE: 31,034
REFEREE: MR JONES

McFarland brace too much for Reds...

26th December 1972, Football League Division One

DERBY COUNTY 3 MANCHESTER UNITED 1

After crashing to 4-0 defeat at Stoke City, County took on United on Boxing Day for the second time in three seasons. The visitors arrived at the Baseball Ground with a squad keen to impress newly-appointed manager Tommy Docherty, but without the "absent" George Best. Brian Clough opted for two changes to the Rams line up, Roger Davies replacing John O'Hare in attack, and Peter Daniel being preferred to Alan Lewis at left back.

Derby opened very strongly and went ahead after just six minutes. John McGovern took a right wing corner and, instead of centring, pulled the ball back for Ron Webster to curl in a great cross which Roy McFarland rose to head home. The Rams' second goal, after twenty minutes, was magnificent; Davies pulled the ball back and Alan Hinton volleyed home past Alex Stepney with the outside of his right foot. Then, instead of finishing their opponents off, County let United back into the game. Bobby Charlton produced his side's first effort on goal after thirty minutes, and Ian Storey Moore, a former Rams "signing", began to run dangerously at their defence from deep positions.

After the interval, McFarland scored his second goal after fifty-eight minutes. With the Reds defence leaving him unmarked, he easily nodded another Hinton free kick past Stepney via the underside of the bar. Within three minutes, Docherty's side pulled back a consolation marker when Moore netted a header from a Brian Kidd cross. The defeat saw United slip to bottom of the table, the victory for Clough's side lifting them three places to 7th and maintaining their unbeaten home record.

DERBY COUNTY: BOULTON, WEBSTER, DANIEL, HENNESSEY, McFARLAND, TODD, McGOVERN, GEMMILL, DAVIES, HECTOR, HINTON. SUBSTITUTE: O'HARE.

MANCHESTER UNITED: STEPNEY, O'NEIL, DUNNE, KIDD, SADLER, BUCHAN, MORGAN, MACDOUGALL, CHARLTON, DAVIES, MOORE. SUBSTITUTE: YOUNG FOR DUNNE (45).

ATTENDANCE: 35,098
REFEREE: MR TINKLER

Davies trio sparks Rams rally...

7th February 1973, FA Cup 4th Round Replay

TOTTENHAM HOTSPUR 3 DERBY COUNTY 5 (AET)

The Rams produced a magnificent fightback in this enthralling contest. After trailing the London side 3-1 with just twelve minutes to play, they levelled the game thanks to the brilliant Roger Davies and then coasted to victory in extra time. After scoring four goals within the space of thirty minutes, it was a recovery to rank alongside any other in the history of the FA Cup competition.

In front of Spurs' biggest crowd of the season, the home side opened the scoring after nineteen minutes, Martin Chivers finishing off a quick-fire, length-of-the-field move. The goal prompted the Rams into action. Kevin Hector hit the bar and Davies glanced a shot off the outside of a post. Despite their pressure, Clough's side fell 2-0 behind before the interval when Alan Gilzean headed in a Chivers long throw-in. Although Hector pulled one back in the sixty-eighth minute, Tottenham again restored their advantage when Mike England netted a penalty, given for a dubious handball offence against John McGovern.

Davies then took centre stage. Within two minutes of England's goal, he reduced the arrears with an edge of the box shot through a crowd of players. The Rams' equaliser after eighty-six minutes was truly remarkable. John O'Hare pulled back a cross to the near post and, in a moment of brilliance, Davies controlled the ball before firing a volley into the net from an almost impossible angle.

After a scoreless first period of extra time, Davies completed his hat trick when he headed home Hector's right wing corner. With the Spurs defence completely bewildered, Hector then completed the late rout when he lashed home the Rams' fifth goal.

TOTTENHAM HOTSPUR: JENNINGS, EVANS, KNOWLES, PRATT, ENGLAND, BEAL, GILZEAN, PERRYMAN, CHIVERS, PETERS, COATES. SUBSTITUTE: PEARCE FOR COATES (EXTRA TIME).

DERBY COUNTY: BOULTON, WEBSTER, NISH, HENNESSEY, McFARLAND, TODD, McGOVERN, GEMMILL, DAVIES, HECTOR, O'HARE. SUBSTITUTE: DURBAN FOR HENNESSEY (45).

ATTENDANCE: 52,736
REFEREE: MR BIDDLE

Roger Davies... Hat-trick hero against Tottenham.

County down by two...lose two...

11th April 1973, European Cup Semi-Final First Leg

JUVENTUS 3 DERBY COUNTY 1

For the first hour of this game, the Rams appeared not to have read the script. Instead of capitulating to their Turin hosts, they gave as good as they got, and scored the first-ever European Cup goal by a British team on Italian soil. Unfortunately, they then discovered the difference between success and failure at this level, two stunningly well taken goals leaving them a colossal mountain to climb in the second leg.

After surviving the expected initial pressure, County settled and began to play with an increasing amount of confidence. Indeed, even after Altafini had swept the home side ahead after twenty-eight minutes, they responded immediately with a magnificent goal from Kevin Hector. The Rams top scorer in the competition exchanged passes with John O'Hare before slipping past Salvadore and Spinosi and firing the ball past Zoff. Although the half-time whistle sounded with the teams still level, County's optimism had been severely dented by the bookings of Roy McFarland and Archie Gemmill - both players, having picked up cautions in an earlier round, were rendered ineligible for the return game at the Baseball Ground. When Juventus introduced Haller in the sixty-fourth minute, they gained an instant reward. A move between right winger Casio and the substitute saw the wide man drive past Colin Boulton from twenty yards out.

However, with the aid of some at times desperate defending, the Rams held on until just seven minutes from time. Altafini then netted a goal of rare quality, the Brazilian easily past two defenders before shooting high into the County net. It was a tremendous individual effort, one which left the Rams needing to win their home game by at least 2-0, and that without the influence of two of their best players. . .

**Kevin Hector, the first British player to score
a European Cup goal in Italy.**

JUVENTUS: ZOFF, SPINOSI, MARCHETTI, FURINO, MORINI, SALVADORE, CASIO, CUCCEREDDU, ANASTAL, CAPELLO, ALTAFINI. SUBSTITUTE: HALLER FOR CUCCEREDDU (64).

DERBY COUNTY: BOULTON, WEBSTER, NISH, DURBAN, McFARLAND, TODD, McGOVERN, HECTOR, O'HARE, GEMMILL, POWELL. SUBSTITUTES: NONE USED.

ATTENDANCE: 72,000
REFEREE: MR SCHULENBURG

Ten man Rams find
Juventus too tough...

25th April 1973, European Cup Semi-Final Second Leg

DERBY COUNTY 0 JUVENTUS 0 (AGGREGATE 1-3)

After the bravest of performances, the Rams exited the European Cup at the hands of the Italian champions. In the final analysis, the conceding of three goals in Turin proved to be too much for Clough's side, the vastly experienced Juventus defence ensuring, through a mixture of skill and aggression, that the contest remained scoreless.

Although Ron Webster sent Zoff sprawling across his line in the opening moments, County were unable to conjure up a repeat of their display against Benfica. When they did manage to create chances, they found the Italian national goalkeeper in superb form, his first half save from an Alan Hinton free kick being of the highest quality. In the fifty-sixth minute, the Rams were presented with a wonderful chance to open the scoring; Kevin Hector skipped clear and was fouled by Spinosi, the referee immediately pointing to the penalty spot. The normally ultra reliable Hinton, back in the line up after an absence of almost a month, unfortunately lost his cool and put the spot kick well wide. In the sixty-second minute the game was decided. Roger Davies, who had fought a long physical battle with the intimidating Morini, suddenly exploded and head-butted the Italian defender. The official had no option but to send the Rams man off, leaving them with ten men against one of the toughest defences in the game.

With about twenty minutes to play, Clough gambled by introducing Sims, the reserve team centre forward, in favour of the excellent Peter Daniel. It was a change which allowed the visitors their only two chances; Boulton saving well from Anastal and Longobucco. The final whistle was greeted by an invasion of Italian supporters waving their enormous black and white chequered flags. County were left to rue what might have been as they trooped off, having won thirteen corners and forced their opponents to concede twenty-nine free kicks - sadly, all to no avail.

DERBY COUNTY: BOULTON, WEBSTER, NISH, POWELL, DANIEL, TODD, McGOVERN, O'HARE, DAVIES, HECTOR, HINTON. SUBSTITUTES: DURBAN FOR POWELL (45), SIMS FOR DANIEL (71).

JUVENTUS: ZOFF, SPINOSI, MARCHETTI, FURINO, MORINI, SALVADORE, CASIO, CUCCEREDDU, ANASTAL, CAPELLO, ALTAFINI. SUBSTITUTE: LONGOBUCCO FOR CUCCEREDDU (67).

ATTENDANCE: 38,350
REFEREE: MR LOBO

8.

THE END OF AN ERA
(1973/74)

OVER THE SUMMER OF 1973, before a ball had again been kicked in earnest, Clough made two decisions which, ultimately, led to his departure from the Baseball Ground. Firstly, always keen to promote his media image, he could not resist accepting the role offered to him by London Weekend Television. With an urgent requirement to replace the departing Jimmy Hill, the company had earmarked him as the ideal person to ensure that the popularity of their football coverage was maintained, especially as the World Cup in West Germany was just twelve months away. A situation ensued where Clough readily agreed to travel to London every Thursday or Friday, and again on Sunday lunchtimes throughout the playing season, travelling back to Derby in between to direct the Rams First Division campaign. Secondly he chose, via his Sunday Express newspaper column, to launch a savage attack on the tactics and professionalism of Leeds United and their manager Don Revie. In an astonishing outburst, Clough suggested that, as a punishment for their methods, the Yorkshire club should be demoted from the top flight of the game, and Revie given a substantial fine.

It was all too much for Longson. As the season got underway, he found himself again being continually bombarded by demands from fellow league club Chairmen to rein his manager in. In a final attempt to curb Clough, he issued a Boardroom ultimatum; curtail the television work and have all newspaper articles vetted by the Directors, or face the consequences. Another uneasy stand-off between the management duo and the Board ensued, hardly then an ideal set of circumstances from which to build the foundations of a fresh challenge for the First Division title.

The Rams opened their campaign with single goal home victories against Chelsea and Manchester City. A hard fought scoreless draw at Birmingham City followed, and although County were defeated at Anfield, they hit back with wins against both Everton and Liverpool at the Baseball Ground. Given all of the uncertainty, it

AGONY! Roger Davies heads wide against Everton, 8th September 1973.

was a solid enough start, the Rams standing in 5th place after the first six games. When Derby were defeated at Coventry City on September 18th, Clough decided the time was ripe to bring in another player. It was an option he had been considering for a while, especially as Terry Hennessey was looking increasingly unlikely to overcome his long term injury problems. There was intense press speculation at the time that Bobby Moore had been approached to undertake the sweeper role that Dave Mackay had earlier performed so well. However, once the West Ham United captain announced he was staying in London, Clough turned his attentions elsewhere and twenty-nine year old Henry Newton arrived from Everton in a £120,000 deal - the experienced former Nottingham Forest performer having been on the "wanted" list for a few seasons. Conscious of impending team changes, the Rams produced their best display of the season four days after the 1-0 reverse at Highfield Road. Southampton were thrashed 6-2, with Kevin Hector netting his third hat trick as a County player. It was a result which lifted Clough's side into 2nd place, three points behind Leeds who remained unbeaten.

The simmering off the pitch tension finally erupted in the Old Trafford boardroom on Saturday October 13th, just minutes after County had secured an impressive 1-0 victory. With a total disregard for the surroundings, but with a sickening sense of predictability, it was Kirkland, now a Director, who lit the fuse on an explosive showdown. Having beckoned Taylor over with a pointed finger, he summoned him to attend a meeting on the following Monday to explain, in detail, exactly what his role at the club was. With all due justification, Taylor felt totally humiliated and stormed away, his anger so deep that on departing Manchester he vowed to Clough that his own Baseball Ground career was over.

And so it proved. After the assistant manager had duly explained himself, Clough attended a board meeting adamant, and buoyed by his colleague's treatment, that he would not submit to what he saw as restrictive demands. On this occasion Longson, with the wounds from their previous confrontations still as deep as ever, was in an equally unyielding frame of mind. He reiterated the Board's position and waited for the manager to respond. With an unshakable conviction that the support of the players and public was with him, Clough tendered his and Taylor's resignations. In an instant, Longson seized his chance and recommended, successfully, that the Board accept the decisions. In an ironic twist, given the nature of the ultimatum issued to them, the duo's formal letters of resignation were later typed out by their long time journalistic confidant, Gerald Mortimer of the Derby Evening Telegraph.

The events of the 15th transformed the Baseball Ground into a hub of media attention. In the days that followed, the town was invaded by reporters from the local, regional and national press, all frantically clamouring for the latest update or quote. A protest movement was also formed, headed by local playwright Don Shaw and former professional player Bill Holmes. Not surprisingly, given that the public's reaction to the departures had been one of outrage, the group's first meeting filled a local theatre to capacity.

With the resignations coming at the start of an important week of World Cup qualification matches, not all of the Rams players had witnessed the initial scenes outside the ground. Of those not away on international duty, one of the most memorable sights was that of Hinton with a tea urn above his head - his proclamation that it represented the club's future silverware sending the assembled photographers into a frenzied overdrive. For the quartet of McFarland, Hector, Todd and Nish it was a particularly distressing time. They had joined up with the England squad to face Poland at

Wembley, the first two of the foursome going on to appear in the infamous 1-1 draw, Hector albeit as a late substitute. It was of course the result which ended the nation's hopes of progressing to the finals of the 1974 tournament in West Germany.

With a home game against Leicester City to prepare for, the Directors announced that Jimmy Gordon, the first team trainer, had been appointed as the club's caretaker manager. Behind the scenes, an approach had already been made to Bobby Robson the Ipswich Town boss, the now Knight of the game subsequently deciding that his immediate future remained in East Anglia. As for the match itself, the ninety or so minutes of the Rams 2-1 win were in reality a support act to the main event; the appearance of both Clough and Longson in the main stand. With the terracing awash with "Clough in - Directors out" banners, the entrance of the people's manager was greeted with thunderous applause. Not to be outdone, Longson also stood to acknowledge the crowd, receiving what at best could be described as a muted response. After the final whistle, Clough headed to London to appear on that night's "Parkinson Show", one of several many media opportunities he took advantage of, the most prominent being the week-long serialisation of his story in the *Daily Mail* newspaper.

Longson's position had not been helped by his ill-advised press statement, issued on Thursday the 18th. It added a more sinister element to what was already an unsavoury affair. He revealed that Clough would be required to attend a Football Association disciplinary enquiry over his continued vociferous criticism of the governing body. Additionally, the chairman alleged that his former manager had developed "a systematic habit of claiming unjustified expenses from the club". The remarkable claim produced an immediate response, with Clough announcing that he had instructed his lawyers to issue a writ for libel against Longson and the Board.

The seventy-two hours after the Leicester game were pivotal. On Monday the 22nd, McFarland handed a letter to Longson within which the players requested the immediate reinstatement of the management duo. On the same day, Clough's legal team duly issued their writ, Clough himself following up the delivery by treating the players to a champagne party at a local hotel. On the following night, several of the team expressed their frustration by staging a sit-in at the Baseball Ground during which they demanded to see the Chairman. In remarkable scenes, they searched the corridors and offices for Longson, only to subsequently learn that he was already elsewhere - about twenty miles down the A52 towards Nottingham to be precise, finalising a deal to bring the illustrious Dave Mackay back to the Baseball Ground, second time around, as the Rams' new manager.

Initially, the players were adamant that they would not play for Mackay. After the sit-in, McFarland even rang his former team mate to plead with him not to accept the Derby job. It was however too late, Mackay's mind was made up and he had been given a healthy four year contract at one of the country's top clubs. Player dispute or no player dispute, it was, for the player-manager of an average Second Division side, too good an opportunity to turn down. The mood of the players remained unrelenting and serious consideration was given to strike action, something which would have seen them break their own contracts with the club. Eventually, Hennessy, the team's Professional Footballers Association (PFA) representative, persuaded his colleagues to see sense and abandon their threat of action, realising that, once Mackay arrived, future protests would be futile.

Clough meanwhile was beginning to regret his actions. Although he held a lingering hope of a possible Boardroom coup, led by one or two of the Directors who had stayed loyal to him, in reality he was an unemployed football manager. To make matters worse, by resigning instead of being sacked, he had forfeited the right to compensation, which for someone with four years of a contract outstanding would have been substantial. At least, later, he did receive a settlement from the club in respect of the libel action which did not go to court, reportedly pocketing around £18,000 plus his legal fees.

And so, the most glorious era in the history of Derby County was over. Clough and Taylor had transformed a mediocre Second Division outfit into a team that was capable of competing with the best, not just at home but in Europe as well - all within the space of just six memorable years. The pair certainly shared a remarkable relationship, which by the time they exited the Baseball Ground had already stretched back almost twenty years to their early days at Middlesbrough. Although page upon page has already been written as to the reasons for their success, the contribution of the camera shy Taylor is often overlooked. His way was more behind the scenes assessing, often instantly, the suitability of a potential recruit. The ability he possessed to spot previously unrecognised talent was exceptional, witnessed by the signings of John Robson and Roger Davies from non-league football, and a young Archie

Gemmill from Preston North End. With their understanding of each other having developed over the years, Taylor also had an almost uncanny knack of being able to take a verbal lead from his outspoken partner. The term "good cop, bad cop" has crept into today's language, usually being descriptive of a person who can change personality from, say, friendly to hostile with apparent ease. By the early Seventies Clough and Taylor had already invented their own unique forerunner, one critical, the other cajoling. It was a ploy seen at its best when a player requested a pay rise. Alan Durban once recalled going in to see the pair adamant he was worth a £20 a week increase. . . and departed feeling he had done exceptionally well to get £8. The tactic, with variations, could disarm even the most determined; an angry Roy McFarland, having once demanded a showdown over being fined, confronted the duo and found himself presented with a couple of airline tickets for a holiday in Spain - anger, what anger?

Although similar gestures from Clough went largely unreported in the press, they were an integral part of his management style. Whether it was flowers for the players' wives, match tickets for the family, even a little extra financial help with whatever, he had a paternalistic aspect which ultimately secured the respect of most of those around him.

Another of Clough's clever ploys was to relax his team prior to kick off. There were no dossiers on the opposition, just a brief reminder of what was expected; play to your strengths, get the simple things right - let them worry about us. . . If after ninety minutes things had not gone well, of course players were criticised, but always in the privacy of the dressing room or office. The fact that the players knew they were safe from any public humiliation simply added to Clough's appeal. With him on the touchline and leaders in the shape of Mackay, McFarland or Gemmill on the pitch, it was in reality perhaps little surprise that the Rams flourished so well.

Just prior to the resignations, County had announced plans for a new stadium. Had Clough and Taylor remained in office they might well have created a "dynasty" alongside the likes of the mid-Seventies Liverpool side, and more recently Manchester United. The prospect of the Rams playing regularly in front of 50,000 crowds is certainly an enthralling thought, but within a week of the stadium news being made public the club had lost its best-ever management team. . . and, as a consequence of its future fortunes, took a further twenty-four years to move to a new home.

With Mackay at the helm, the Rams initially struggled for any real form at all. They failed to win any of their next eight league and cup games and by December 8th had slipped down to 9th place in the table. The new manager refused however to rush headlong into panic buying, and in a tremendous display of his own strength of character set about turning the season around. Remarkably, after such an ominous period, County were beaten just five times in their remaining twenty-two league fixtures, a 2-0 home victory on the last day of the season against Wolverhampton Wanderers confirming a 3rd place finish - and more importantly a place in the UEFA Cup. For the record, Mackay's managerial contribution to Derby County was outstanding. In season 1974/75 the Rams again were First Division champions ahead of Liverpool and Ipswich Town. In the following year, they finished 4th in the league and also reached the semi-final of the FA Cup. Indeed when Mackay left the club, resigning in November 1976 after a disagreement with the Board, his departure coincided precisely with the end of the Rams as a real First Division force.

Clough did not stay out of work for very long. By the beginning of November 1973 he had agreed, along with Taylor, to manage Third Division Brighton and Hove Albion. It was an appointment which lasted until the end of the 1973/74 season and, in the circumstances, his absence away from Derby probably aided Mackay's integration back into the unsettled Rams set-up as much as anything else. In the summer of 1974 Clough returned to the First Division with Leeds United, a job he held for just 44 days. He had arrived at Elland Road determined to stamp his authority on a group of international stars who were used to the Revie style of management and resented Clough from the outset. When the end came for Clough he made sure, second time around, that he was sacked - and promptly pocketed a cheque for over £100,000 in compensation. The money was nice, but Clough was stung by the criticism he received in the press, and the remainder of 1974 passed by without him having any managerial involvement.

In January 1975 Brian Clough was appointed manager of Second Division Nottingham Forest, a side playing mediocre football in front of dwindling attendances. The rest, as they say, is history. . .

John McGovern and Archie Gemmill, who, along with John O'Hare, all rejoined Clough at Nottingham Forest.

KEY MATCHES OF 1972/73

Rams no match for Keegan-inspired Liverpool...

4th September 1973, Football League Division One

LIVERPOOL 2 DERBY COUNTY 0

After two wins and a draw from their opening three games, the Rams slipped to defeat at Anfield, Bill Shankly's side fully deserving what in the end proved to be an easy victory. As a consequence of their defeat County dropped two places in the standings to 7th, that on a night when the shock result in the First Division was Sheffield United's 5-0 rout of Arsenal at Bramall Lane.

DEFEAT HURTS! The Rams players troop off at Anfield.

Although Ray Clemence was forced to make early saves from Steve Powell and John McGovern, the Reds soon took control with "KK" (Kevin Keegan) proving to be an almost constant threat to the overworked County defence. The home side opened the scoring ten minutes from half time when Phil Thompson, normally more adept at preventing goals, smashed a marvellous right foot volley past Colin Boulton from fully thirty yards out - it was the nineteen year old's first senior strike for the Merseyside club.

Prompted by Archie Gemmill, the Rams rallied briefly after the interval but found the Liverpool defence, boosted by the return of Tommy Smith from suspension, in commanding form. The points were secured in the eighty-fifth minute when Keegan thumped home an unstoppable penalty, Colin Todd having upended John Toshack. Indeed, the foul summed up Todd's night; he never looked comfortable against the speed and enthusiasm of Keegan and, after picking the ball up after a whistle, was also booked for dissent.

The goal from Thompson was the first Clough's side had conceded in 305 minutes of First Division football, and yet on this occasion the back four never looked anything like a strong organised unit.

LIVERPOOL: CLEMENCE, LAWLER, THOMPSON, SMITH, LLOYD, HUGHES, KEEGAN, CORMACK, HEIGHWAY, TOSHACK, CALLAGHAN. SUBSTITUTE: BOERSMA.

DERBY COUNTY: BOULTON, WEBSTER, NISH, POWELL, McFARLAND, TODD, McGOVERN, GEMMILL, O'HARE, HECTOR, HINTON. SUBSTITUTE: DANIEL.

ATTENDANCE: 45,237
REFEREE: MR RABY

Sweet revenge for brilliant County...

12th September 1973, Football League Division One

DERBY 3 LIVERPOOL 1

They say a week is a long time in politics. In Derby County's case, their performance at the Baseball Ground against Liverpool was almost unrecognisable from the one they returned at Anfield on

September 4. The Rams scored three, had another disallowed and in honesty on any other night might have accumulated six or seven - such was their dominance.

Whatever Brian Clough said to his players before the kick off certainly had the desired effect. With revenge clearly in mind, they took the lead after just ten minutes when Roger Davies stabbed home a rebound after Kevin Hector's shot had been blocked. Although Liverpool equalised sixteen minutes later, Phil Boersma's goal from a Kevin Keegan pass was definitely scored against the run of play. Roy McFarland, who had allowed Boersma to go past him for the Reds marker, fully redeemed himself after forty minutes, the Rams centre half exchanging passes with Hector before firing in a well taken strike.

Hector put the contest well beyond the visitors reach ten minutes into the second half. Although his shot looped past Ray Clemence after taking a deflection, it came after a great move instigated by David Nish and involving both Davies and Archie Gemmill. After that the Liverpool shot stopper kept the scoreline respectable by making fine saves from a fine Davies effort and a John McGovern volley.

In the days following the victory, Clough was rumoured to be about to announce a major signing. On the evidence of this performance, any quality addition to the Rams squad would strengthen even more their aspiration of regaining the championship crown.

DERBY COUNTY: BOULTON, WEBSTER, NISH, POWELL, McFARLAND, TODD, McGOVERN, GEMMILL, DAVIES, HECTOR, HINTON. SUBSTITUTE: O'HARE.

LIVERPOOL: CLEMENCE, LAWLER, THOMPSON, SMITH, LLOYD, HUGHES, KEEGAN, CORMACK, HEIGHWAY, BOERSMA, CALLAGHAN. SUBSTITUTE: HALL.

ATTENDANCE: 32,867
REFEREE: MR HOWELL

Hector hits three as Derby crush Saints...

22nd September 1973, Football League Division One

DERBY COUNTY 6 SOUTHAMPTON 2

With £120,000 new signing Henry Newton still to make his debut, the Rams demolished Southampton and scored six for the first time since they beat Scunthorpe United by a similar scoreline in April 1963. Kevin Hector wreaked havoc in the Saints defence and his hat trick took his league tally for the club to 107 goals in 287 matches - a performance which places him fourth on the Rams all-time scoring list behind Steve Bloomer, Jack Bowers and Harry Bedford.

The rout started after seven minutes. Hector was fouled in the penalty area and although Eric Martin saved Alan Hinton's spot kick, the referee ordered a retake and second time around the Rams winger made no mistake. It was 2-0 after twenty-six minutes as Roger Davies controlled Hinton's cross on his chest before steering the ball wide of the Southampton goalkeeper. Hector scored his first of the afternoon nine minutes before half time, the Rams striker converting a low Hinton centre to the far post. The visitors pulled one back almost immediately when Ron Webster mistimed a back pass to Colin Boulton and Brian O'Neil nipped in to score.

With Hinton in unstoppable form, County's fourth goal was brilliant. The winger left two men in his wake before looking up and crossing in the 56th minute for Hector to make it 4-1. Although O'Neil again reduced the arrears, Clough's side finished in style. Hector set up Davies for number five on seventy-seven minutes, and the favour was returned just before the final whistle when Hector completed his triple blast from a neat Davies pass. County moved up into 2nd place in the table behind Leeds United, the Yorkshire side along with fifth placed Leicester City being the only two unbeaten teams in the division.

DERBYCOUNTY: BOULTON, WEBSTER, NISH,POWELL, McFARLAND, TODD, McGOVERN, GEMMILL, DAVIES, HECTOR, HINTON. SUBSTITUTE: O'HARE.

SOUTHAMPTON: MARTIN, McCARTHY, WALKER, FISHER, BENNETT, BYRNE, PAINE, CHANNON, GILCHRIST, O'NEIL, STOKES. SUBSTITUTE: TALKES.

ATTENDANCE:25,500
REFEREE:MR GOW

Hector strike sets up Rams victory...

13th October 1973, Football League Division One

MANCHESTER UNITED 0 DERBY COUNTY 1

The Rams achieved their first away win of the season, although the significance of their performance was nullified by the events which surrounded the club in the immediate days that followed. The home defeat for Tommy Docherty's United saw them drop to 18th place in the table, and on the evidence of this performance, the lowly position was a fair reflection of the Reds' level of ability.

County started well and were gifted an early goal. Alex Forsyth, back in the Reds side after a seven month absence, under hit a 4th minute back pass and Kevin Hector nipped in to tuck the ball into the corner of the net. The Rams remained well on top and indeed United did not create a real chance until just before the interval. At least,much to the relief of the 43,724 Old Trafford crowd, the home side had more of the game in the second half.Colin Boulton saved efforts from Brian Kidd and Jimmy Greenhoff. At the other end Hector got clear, his break only being ended by a crude foul by Jim Holton, an offence which earned the Scottish international his third booking of the season.

With the United diehards streaming away from the ground, the home side enjoyed their best spell of the game. Boulton was beaten

Kevin Hector scores the only goal at Old Trafford.

twice within the space of a minute, but both the efforts that went past him, from Kidd and Tony Young, came back off the crossbar. The Rams kept their composure and on the balance of play deserved their victory. The midfield trio of Archie Gemmill, Henry Newton and John McGovern controlled proceedings well, with Gemmill in particular having a fine game.

MANCHESTER UNITED: STEPNEY, BUCHAN(MARTIN) , FORSYTH, GREENHOFF, HOLTON, JAMES, MORGAN, YOUNG, KIDD, ANDERSON, GRAHAM. SUBSTITUTE: BUCHAN(GEORGE).

DERBY COUNTY: BOULTON, WEBSTER, NISH, NEWTON, McFARLAND, TODD, McGOVERN, GEMMILL, DAVIES, HECTOR, HINTON. SUBSTITUTE: O'HARE.

ATTENDANCE:43,724
REFEREE:MR WALLACE

APPENDIX

INTRODUCTION TO APPENDICES

GENERAL:

All competitive games played under the management of Brian Clough are reviewed on a seasonal basis. For each season therefore, League, League Cup and FA Cup fixtures are included - and for season 1971/72 the Texaco Cup is reviewed, as is the European Cup competition of season 1972/73.

N.B. For this analysis the Rams involvement in the 1970/71 Watney Cup is ignored as this was a pre-season competition.

Information provided for each game played:

DATE: DATE/MONTH/YEAR FORMAT

VENUE: HOME OR AWAY

OPPOSITION: AS STATED

RESULT: DERBY COUNTY SCORE FIRST IN ALL CASES

ATTENDANCE: AS STATED

POSITION: POST-MATCH LEAGUE POSITIONS OF BOTH TEAMS WHERE APPROPRIATE - DERBY COUNTY ALWAYS STATED FIRST

FOR CUP FIXTURES THE APPROPRIATE ROUND IS SHOWN IN THE POSITION COLUMN WITH THE LETTERS R AND L REPRESENTING REPLAY AND LEG AS APPROPRIATE.

TEAM LINEUPS

Both teams are shown across the page from numbers 1 to 11. A player name marked with an * indicates that player was substituted in favour of the player shown in column 12. The notation NA indicates that a substitute was not used.

N.B. For line-ups and goalscorers the Derby County players are in the "C" rows whilst the opposition are in the "O" rows.

MILESTONES

THE FOLLOWING MILESTONES ARE SHOWN:

1 DEBUT GAME.

2 LAST GAME.

3 FIRST GOAL.

4 MILESTONE RAMS LEAGUE APPEARANCES AS SHOWN.

5 MILESTONE OVERALL LEAGUE APPEARANCES AS SHOWN - I.E. THOSE PLAYERS WHO PLAYED LEAGUE FOOTBALL BEFORE JOINING DERBY COUNTY.

6 MISCELLANEOUS MILESTONES AS INDICATED.

1967/68

DIVISION 2		1	2	3	4	5	6	7	8	9	10	11	12
DATE	19.8.67	MATTHEWS	DANIEL	HOPKINSON	WEBSTER	SAXTON	WALLER	HUGHES	DURBAN	O'HARE	HECTOR	HODGSON	NA
VENUE	HOME	WRIGHT	CURTIS	KINSEY	REEVES	KING	HALOM	PEACOCK	CAMPBELL	WENT	MOORE	GLOVER	NA
OPPOS	CHARLTON ATHLETIC												
RESULT	3-2	O'HARE, HECTOR, KING (OG)											
ATTND	19412	CURTIS, CAMPBELL											
POS	2-15	MILESTONES:		SCORING DEBUT FOR O'HARE									
DATE	26.8.67	MATTHEWS	DANIEL	HOPKINSON	WEBSTER	SAXTON	WALLER*	HUGHES	DURBAN	O'HARE	HECTOR	HODGSON	THOMAS
VENUE	AWAY	JACKSON	SEWELL	PRESLAND	PAYNE	STEPHENSON	BANNISTER	KEMBER	BRYNE	WHITE	WOODRUFF	JACKSON	NA
OPPOS	CRYSTAL PALACE												
RESULT	0-1	NA											
ATTND	17875	WOODRUFF											
POS	14-6	MILESTONES:		LAST APPEARANCE FOR THOMAS									
DATE	28.8.67	MATTHEWS	DANIEL	RICHARDSON	WEBSTER	McFARLAND	SAXTON	HUGHES	BUXTON	O'HARE	HECTOR	HODGSON	NA
VENUE	AWAY	HILL	WILCOOKSON	CLISH	HASELDEN	THOMPSON	TILER	CHAPPELL	RABJOHN	SHEFFIELD	BRADD	PRING	NA
OPPOS	ROTHERHAM UNITED												
RESULT	3-1	HECTOR (P), O'HARE, BUXTON											
ATTND	11088	SHEFFIELD											
POS	7-21	MILESTONES:		DEBUT FOR McFARLAND									
DATE	2.9.67	MATTHEWS	DANIEL	RICHARDSON	WEBSTER	McFARLAND	SAXTON	HUGHES	DURBAN	O'HARE	HECTOR	HODGSON	NA
VENUE	HOME	WITHERS	WRIGHT	AITKEN	CHATTERLEY	SLEEUWENHOEK	POUNTNEY	MACLEOD	RUDGE	STOBART	MITCHINSON	ANDERSON	NA
OPPOS	ASTON VILLA												
RESULT	3-1	DURBAN (2), HECTOR (P)											
ATTND	22967	STOBART											
POS	6-19	MILESTONES:											
DATE	6.9.67	MATTHEWS	DANIEL	RICHARDSON	WEBSTER	McFARLAND	SAXTON	HUGHES	DURBAN	O'HARE	HECTOR	HODGSON	NA
VENUE	AWAY	KEELAN	STRINGER	GLADWIN	LUCAS	BROWN	SHARPE	MANNION	BRYCELAND	BOLLAND	CURRAN	KENNING	NA
OPPOS	NORWICH CITY												
RESULT	2-3	HUGHES, DURBAN											
ATTND	14933	CURRAN, BROWN, KENNING											
POS	9-11	MILESTONES:											
DATE	9.9.67	MATTHEWS	DANIEL	RICHARDSON	WEBSTER	McFARLAND	SAXTON	HUGHES	DURBAN	O'HARE	HECTOR	HODGSON	NA
VENUE	HOME	SPRINGETT	CLEMENT	HARRIS	KEEN	HUNT	HAZELL	LAZARUS	MORGAN	SANDERSON	LEACH	MORGAN*	ALLEN
OPPOS	QUEENS PARK RANGERS												
RESULT	1-0	HECTOR											
ATTND	18431	NA											
POS	9-1	MILESTONES:											

DATE	16.9.67	23.9.67	27.9.67	30.9.67	7.10.67	14.10.67
VENUE	HOME	AWAY	HOME	HOME	HOME	AWAY
OPPOS	PLYMOUTH ARGYLE	CARDIFF CITY	ROTHERHAM UNITED	PORTSMOUTH	MILLWALL	IPSWICH TOWN
RESULT	1-0	5-1	4-1	0-1	3-3	0-4
ATTND	21516	15375	28161	27043	23609	15785
POS	8-17	5-13	4-18	5-4	5-19	7-5
1	MATTHEWS / DUNNE	MATTHEWS / WILSON	MATTHEWS / HILL	MATTHEWS / MILKENS	MATTHEWS / LESLIE	MATTHEWS / HANCOCK
2	DANIEL / EVERITT	DANIEL / COLDRICK	DANIEL / WILCOCKSON	DANIEL / TINDALL	WRIGHT / GILCHRIST	WRIGHT / CARROLL
3	RICHARDSON / BAIRD	RICHARDSON / FERGUSON	RICHARDSON / HARRITY	RICHARDSON / LEY	RICHARDSON / BURNETT	RICHARDSON / HOUGHTON
4	WEBSTER / HORE	WEBSTER / WILLIAMS	WEBSTER / HASELDEN	WEBSTER / SMITH	WEBSTER / JONES	WEBSTER* / VILJOEN
5	McFARLAND / NELSON	McFARLAND / MURRAY	McFARLAND / THOMPSON	McFARLAND / HAYDOCK	McFARLAND / KITCHENER	McFARLAND / BAXTER
6	SAXTON / NEWMAN	WALLER / HARRIS	WALLER / TILER*	SAXTON / HARRIS	SAXTON / WILSON	SAXTON / MILLS
7	HUGHES / DAVEY	HUGHES / JONES	HUGHES / CHAMBERS	HUGHES / PORTWOOD	HUGHES / POSSEE	HUGHES / SPEARITT
8	DURBAN / TEDESCO*	DURBAN / ALLEN	DURBAN / GALLEY	DURBAN / POINTER	DURBAN / NEIL	DURBAN / HEGAN
9	O'HARE / SILLETT	O'HARE / TOSHACK	O'HARE / SHEFFIELD	O'HARE / HIRON	O'HARE / HUNT	O'HARE / CRAWFORD
10	HECTOR / PIPER	HECTOR / KING	HECTOR / CHAPPELL	HECTOR / KELLARD	HECTOR / DUNPHY	HECTOR / BAKER
11	HODGSON / MITTEN	HODGSON / BIRD	HINTON / PRING	HINTON / JENNINGS	HINTON / WELLER	HINTON / BROGAN
12	NA / ROUNSEVELL	NA / NA	NA / BURGIN	NA / NA	NA / NA	HOPKINSON / NA
Goals (Derby)	EVERITT (OG)	HECTOR (3), O'HARE (2)	HECTOR (2), O'HARE, HUGHES	NA	HECTOR, SAXTON, GILCHRIST (OG)	NA
Goals (Opp)	NA	BIRD	SHEFFIELD	SMITH	HUNT (2), WELLER	BROGAN (2), SPEARITT, CRAWFORD
MILESTONES		100TH RAMS LEAGUE GAME FOR WALLER / LAST GAME FOR HODGSON / FIRST HAT TRICK FOR HECTOR	DEBUT FOR HINTON	NA	300TH OVERALL LEAGUE GAME FOR HUGHES / DEBUT FOR WRIGHT / FIRST AND ONLY GOAL FOR SAXTON	200TH RAMS LEAGUE GAME FOR MATTHEWS

DATE	21.10.67
VENUE	HOME
OPPOS	HUDDERSFIELD TOWN
RESULT	1-0
ATTND	23950
POS	6-15
1	MATTHEWS / OLDFIELD
2	WRIGHT / PARKIN
3	RICHARDSON* / CATTLIN
4	WEBSTER / McGILL
5	McFARLAND / MELCZAREK
6	HOPKINSON / MEAGAN
7	HUGHES / HELLAWELL
8	BARKER / WORTHINGTON
9	O'HARE / CLARKE*
10	HECTOR / DOBSON
11	HINTON / HILL
12	SAXTON / CHERRY
Goals (Derby)	BARKER
Goals (Opp)	NA
MILESTONES	SCORING DEBUT FOR BARKER

BOLTON WANDERERS — 28.10.67 — AWAY — RESULT 3-5 — ATTND 12631 — POS 7-11

Position	MATTHEWS	WRIGHT	DANIEL	WEBSTER	McFARLAND	SAXTON	HUGHES	DURBAN	O'HARE	HECTOR	HINTON	NA
Derby	MATTHEWS	WRIGHT	DANIEL	WEBSTER	McFARLAND	SAXTON	HUGHES	DURBAN	O'HARE	HECTOR	HINTON	NA
Opp	HOPKINSON	HATTON	FARRIMOND	WILLIAMS	HULME	RIMMER	BROMLEY	GREAVES	BYROM	HILL	TAYLOR	NA

MILESTONES: HECTOR, O'HARE, DURBAN / BYROM (2), WILLIAMS (2), GREAVES

BIRMINGHAM CITY — 4.11.67 — HOME — RESULT 2-2 — ATTND 25484 — POS 7-6

Position	MATTHEWS	WRIGHT	DANIEL	WEBSTER	McFARLAND	SAXTON	HUGHES	DURBAN	O'HARE	HECTOR	HINTON	NA
Derby	MATTHEWS	WRIGHT	HOPKINSON	WEBSTER	McFARLAND	SAXTON	HUGHES	BARKER	O'HARE	HECTOR	BARKER	NA
Opp	HERRIOT	MURRAY	GREEN	THOMSON	SLEEUWENHOEK	BEARD	BRIDGES	VINCENT	PICKERING	VOWDEN	HOCKEY	NA

MILESTONES: DURBAN, BARKER / VINCENT, BRIDGES

BRISTOL CITY — 10.11.67 — AWAY — RESULT 0-1 — ATTND 15919 — POS 7-21

Position	MATTHEWS	WRIGHT	DANIEL	WEBSTER	McFARLAND	SAXTON	HUGHES	DURBAN	O'HARE	HECTOR	HINTON	NA
Derby	MATTHEWS	WRIGHT	HOPKINSON	WEBSTER*	McFARLAND	SAXTON	HUGHES	DURBAN	O'HARE	HECTOR	WALLER	BARKER
Opp	GIBSON	BRIGGS	DAVIES	WIMSHURST	CONNOR	PARR	DERRICK	CROWE	GARLAND	QUIGLEY	BARTLEY	NA

MILESTONES: GARLAND

CARLISLE UNITED — 18.11.67 — HOME — RESULT 0-1 — ATTND 20850 — POS 9-7

Position	MATTHEWS	WRIGHT	DANIEL	WEBSTER	McFARLAND	SAXTON	HUGHES	DURBAN	O'HARE	HECTOR	HINTON	NA
Derby	MATTHEWS	WRIGHT	HOPKINSON	WEBSTER	McFARLAND	WALLER	HUGHES	BUTLIN*	O'HARE	HECTOR	DURBAN	HINTON
Opp	ROSS	NEIL	CALDWELL	McCONNELL	PASSMOOR	GARBUTT	MURRAY	RUDGE	McILMOYLE	BALDERSTONE	SHARPE*	McVITIE

450TH OVERALL LEAGUE GAME FOR MATTHEWS
MILESTONES: BALDERSTONE

HULL CITY — 25.11.67 — AWAY — RESULT 0-3 — ATTND 14767 — POS 10-9

Position	MATTHEWS	WRIGHT	DANIEL	WEBSTER	McFARLAND	SAXTON	HUGHES	DURBAN	O'HARE	HECTOR	HINTON	NA
Derby	MATTHEWS	WRIGHT	HOPKINSON	WEBSTER	McFARLAND	SAXTON	HUGHES*	DURBAN	O'HARE	HECTOR	HINTON	BARKER
Opp	McKECHNIE	GREENWOOD	BUTLER	BANKS	WILSON	SIMPKIN	HENDERSON	WAGSTAFF	CHILTON	HOUGHTON*	WILKINSON	HEATH

100TH RAMS LEAGUE GAME FOR HOPKINSON
MILESTONES: WILKINSON (2), CHILTON

MIDDLESBROUGH — 2.12.67 — HOME — RESULT 2-4 — ATTND 20381 — POS 12-11

Position	MATTHEWS	WRIGHT	DANIEL	WEBSTER	McFARLAND	SAXTON	HUGHES	DURBAN	O'HARE	HECTOR	HINTON	NA
Derby	BOULTON	WRIGHT	RICHARDSON	WEBSTER	McFARLAND	STEWART	HUGHES	DURBAN	O'HARE	HECTOR	HINTON	NA
Opp	WHIGHAM	HICKTON	JONES	HORNER	ROOKS	SPRAGGON	KEAR	McMORDIE	O'ROURKE	CROSSAN	CHADWICK	NA

DEBUT FOR STEWART
MILESTONES: HECTOR, O'HARE / O'ROURKE (3), HICKTON

BLACKPOOL — 9.12.67 — AWAY — RESULT 1-1 — ATTND 11113 — POS 14-3

Position	MATTHEWS	WRIGHT	DANIEL	WEBSTER	McFARLAND	SAXTON	HUGHES	DURBAN	O'HARE	HECTOR	HINTON	NA
Derby	MATTHEWS	WEBSTER	RICHARDSON	SAXTON	McFARLAND	STEWART	HUGHES	BARKER	O'HARE	HECTOR	DURBAN	NA
Opp	TAYLOR	ARMFIELD	MOWBRAY	MILNE	JAMES	McPHEE	SKIRTON*	CRAVEN	INGRAM	BROWN	OATES	SUDDICK

MILESTONES: O'HARE / McPHEE

CHARLTON ATHLETIC

DATE	16.12.67	MATTHEWS	WEBSTER	RICHARDSON	SAXTON	McFARLAND	STEWART	HUGHES	BARKER	O'HARE	HECTOR	DURBAN	NA
VENUE	AWAY	WRIGHT	CURTIS	KINSEY	MOORE	WENT	REEVES	CAMPBELL	TEES	GREGORY	BOLLAND	PEACOCK	NA
OPPOS	CHARLTON ATHLETIC												
RESULT	2-1	BARKER, CURTIS (OG)											
ATTND	12078	TEES											
POS	12-17	MILESTONES:											

DATE	23.12.67	MATTHEWS	WEBSTER	WRIGHT	SAXTON	McFARLAND	STEWART	HUGHES	BARKER	O'HARE	HECTOR	DURBAN	NA
VENUE	HOME	JACKSON	PRESLAND	McCORMICK	PAYNE	STEPHENSON	BANNISTER	LAZARUS	KEMBER	WHITE	BRYNE	WOODRUFF	NA
OPPOS	CRYSTAL PALACE	DURBAN											
RESULT	1-1	WHITE											
ATTND	20224	MILESTONES:											
POS	12-6												

DATE	26.12.67	MATTHEWS	WEBSTER	WRIGHT	SAXTON	McFARLAND	STEWART	HUGHES	BARKER	O'HARE	HECTOR	DURBAN	NA
VENUE	AWAY	BLACKLAW	NEWTON	WILSON	SHARPLES	CODDINGTON	HOLE	FERGUSON	ROGERS	GILLIVER	DARLING	CONNELLY	NA
OPPOS	BLACKBURN ROVERS	NA											
RESULT	0-3	FERGUSON, DARLING, GILLIVER											
ATTND	17902	MILESTONES:											
POS	13-8												

DATE	30.12.67	MATTHEWS	WEBSTER	DANIEL	SAXTON	McFARLAND	STEWART	HUGHES	BARKER	O'HARE	HECTOR	DURBAN	NA
VENUE	HOME	BLACKLAW	NEWTON	WILSON	SHARPLES	CODDINGTON	HOLE	FERGUSON	ROGERS	GILLIVER	DARLING	CONNELLY	NA
OPPOS	BLACKBURN ROVERS	HECTOR, BARKER											
RESULT	2-2	DARLING, CONNELLY											
ATTND	19064	MILESTONES:											
POS	12-9												

ASTON VILLA

DATE	6.1.68	MATTHEWS	WEBSTER	RICHARDSON	SAXTON	McFARLAND	STEWART	HUGHES	BARKER	O'HARE	HECTOR	DURBAN	NA
VENUE	AWAY	WITHERS	WRIGHT	AITKEN	PARK	CHATTERLEY	DEAKIN	MACLEOD	MITCHINSON	GREENHALGH	GODFREY	ANDERSON	NA
OPPOS	ASTON VILLA	HECTOR											
RESULT	1-2	GREENHALGH, MACLEOD											
ATTND	23805	MILESTONES:											
POS	15-16												

PLYMOUTH ARGYLE

DATE	20.1.68	MATTHEWS	DANIEL	RICHARDSON	WEBSTER	McFARLAND	STEWART	HUGHES	DURBAN*	O'HARE	HECTOR	HINTON	BARKER
VENUE	AWAY	DUNNE	SILLETT	BAIRD	NEALE	NELSON	PIPER	DAVEY	BICKLE	PEACOCK	MITTEN	HARRISON	NA
OPPOS	PLYMOUTH ARGYLE	HINTON (2), O'HARE, BARKER											
RESULT	4-3	MITTEN (2), BICKLE											
ATTND	9026	MILESTONES:		FIRST GOALS FOR HINTON									
POS	13-21												

CARDIFF CITY

DATE	3.2.68	MATTHEWS	DANIEL	RICHARDSON	WEBSTER	McFARLAND	STEWART	HUGHES	DURBAN	O'HARE*	HECTOR	HINTON	BARKER
VENUE	HOME	DAVIES	BELL*	FERGUSON	DERRETT	MURRAY	CLARKE	JONES	CLARK	KING	TOSHACK	LEA	PHILLIPS
OPPOS	CARDIFF CITY	DURBAN, HECTOR, HINTON											
RESULT	3-4	CLARK (2), KING (2)											
ATTND	18096	MILESTONES:											
POS	15-13												

10.2.68 — PORTSMOUTH (AWAY) — 2-3 — Att. 26567 — Pos. 15-2

MATTHEWS	DANIEL	RICHARDSON	WEBSTER	McFARLAND	STEWART	DURBAN	BARKER	O'HARE	HECTOR	HINTON	NA
MILKENS	PACK	LEY	SMITH	TINDALL	HARRIS	McCANN	POINTER	HIRON	KELLARD	TREBILCOCK	NA

MILESTONES:
(C) HECTOR, BARKER
(O) TREBILCOCK, POINTER, KELLARD

17.2.68 — QUEENS PARK RANGERS (HOME) — 4-0 — Att. 22854 — Pos. 14-1

MATTHEWS	RICHARDSON	HOPKINSON	WEBSTER	McFARLAND	STEWART	DURBAN	BARKER	O'HARE	HECTOR	HINTON	WALLER
SPRINGETT	CLEMENT	HARRIS	KEEN	KEETCH	HAZELL	MORGAN	SANDERSON	LEACH	MARSH	MORGAN	NA

MILESTONES:
(C) HECTOR, McFARLAND, HINTON, STEWART
FIRST GOAL FOR McFARLAND / LAST APPEARANCE FOR WALLER

24.2.68 — MILLWALL (AWAY) — 1-1 — Att. 12258 — Pos. 12-6

MATTHEWS	RICHARDSON	HOPKINSON	WEBSTER*	McFARLAND	STEWART	DURBAN	BARKER	O'HARE	HECTOR	HINTON	WRIGHT
LESLIE	GILCHRIST	CRIPPS	JONES	KITCHENER	BURNETT	POSSEE	WELLER	CONLON	JACKS	NEIL	NA

MILESTONES:
(C) DURBAN
(O) GILCHRIST

2.3.68 — IPSWICH TOWN (HOME) — 2-3 — Att. 20723 — Pos. 15-4

MATTHEWS	RICHARDSON	HOPKINSON	ROBSON	McFARLAND	STEWART	DURBAN	BARKER	O'HARE	HECTOR	HINTON	NA
HANCOCK	CARROLL	HOUGHTON	MORRIS	BAXTER	JEFFERSON	HEGAN	VILJOEN	CRAWFORD	O'ROURKE	BROGAN	NA

MILESTONES:
(C) HECTOR, BARKER
(O) BROGAN (2), O'ROURKE
DEBUT FOR ROBSON

9.3.68 — NORWICH CITY (HOME) — 1-1 — Att. 18644 — Pos. 14-11

MATTHEWS	RICHARDSON	HOPKINSON	ROBSON	McFARLAND	STEWART	DURBAN	BARKER	O'HARE	HECTOR	HINTON	NA
VASPER	STRINGER	BLACK	LUCAS	BROWN	HOWSHALL	FOGGO	BRYCELAND	MANNING	CURRAN	CRICKMORE	NA

MILESTONES:
(C) BARKER
(O) BRYCELAND

16.3.68 — HUDDERSFIELD TOWN (AWAY) — 1-3 — Att. 9326 — Pos. 14-17

MATTHEWS	RICHARDSON	HOPKINSON	WEBSTER	McFARLAND	STEWART	DURBAN	BARKER	O'HARE	HECTOR	HINTON	NA
OLDFIELD	McGILL	LEGG	NICHOLSON	ELLAM	CHERRY	HARPER	SHAW	AIMSON	DOBSON	HILL	NA

MILESTONES:
(C) McFARLAND
(O) HARPER, AIMSON, DOBSON

23.3.68 — BOLTON WANDERERS (HOME) — 2-1 — Att. 16054 — Pos. 13-12

BOULTON	RICHARDSON	WEBSTER	STEWART	HOPKINSON	HINTON	HINTON	DURBAN	BARKER	O'HARE	HECTOR	NA
HOPKINSON	COOPER	FARRIMOND	WILLIAMS	HULME	HATTON	RITSON	BROMLEY	GREAVES	LENNARD	TAYLOR	

MILESTONES:
(C) O'HARE, HINTON
(O) GREAVES
100TH RAMS LEAGUE GAME FOR RICHARDSON

BIRMINGHAM CITY

	Derby	Opposition
DATE	2.4.68	
VENUE	AWAY	
RESULT	1-3	
ATTND	29327	
POS	13-5	

BOULTON	WEBSTER	RICHARDSON	STEWART	McFARLAND	HOPKINSON	DURBAN	BARKER	O'HARE	HECTOR	HINTON	NA
HERRIOT	MURRAY	GREEN	WYLIE	FOSTER	BEARD	VOWDEN	HOCKEY*	PICKERING	PAGE	BRIDGES	MARTIN

MILESTONES: O'HARE / VOWDEN, BRIDGES, RICHARDSON (OG)

BRISTOL CITY

	Derby	Opposition
DATE	6.4.68	
VENUE	HOME	
RESULT	3-1	
ATTND	16028	
POS	12-9	

BOULTON	WEBSTER	RICHARDSON	STEWART	McFARLAND	HOPKINSON	DURBAN	BARKER	O'HARE	HECTOR	HINTON	NA
GIBSON	JACOBS	BRIGGS	WIMSHURST	CONNOR	PARR	DERRICK	GARLAND	GALLEY	BUSH*	QUIGLEY	BARTLEY

MILESTONES: BARKER (2), HECTOR (P) / BRIGGS

CARLISLE UNITED

	Derby	Opposition
DATE	13.4.68	
VENUE	AWAY	
RESULT	1-1	
ATTND	8009	
POS	12-9	

BOULTON	WEBSTER	RICHARDSON	STEWART	McFARLAND	HOPKINSON	DURBAN	BARKER	O'HARE	HECTOR	HINTON	NA
ROSS	McCARRON	CALDWELL	McCONNELL	PASSMOOR	MARSLAND	BARTON	GARBUTT	McILMOYLE	BALDERSTONE	McVITIE	NA

MILESTONES: DURBAN / McILMOYLE

PRESTON NORTH END

	Derby	Opposition
DATE	15.4.68	
VENUE	HOME	
RESULT	1-2	
ATTND	17783	
POS	11-19	

MATTHEWS	WEBSTER	RICHARDSON	STEWART	McFARLAND	HOPKINSON	DURBAN	BARKER	O'HARE	HECTOR	HINTON	NA
KELLY	PATRICK	ROSS	SMITH	HAWKINS	KNIGHTON	TEMPLE	IRVINE	CHARNLEY	McNAB	GEMMILL	NA

MILESTONES: HINTON (P) / TEMPLE, WEBSTER (OG)

PRESTON NORTH END

	Derby	Opposition
DATE	16.4.68	
VENUE	AWAY	
RESULT	1-1	
ATTND	17871	
POS	13-19	

MATTHEWS	WEBSTER	RICHARDSON	STEWART	McFARLAND	HOPKINSON	DURBAN	BARKER	O'HARE	HECTOR	HINTON	NA
KELLY	PATRICK	ROSS	SMITH*	HAWKINS	KNIGHTON	TEMPLE	IRVINE	CHARNLEY	McNAB	GEMMILL	LYALL

MILESTONES: O'HARE / CHARNLEY

HULL CITY

	Derby	Opposition
DATE	20.4.68	
VENUE	HOME	
RESULT	1-2	
ATTND	15711	
POS	15-17	

MATTHEWS	RICHARDSON	HOPKINSON	WEBSTER	McFARLAND	STEWART	O'HARE	BARKER	BUTLIN	DURBAN	HINTON	NA
McKECHNIE	BANKS	GREENWOOD	JARVIS	WILSON	SIMPKIN	HENDERSON	WAGSTAFF*	CHILTON	HOUGHTON	BUTLER	LORD

MILESTONES: RICHARDSON / LORD, BUTLER

MIDDLESBROUGH

	Derby	Opposition
DATE	27.4.68	
VENUE	AWAY	
RESULT	2-2	
ATTND	13123	
POS	16-8	

MATTHEWS	WEBSTER	ROBSON	STEWART	McFARLAND	STEWART	DURBAN	BARKER	O'HARE	HECTOR	HINTON	NA
SHORT	SMITH	JONES	HORNER	ROOKS	SPRAGGON	KEAR	McMORDIE	HICKTON	HORSFIELD	CHADWICK	NA

MILESTONES: HECTOR (2) / HICKTON (2)
150TH OVERALL LEAGUE GOAL FOR HECTOR (2ND GOAL)

Player columns (Derby / "C"): MATTHEWS | WRIGHT | HOPKINSON | ROBSON | McFARLAND | STEWART | HINTON | BARKER | O'HARE | HECTOR | WALKER | NA

Match — BLACKPOOL

		DATE 4.5.68	VENUE HOME	OPPOS BLACKPOOL	RESULT 1-3	ATTND 20635	POS 18-3

	MATTHEWS	WRIGHT	HOPKINSON	ROBSON	McFARLAND	STEWART	HINTON	BARKER	O'HARE	HECTOR	WALKER	NA
C	MATTHEWS	WRIGHT	HOPKINSON	ROBSON	McFARLAND	STEWART	HINTON	BARKER	O'HARE	HECTOR	WALKER	NA
O	TAYLOR	ARMFIELD	MOWBRAY	CRAVEN	JAMES	McPHEE	SKIRTON	GREEN	WHITE	SUDDICK	HUTCHINSON	NA

ROBSON
WHITE, SKIRTON, SUDDICK

MILESTONES: FIRST GOAL FOR ROBSON / DEBUT FOR WALKER / LAST APPEARANCE FOR MATTHEWS, WRIGHT AND HOPKINSON / O'HARE EVER-PRESENT

AFTER ALL TEAMS HAD PLAYED 42 GAMES, DERBY REMAINED IN 18TH PLACE

LEAGUE CUP

Match — HARTLEPOOLS UNITED

DATE 13.9.67	VENUE HOME	OPPOS HARTLEPOOLS UNITED	RESULT 4-0	ATTND 17810	ROUND 2ND

	MATTHEWS	WRIGHT	HOPKINSON	ROBSON	McFARLAND	STEWART	HINTON	BARKER	O'HARE	HECTOR	WALKER	NA
C	MATTHEWS	RICHARDSON	HOPKINSON	WEBSTER	SAXTON	BUXTON	HUGHES	DURBAN	O'HARE	HECTOR	HOPKINSON	NA
O	SMITH	GOAD	DRYSDALE	SHERIDAN*	GILL	PARRY	McGOVERN	HEPPLEWHITE	PYTHIAN	BROADBENT	SOMERS	WRIGHT

O'HARE (3), HODGSON

MILESTONES: NA

Match — BIRMINGHAM CITY

DATE 11.10.67	VENUE HOME	OPPOS BIRMINGHAM CITY	RESULT 3-1	ATTND 24827	ROUND 3RD

	MATTHEWS	WRIGHT	HOPKINSON	ROBSON	McFARLAND	STEWART	HINTON	BARKER	O'HARE	HECTOR	WALKER	NA
C	MATTHEWS	DANIEL	RICHARDSON	WEBSTER	SAXTON	WALLER	HUGHES	DURBAN	O'HARE	HECTOR	HOPKINSON	NA
O	HERRIOT	MURRAY	WYLIE	PAGE	BEARD	BRIDGES	VINCENT	PICKERING	VOWDEN	HOCKEY		NA

HECTOR, HOPKINSON, O'HARE
BRIDGES

MILESTONES: LAST APPEARANCE FOR BUXTON / FIRST AND ONLY HAT TRICK FOR O'HARE

Match — LINCOLN CITY

DATE 1.11.67	VENUE HOME	OPPOS LINCOLN CITY	RESULT 1-1	ATTND 25079	ROUND 4TH

	MATTHEWS	WRIGHT	HOPKINSON	ROBSON	McFARLAND	STEWART	HINTON	BARKER	O'HARE	HECTOR	WALKER	NA
C	MATTHEWS	DANIEL	HOPKINSON	WEBSTER	SAXTON	WALLER	HUGHES	DURBAN	O'HARE	HECTOR	BARKER	NA
O	KENNEDY	BROWN	PEDEN	COBB*	HARTFORD	GRUMMETT	GREGSON	FORD	LEWIS	HOLMES	THOM	NA

BARKER
THOM

MILESTONES:

Match — LINCOLN CITY

DATE 15.11.67	VENUE AWAY	OPPOS LINCOLN CITY	RESULT 3-0	ATTND 23196	ROUND 4TH R

	MATTHEWS	WRIGHT	HOPKINSON	ROBSON	McFARLAND	STEWART	HINTON	BARKER	O'HARE	HECTOR	WALKER	NA
C	MATTHEWS	DANIEL	HOPKINSON	WEBSTER	SAXTON	WALLER	HUGHES	BUTLIN	O'HARE	HECTOR*	DURBAN	RHODES
O	KENNEDY	BROWN	PEDEN	COBB*	HARTFORD	GRUMMETT	GREGSON	FORD	CORNER	HOLMES	THOM	BROOKES

O'HARE (2), HECTOR

MILESTONES: DEBUT FOR BUTLIN

Match — DARLINGTON

DATE 29.11.67	VENUE HOME	OPPOS DARLINGTON	RESULT 5-4	ATTND 23631	ROUND 5TH

	MATTHEWS	WRIGHT	HOPKINSON	ROBSON	McFARLAND	STEWART	HINTON	BARKER	O'HARE	HECTOR	WALKER	NA
C	MATTHEWS	DANIEL	RICHARDSON	WEBSTER	SAXTON	WALLER	HUGHES	BARKER	O'HARE	HECTOR	DURBAN	NA
O	MOOR	PEVERILL	KEEBLE	DAVIDSON	ATKINSON	ALBESON	RATCLIFFE	O'NEIL	CUMMINGS	SPROATES	O'NEIL	JACQUES

DURBAN (2), HUGHES, BARKER, O'NEIL (OG)

MILESTONES: O'NEIL, CUMMINGS, RATCLIFFE, JACQUES

DATE	17.1.68	MATTHEWS	DANIEL	RICHARDSON	WEBSTER	SAXTON	STEWART	HUGHES	BARKER	O'HARE	HECTOR	DURBAN	NA
VENUE	HOME	SPRAKE	REANEY	COOPER	BREMNER	CHARLTON	HUNTER	GREENHOFF	LORIMER	MADELEY	GILES	GRAY	NA
OPPOS	LEEDS UNITED												
RESULT	0-1	NA											
ATTND	31904	GILES (P)											
ROUND	SF L1	MILESTONES:											

DATE	7.2.68	MATTHEWS	DANIEL	RICHARDSON	WEBSTER	WALLER	STEWART	HUGHES	BARKER	O'HARE	HECTOR	DURBAN	NA
VENUE	AWAY	SPRAKE	REANEY	COOPER*	BREMNER	MADELEY	HUNTER	GREENHOFF	LORIMER	BELFITT	GILES	GRAY	BATES
OPPOS	LEEDS UNITED												
RESULT	2-3	HECTOR,STEWART											
ATTND	29367	BELFITT (2), GRAY											
ROUND	SF L2	MILESTONES: 1ST GOAL FOR STEWART /LAST APPEARANCE FOR HUGHES											

FA CUP

DATE	27.1.68	MATTHEWS	DANIEL	RICHARDSON	WEBSTER	SAXTON	McFARLAND	HUGHES	STEWART	O'HARE	HECTOR	HINTON	NA
VENUE	AWAY	SPRAKE	REANEY	COOPER	BREMNER	CHARLTON*	HUNTER	GREENHOFF	LORIMER	JONES	GILES	GRAY	MADELEY
OPPOS	LEEDS UNITED												
RESULT	0-2	NA											
ATTND	39753	CHARLTON, LORIMER											
ROUND	3RD	MILESTONES: LAST APPEARANCE FOR SAXTON											

DIVISION 2

10.8.68 — AWAY — BLACKBURN ROVERS — RESULT 1-1 — ATTND 13686 — POS 11-9

	1	2	3	4	5	6	7	8	9	10	11	12
C	GREEN	RICHARDSON	ROBSON	STEWART	McFARLAND	MACKAY	WALKER	BARKER	O'HARE	HECTOR	HINTON	NA
O	BLACKLAW	NEWTON	WILSON	SHARPLES	CODDINGTON	HOLE	METCALFE	ROGERS	MARTIN	DARLING	CONNELLY	NA

Scorers: McFARLAND — ROGERS (P)
MILESTONES: DEBUTS FOR GREEN / MACKAY

17.8.68 — HOME — BLACKPOOL — RESULT 1-1 — ATTND 24760 — POS 12-6

	1	2	3	4	5	6	7	8	9	10	11	12
C	GREEN	RICHARDSON	ROBSON	STEWART	McFARLAND	MACKAY	WALKER	BARKER	O'HARE	HECTOR	HINTON	NA
O	TAYLOR	ARMFIELD	MOWBRAY	MILNE	JAMES	McPHEE	SKIRTON	JAMES	GREEN	SUDDICK	HUTCHINSON	NA

Scorers: O'HARE — GREEN
MILESTONES:

20.8.68 — AWAY — SHEFFIELD UNITED — RESULT 0-2 — ATTND 23609 — POS 18-3

	1	2	3	4	5	6	7	8	9	10	11	12
C	GREEN	WEBSTER	ROBSON	STEWART	McFARLAND	MACKAY	WALKER	BARKER	O'HARE	HECTOR	HINTON	NA
O	HODGKINSON	BADGER	SHAW	MUNKS	MALLANDER	WAGSTAFF	WOODWARD	CARLIN	ADDISON	CURIE	REECE	NA

Scorers: NA — ADDISON (P), CARLIN
MILESTONES: 250TH OVERALL LEAGUE GAME FOR HECTOR

24.8.68 — AWAY — HUDDERSFIELD TOWN — RESULT 0-2 — ATTND 10442 — POS 21-11

	1	2	3	4	5	6	7	8	9	10	11	12
C	GREEN	WEBSTER	ROBSON	STEWART	McFARLAND	MACKAY	WALKER	HECTOR	O'HARE	BARKER	HINTON	NA
O	OLDFIELD	SMITH	LEGG	NICHOLSON	ELLAM	CHERRY	DOBSON	SHAW	AIMSON	McGILL	HILL	NA

Scorers: NA — AIMSON (2)
MILESTONES:

28.8.68 — HOME — HULL CITY — RESULT 2-2 — ATTND 24650 — POS 19-20

	1	2	3	4	5	6	7	8	9	10	11	12
C	GREEN	WEBSTER	ROBSON	CARLIN	McFARLAND	MACKAY	WALKER	BARKER	O'HARE	BARKER	HINTON	NA
O	McKECHNIE	BANKS	BEARDSLEY	PETIT	WILSON	GREENWOOD	JARVIS	WAGSTAFF	CHILTON	SIMPKIN	BUTLER	NA

Scorers: BARKER, HECTOR — JARVIS, WAGSTAFF
MILESTONES: DEBUT FOR CARLIN

31.8.68 — HOME — OXFORD UNITED — RESULT 2-0 — ATTND 21737 — POS 17-16

	1	2	3	4	5	6	7	8	9	10	11	12
C	GREEN	WEBSTER	ROBSON	DURBAN	McFARLAND	MACKAY	HINTON	CARLIN	O'HARE	HECTOR	WALKER	NA
O	BARRON	GLADWIN*	LLOYD	ATKINSON	KYLE	CLARKE	SLOAN	ATKINSON	BULLOCK	HATCH	HARRINGTON	LUCAS

Scorers: McFARLAND, O'HARE — NA
MILESTONES:

Match info		GREEN	WEBSTER	ROBSON	DURBAN	McFARLAND	MACKAY	WALKER*	CARLIN	O'HARE	HECTOR	HINTON	BARKER
ASTON VILLA — DATE 7.9.68, VENUE HOME, RESULT 3-1, ATTND 23723, POS 12-20	C	GREEN	WEBSTER	ROBSON	DURBAN	McFARLAND	MACKAY	WALKER*	CARLIN	O'HARE	HECTOR	HINTON	BARKER
	O	DUNN	WRIGHT	AITKEN	EDWARDS	TURNBULL	DEAKIN	FERGUSON	MITCHINSON	GREENHALGH	MARTIN	ANDERSON*	WOODWARD
MILESTONES: HECTOR (2), HINTON / FERGUSON													
BRISTOL CITY — DATE 14.9.68, VENUE AWAY, RESULT 0-0, ATTND 15850, POS 13-17	C	GREEN	WEBSTER	ROBSON	DURBAN	McFARLAND	MACKAY	WALKER	CARLIN	O'HARE	HECTOR	HINTON	NA
	O	GIBSON	JACOBS	BRIGGS	WIMSHURST	CONNOR	PARR	CROWE	GARLAND	GALLEY	KELLAND	SHARPE	NA
MILESTONES: NA / NA — RAMS FIRST 0-0 LEAGUE GAME SINCE 22-4-67 V PORTSMOUTH (51 MATCHES)													
FULHAM — DATE 18.9.68, VENUE HOME, RESULT 1-0, ATTND 26771, POS 9-18	C	GREEN	WEBSTER	ROBSON	DURBAN	McFARLAND	MACKAY	WALKER	CARLIN	O'HARE	HECTOR	HINTON	BARKER
	O	SEYMOUR	PENTECOST	DEMPSEY	MATTHEWSON	CALLAGHAN	BROWN	HAYNES	CONWAY	LARGE	MACDONALD	BARRETT	NA
MILESTONES: HINTON / NA													
MILLWALL — DATE 21.9.68, VENUE HOME, RESULT 1-0, ATTND 25000, POS 6-5	C	GREEN	WEBSTER	ROBSON	DURBAN	McFARLAND	MACKAY	WALKER*	CARLIN	O'HARE	HECTOR	HINTON	BARKER
	O	KING	GILCHRIST	CRIPPS	JONES	KITCHENER	BURNETT	POSSEE	WELLER	CONLON	JACKS	DUNPHY	NA
MILESTONES: DURBAN / NA													
BOLTON WANDERERS — DATE 28.9.68, VENUE AWAY, RESULT 2-1, ATTND 15202, POS 5-12	C	GREEN	WEBSTER	ROBSON	DURBAN	McFARLAND	MACKAY	WALKER	CARLIN	BARKER	HECTOR	HINTON	
	O	HOPKINSON	RITSON	FARRIMOND	WILLIAMS	HULME	HATTON	WHARTON	HILL	GREAVES	BROMLEY	PHILLIPS	
MILESTONES: WALKER, BARKER, WHARTON — DURBAN SCORES IN 250TH OVERALL LEAGUE GAME — FIRST GOAL FOR WALKER													
MIDDLESBROUGH — DATE 5.10.68, VENUE AWAY, RESULT 0-0, ATTND 28636, POS 4-2	C	GREEN	WEBSTER	ROBSON	DURBAN	McFARLAND	MACKAY	WALKER	CARLIN	O'HARE	HECTOR	HINTON	NA
	O	WHIGHAM	SMITH	JONES	GATES	ROOKS	SPRAGGON	LUGG	HICKTON	WEBB	HORSFIELD	DOWNING	NA
MILESTONES: NA / NA — 200TH RAMS LEAGUE GAME FOR WEBSTER													
HULL CITY — DATE 9.10.68, VENUE AWAY, RESULT 0-1, ATTND 24307, POS 7-3	C	GREEN	WEBSTER	ROBSON	DURBAN	McFARLAND	MACKAY	WALKER	CARLIN	O'HARE	HECTOR	HINTON	NA
	O	McKECHNIE	BUTLER	BEARDSLEY	JARVIS	GREENWOOD	SIMPKIN	LORD	WAGSTAFF	CHILTON	HOUGHTON	BUTLER	NA
MILESTONES: NA / NA — 200TH RAMS LEAGUE GAME FOR DURBAN													

		1	2	3	4	5	6	7	8	9	10	11	12
DATE	12.10.68	C	GREEN	WEBSTER	ROBSON	DURBAN	McFARLAND	MACKAY	WALKER	CARLIN	O'HARE	HECTOR	HINTON	NA
VENUE	HOME	O	KELLY	ROSS	RITCHIE	SMITH	HAWKINS	KNIGHTON	WILSON*	SPAVIN	IRVINE	INGRAM	TEMPLE	GEMMILL
OPPOS	PRESTON NORTH END													
RESULT	**1-0**		HINTON											
ATTND	27146		NA											
POS	4-12		MILESTONES:											
DATE	19.10.68	C	GREEN	WEBSTER	ROBSON	DURBAN	McFARLAND	MACKAY	O'HARE	CARLIN	BARKER	HECTOR	HINTON	NA
VENUE	AWAY	O	MILKENS	YOULDEN	LEY	McCANN	TINDALL	HARRIS	TREBILCOCK	POINTER	HIRON	TRAVERS	JENNINGS	NA
OPPOS	PORTSMOUTH													
RESULT	**1-0**		HECTOR											
ATTND	22041		NA											
POS	4-18		MILESTONES:											
DATE	26.10.68	C	GREEN	WEBSTER	ROBSON	DURBAN	McFARLAND	MACKAY	WALKER	CARLIN	O'HARE	HECTOR	HINTON*	BARKER
VENUE	HOME	O	HERRIOT	MARTIN	FOSTER	PAGE	ROBINSON	BEARD	HOCKEY	GREENHOFF	VOWDEN	VINCENT	SUMMERILL*	MURRAY
OPPOS	BIRMINGHAM CITY													
RESULT	**1-0**		CARLIN											
ATTND	34218		NA											
POS	3-17		MILESTONES:	FIRST GOAL FOR CARLIN										
DATE	9.11.68	C	GREEN	DANIEL	ROBSON	DURBAN	McFARLAND	MACKAY	McGOVERN	CARLIN	O'HARE	HECTOR	WALKER	NA
VENUE	HOME	O	WRIGHT	BURKETT	KINSEY	CAMPBELL	WENT	REEVES	GREGORY	TEES	TREACEY	MOORE	PEACOCK	NA
OPPOS	CHARLTON ATHLETIC													
RESULT	**2-1**		O'HARE, HECTOR											
ATTND	25176		GREGORY											
POS	2-8		MILESTONES:	DEBUT FOR McGOVERN										
DATE	16.11.68	C	GREEN	DANIEL	ROBSON	DURBAN	McFARLAND	MACKAY	WALKER	CARLIN	O'HARE	HECTOR	HINTON	NA
VENUE	AWAY	O	DAVIES	CARVER	BELL*	SUTTON	MURRAY	DERRETT	JONES	CLARK	LEA	TOSHACK	BIRD	PHILLIPS
OPPOS	CARDIFF CITY													
RESULT	**1-1**		DURBAN											
ATTND	17328		CLARK											
POS	2-10		MILESTONES:											
DATE	23.11.68	C	GREEN	WEBSTER	ROBSON	DURBAN	McFARLAND	MACKAY	McGOVERN	CARLIN	O'HARE	HECTOR	HINTON	NA
VENUE	HOME	O	ROSS	McCONNELL	CALDWELL	TENNENT	PASSMOOR	GARBUTT	BARTON	MURRAY	McILMOYLE	BALDERSTONE	McVITIE	NA
OPPOS	CARLISLE UNITED													
RESULT	**3-3**		MACKAY, O'HARE, CARLIN											
ATTND	23395		McVITIE, McILMOYLE											
POS	3-14		MILESTONES:											
DATE	30.11.68	C	GREEN	WEBSTER	ROBSON	DURBAN	McFARLAND	MACKAY	WALKER	CARLIN	O'HARE	HECTOR	HINTON	NA
VENUE	AWAY	O	JACKSON	SEWELL	LOUGHLAN	HOY	McCORMICK	BLYTH	LAZARUS	KEMBER	JACKSON	WOODRUFF	TAYLOR	NA
OPPOS	CRYSTAL PALACE													
RESULT	**2-1**		McFARLAND, CARLIN											
ATTND	20751		McCORMICK											
POS	1-3		MILESTONES:											

DATE	VENUE	OPPOS	RESULT	ATTND	POS	Team (Derby / Opposition by position)	MILESTONES
7.12.68	HOME	NORWICH CITY	1-1 (C/O)	24719	1-16	GREEN/KEELAN · WEBSTER/STRINGER · ROBSON/BUTLER · DURBAN/HOWSHALL · McFARLAND/MALLANDER · MACKAY/ANDERSON · WALKER*/FOGGO · CARLIN/O'DONNELL · O'HARE/MANNING · HECTOR/CURRAN · HINTON/FORBES · BARKER/NA	McFARLAND ANDERSON
14.12.68	AWAY	PRESTON NORTH END	0-0 (C/O)	12714	1-14	GREEN/KELLY · WEBSTER/ROSS · ROBSON/McNAB* · DURBAN/SPARK · McFARLAND/HAWKINS · MACKAY/HEPPOLETTE · WALKER/TEMPLE · CARLIN/KNIGHTON · O'HARE/IRVINE · HECTOR/INGRAM · HINTON/LEE · BARKER/GEMMILL (NA)	NA
21.12.68	HOME	PORTSMOUTH	2-1 (C/O)	22061	1-15	GREEN/MILKENS · WEBSTER/PARK · RICHARDSON/LEY · DURBAN/SMITH · McFARLAND/HAND · MACKAY/HARRIS · WALKER/McCANN · CARLIN/TREBILCOCK · O'HARE/POINTER · HECTOR/BROMLEY · HINTON/JENNINGS	HECTOR (2) SMITH
26.12.68	HOME	MIDDLESBROUGH	3-2 (C/O)	34481	1-2	GREEN/WHIGHAM · WEBSTER/GATES · ROBSON/JONES · DURBAN/SPRAGGON · McFARLAND/ROOKS · MACKAY/KINNELL · WALKER/ALLEN · CARLIN/HICKTON · O'HARE/CHADWICK · HECTOR/McMORDIE · HINTON/DOWNING · BARKER/NA	HINTON (2) (1P), McFARLAND / HICKTON (2) (1P)
11.1.69	HOME	BURY	2-0 (C/O)	24578	1-20	GREEN/RAMSBOTTOM · WEBSTER/PARNELL · RICHARDSON/SALE · ROBSON/KERR · McFARLAND/TURNER · MACKAY*/LINDSAY · McGOVERN/TOWERS · CARLIN/JONES · O'HARE/ARROWSMITH · DURBAN/COLLINS · HINTON/HINCE · WALKER/NA	McFARLAND, O'HARE
14.1.69	AWAY	BIRMINGHAM CITY	1-1 (C/O)	39977	1-14	GREEN/HERRIOT · WEBSTER/MARTIN · ROBSON/BEARD · DURBAN/WYLIE · McFARLAND/SLEEUWENHOEK · MACKAY/ROBINSON · McGOVERN/HOCKEY · WALKER/GREENHOFF · O'HARE/PICKERING · HECTOR/VINCENT · HINTON/SUMMERILL · BARKER/NA	HECTOR PICKERING
18.1.69	AWAY	CHARLTON ATHLETIC	0-2 (C/O)	30115	1-2	GREEN/WRIGHT · WEBSTER/CURTIS · ROBSON/KINSEY · DURBAN/CAMPBELL · McFARLAND/WENT · MACKAY/REEVES · McGOVERN/GREGORY · CARLIN/TREACEY · O'HARE/TEES · HECTOR/MOORE · HINTON/MULLEN · BARKER/NA	TREACEY, TEES

LAST APPEARANCE FOR BARKER

FIRST LEAGUE DEFEAT IN FOURTEEN GAMES

		GREEN	WEBSTER	ROBSON	DURBAN	McFARLAND	MACKAY*	McGOVERN	CARLIN	O'HARE	HECTOR	HINTON	WALKER
DATE	25.1.69												
VENUE	AWAY	C											
OPPOS	BURY	O	RAMSBOTTOM	ECCLESHARE	TINNEY	KERR	TURNER	ANDERSON	FARRELL	JONES	ARROWSMITH	COLLINS	HINCE	NA
RESULT	1-0												
ATTND	15361												
POS	1-19												

MILESTONES: O'HARE

		GREEN	WEBSTER	ROBSON	DURBAN	McFARLAND	MACKAY	McGOVERN	CARLIN	O'HARE	HECTOR	HINTON	WALKER
DATE	1.2.69												
VENUE	HOME	C											
OPPOS	CARDIFF CITY	O	DAVIES	CARVER	BELL	SUTTON	MURRAY	DERRETT	JONES	CLARK	LEA	TOSHACK	KING	NA
RESULT	2-0												
ATTND	34589												
POS	1-4												

MILESTONES: HECTOR (2)

BLACKBURN ROVERS

		GREEN	WEBSTER	ROBSON	DURBAN	McFARLAND	MACKAY	McGOVERN	CARLIN*	O'HARE	HECTOR	HINTON	WIGNALL
DATE	1.3.69												
VENUE	HOME	C											
OPPOS	BLACKBURN ROVERS	O	BLACKLAW	MULVENEY	GALLOWAY	MARTIN	CODDINGTON	SHARPLES	METCALFE	DARLING	FRYETT	HELLIWELL*	CONNELLY	CLAYTON
RESULT	4-2												
ATTND	26492												
POS	1-12												

MILESTONES: HECTOR, O'HARE, CARLIN, WIGNALL DARLING, CONNELLY

100TH LEAGUE GOAL FOR HECTOR / SCORING DEBUT FOR WIGNALL / 250TH OVERALL LEAGUE GAME FOR CARLIN.

		GREEN	WEBSTER	ROBSON	DURBAN	McFARLAND	MACKAY	McGOVERN*	CARLIN	O'HARE	WIGNALL	HINTON	WALKER
DATE	5.3.69												
VENUE	HOME	C											
OPPOS	CRYSTAL PALACE	O	JACKSON	SEWELL	LOUGHLAN	HOY	McCORMICK	BLYTH	LAZARUS	KEMBER	WOODRUFF	TAYLOR	TAYLOR	WALKER
RESULT	0-1												
ATTND	31748												
POS	1-5												

WOODRUFF

MILESTONES: NA

BLACKPOOL

		GREEN	WEBSTER	ROBSON	DURBAN	McFARLAND	MACKAY	McGOVERN	CARLIN	O'HARE	HECTOR	HINTON	NA
DATE	8.3.69												
VENUE	AWAY	C											
OPPOS	BLACKPOOL	O	TAYLOR	ARMFIELD	BENTLEY	CRAVEN	JAMES	ALCOCK	BROWN	GREEN	SUDDICK	JOHNSTON*	HUTCHINSON	McPHEE
RESULT	3-2												
ATTND	18853												
POS	1-11												

McFARLAND, O'HARE, HINTON (P)

BROWN, CRAVEN

MILESTONES:

CARLISLE UNITED

		GREEN	WEBSTER	ROBSON	DURBAN	McFARLAND	MACKAY	McGOVERN	CARLIN	O'HARE	HECTOR	HINTON	NA
DATE	11.3.69												
VENUE	AWAY	C											
OPPOS	CARLISLE UNITED	O	ROSS	MARSLAND	BALDERSTONE	TENNENT	PASSMOOR	GARBUTT	WELSH	MURRAY	McILMOYLE	BARTON	McVITIE	NA
RESULT	1-1												
ATTND	12844												
POS	1-7												

HECTOR

WELSH

MILESTONES:

300TH OVERALL LEAGUE GAME FOR MACKAY

HUDDERSFIELD TOWN

		GREEN	WEBSTER	ROBSON	DURBAN	McFARLAND	MACKAY	McGOVERN	CARLIN	O'HARE	HECTOR	HINTON	NA
DATE	15.3.69												
VENUE	HOME	C											
OPPOS	HUDDERSFIELD TOWN	O	POOLE	CLARK	HUTT	NICHOLSON	ELLAM	CHERRY	SMITH	LAWSON	WORTHINGTON	McGILL	DOBSON	NA
RESULT	1-0												
ATTND	28293												
POS	1-10												

McFARLAND

MILESTONES:

22.3.69 — AWAY — OXFORD UNITED — RESULT 2-0 — ATTND 18020 — POS 1-20

Derby	Opposition
GREEN	BARRON
WEBSTER	BEAVON
ROBSON	GLADWIN
DURBAN	ATKINSON
McFARLAND	CLARKE
MACKAY	SMITHSON
McGOVERN	SLOAN
CARLIN	SHUKER
O'HARE	SKEEN
HECTOR	ATKINSON
HINTON	HARRINGTON
NA	NA

MILESTONES: HECTOR (2), NA

29.3.69 — AWAY — ASTON VILLA — RESULT 1-0 — ATTND 49188 — POS 1-16

Derby	Opposition
GREEN	DUNN
WEBSTER	WRIGHT
ROBSON	AITKEN
DURBAN	HOLE
McFARLAND	EDWARDS
MACKAY	TILER
McGOVERN	RUDGE
CARLIN	GODFREY*
O'HARE	SIMMONS
HECTOR	TURNBULL
HINTON	ANDERSON
NA	MARTIN

MILESTONES: SIMMONS (OG), NA

2.4.69 — AWAY — FULHAM — RESULT 1-0 — ATTND 18173 — POS 1-22

Derby	Opposition
GREEN	SUNDERLAND
WEBSTER	TRANTER
ROBSON	CALLAGHAN
DURBAN	LLOYD
McFARLAND	HAYES
MACKAY	ROBERTS
McGOVERN*	CONWAY
CARLIN	EARLE
O'HARE	DEALE
HECTOR	BROWN
HINTON	BARRETT
WIGNALL	NA

MILESTONES: WIGNALL, NA

5.4.69 — HOME — BOLTON WANDERERS — RESULT 5-1 — ATTND 30684 — POS 1-20

Derby	Opposition
GREEN	HOPKINSON
WEBSTER	COOPER
ROBSON	FARRIMOND
DURBAN	WILLIAMS
McFARLAND	MARSH
MACKAY	RIMMER
WIGNALL	PHILLIPS
CARLIN	HILL
O'HARE	BYROM
HECTOR	GREAVES
HINTON	TAYLOR
NA	NA

MILESTONES: McFARLAND, O'HARE, HECTOR, CARLIN, WIGNALL / GREAVES
250TH OVERALL LEAGUE GAME FOR HINTON

7.4.69 — HOME — SHEFFIELD UNITED — RESULT 1-0 — ATTND 34976 — POS 1-8

Derby	Opposition
GREEN	HODGKINSON
WEBSTER	BADGER
ROBSON	SHAW
DURBAN	HODGE
McFARLAND	COLQUHOUN
MACKAY	BARLOW
McGOVERN	WOODWARD
CARLIN	CURRIE
O'HARE	TUDOR
HECTOR	POWELL
HINTON	REECE
NA	NA

MILESTONES: DURBAN, NA

12.4.69 — AWAY — MILLWALL — RESULT 1-0 — ATTND 13735 — POS 1-7

Derby	Opposition
GREEN	KING
WEBSTER	BROWN
ROBSON	BURNETT
DURBAN	JACKS
McFARLAND	KITCHENER
MACKAY	DORLEY
McGOVERN	POSSEE
CARLIN	JONES
O'HARE	PETERSON
HECTOR	WELLER
HINTON	DUNPHY*
NA	CRIPPS

MILESTONES: CARLIN, NA

16.4.69 — AWAY — NORWICH CITY — RESULT 4-1 — ATTND 13804 — POS 1-18

Derby	Opposition
GREEN	VASPER
WEBSTER	STRINGER
ROBSON	PANE
McGOVERN	LUCAS
McFARLAND	FORBES
MACKAY	ANDERSON
WIGNALL	FOGGO
CARLIN	BRYCELAND
O'HARE	ALLCOCK
HECTOR	O'DONNELL
HINTON	HOWARD
NA	NA

MILESTONES: CARLIN (2), O'HARE, WIGNALL / FOGGO (P)
CLOUGH'S 100TH COMPETITIVE GAME IN CHARGE

BRISTOL CITY — DATE 19.4.69 · VENUE HOME · RESULT 5-0 · ATTND 31644 · POS 1-16

Pos	1	2	3	4	5	6	7	8	9	10	11	12
Derby	GREEN	WEBSTER	ROBSON	DURBAN	McFARLAND	MACKAY	McGOVERN	CARLIN	O'HARE	HECTOR	HINTON	NA
Bristol City	WATLING	JACOBS	BRIGGS	WIMSHIRST	CONNOR	PARR	SKIRTON	KELLARD	BARTLEY	GARLAND	SHARPE	NA

MILESTONES: DURBAN (3), HINTON, HECTOR
MILESTONES: GREEN, ROBSON AND McFARLAND ALL EVER-PRESENTS
AFTER ALL TEAMS HAD PLAYED 42 GAMES, DERBY REMAINED IN 1ST PLACE

LEAGUE CUP

CHESTERFIELD — DATE 14.8.68 · VENUE HOME · RESULT 3-0 · ATTND 21847 · ROUND 1ST

Pos	1	2	3	4	5	6	7	8	9	10	11	12
Derby	GREEN	WEBSTER	ROBSON	STEWART	McFARLAND	MACKAY	WALKER	BARKER	O'HARE	HECTOR	HINTON	NA
Chesterfield	HUMPHREYS	HOLMES	LAMSDEN	KETTLEBOROUGH	PHELAN	HUGHES	WARNOCK	RANDALL	HOLLETT	PUGH	MARTIN	NA

MILESTONES: HECTOR, HINTON, HUMPHREYS (OG)

STOCKPORT COUNTY — DATE 4.9.68 · VENUE HOME · RESULT 5-1 · ATTND 21549 · ROUND 2ND

Pos	1	2	3	4	5	6	7	8	9	10	11	12
Derby	GREEN	WEBSTER	ROBSON	STEWART	McFARLAND	MACKAY	WALKER	CARLIN	O'HARE	HECTOR	HINTON	NA
Stockport County	LLOYD	HAYDOCK	HARTLE	GOODWIN	MILNER	LOW	ALLCHURCH	MORRIN*	FRYATT	HARLEY	PRICE	LEDGARD

MILESTONES: HINTON (4), HECTOR
LEDGARD
FIRST 4-GOAL TALLY SINCE 1956

CHELSEA — DATE 25.9.68 · VENUE AWAY · RESULT 0-0 · ATTND 26975 · ROUND 3RD

Pos	1	2	3	4	5	6	7	8	9	10	11	12
Derby	GREEN	WEBSTER	ROBSON	DURBAN	McFARLAND	MACKAY	WALKER	CARLIN	O'HARE	HECTOR	HINTON	NA
Chelsea	BONETTI	HARRIS	McCREADIE	HOLLINS	WEBB	BOYLE	BALDWIN	COOKE*	OSGOOD	BIRCHENALL	TAMBLING	HINTON

MILESTONES: NA, NA

CHELSEA — DATE 2.10.68 · VENUE HOME · RESULT 3-1 · ATTND 34346 · ROUND 3RD R

Pos	1	2	3	4	5	6	7	8	9	10	11	12
Derby	GREEN	WEBSTER	ROBSON	DURBAN	McFARLAND	MACKAY	WALKER	CARLIN	O'HARE	HECTOR	HINTON	NA
Chelsea	BONETTI	HINTON	McCREADIE	HOLLINS	WEBB	HARRIS	BIRCHENALL	TAMBLING	OSGOOD	HUTCHINSON	HOUSEMAN	HOUSEMAN

MILESTONES: MACKAY, DURBAN, HECTOR
HOUSEMAN
FIRST GOAL FOR MACKAY

EVERTON — DATE 16.10.68 · VENUE AWAY · RESULT 0-0 · ATTND 44795 · ROUND 4TH

Pos	1	2	3	4	5	6	7	8	9	10	11	12
Derby	GREEN	WEBSTER	ROBSON	DURBAN	McFARLAND	MACKAY	WALKER	CARLIN	O'HARE	HECTOR	HINTON	NA
Everton	WEST	WRIGHT	BROWN	KENDALL	LABONE	HARVEY	HUSBAND*	BALL	ROYLE	HURST	MORRISSEY	KENYON

MILESTONES: NA, NA

DATE	VENUE	OPPOS	RESULT	ATTND	ROUND	1	2	3	4	5	6	7	8	9	10	11	12
23.10.68	HOME	EVERTON	1-0	34370	4TH R	GREEN	WEBSTER	ROBSON	DURBAN	McFARLAND	MACKAY	HINTON	CARLIN	O'HARE	HECTOR	WALKER	NA
						WEST	WRIGHT	BROWN	KENDALL	LABONE	HARVEY	HUMPHREYS*	BALL	ROYLE	HURST	MORRISSEY	WILSON

MILESTONES: HECTOR / NA

DATE	VENUE	OPPOS	RESULT	ATTND	ROUND	1	2	3	4	5	6	7	8	9	10	11	12
30.10.68	HOME	SWINDON TOWN	0-0	35014	5TH	GREEN	WEBSTER	ROBSON	DURBAN	McFARLAND	MACKAY	BARKER	CARLIN	O'HARE	HECTOR	WALKER	NA
						DOWNSBOROUGH	BUTLER*	THOMAS	PENMAN	BURROWS	HARLAND	HEATH	SMART	SMITH	NOBLE	ROGERS	DAWSON

MILESTONES: NA / NA

DATE	VENUE	OPPOS	RESULT	ATTND	ROUND	1	2	3	4	5	6	7	8	9	10	11	12
5.11.68	AWAY	SWINDON TOWN	0-1	26449	5TH R	GREEN	WEBSTER	ROBSON	DURBAN	McFARLAND	MACKAY	WALKER	CARLIN	BUTLIN	HECTOR	WALKER	NA
						DOWNSBOROUGH	BUTLER	THOMAS	PENMAN	BURROWS	HARLAND	HEATH	SMART	SMITH	NOBLE	ROGERS	NA

MILESTONES: ROGERS

FA CUP

DATE	VENUE	OPPOS	RESULT	ATTND	ROUND	1	2	3	4	5	6	7	8	9	10	11	12
4.1.69	AWAY	BURNLEY	1-3	22842	3RD	GREEN	WEBSTER	RICHARDSON	DURBAN	McFARLAND	ROBSON	McGOVERN	CARLIN	O'HARE	HECTOR	HINTON	NA
						THOMSON	SMITH	LATCHAM	MERRINGTON	WALDRON	BLANT	THOMAS	COATES	CASPER	BELLAMY	COLLINS	NA

MILESTONES: DURBAN / CASPER (2), THOMAS

DIVISION 1

		1	2	3	4	5	6	7	8	9	10	11	12
DATE	9.8.69	GREEN	WEBSTER	ROBSON	DURBAN	McFARLAND	MACKAY	McGOVERN	CARLIN	O'HARE	HECTOR	HINTON	NA
VENUE	HOME C	MELLOR*	ANGUS	LATCHAM	O'NEIL	WALDRON	TODD	THOMAS	COATES	CASPER	DOCHERTY	KINDON	PROBERT
OPPOS	BURNLEY O												
RESULT	0-0 C												
ATTND	29451 O	NA											
POS	12-10	NA											
		MILESTONES:											
DATE	12.8.69	GREEN	WEBSTER	ROBSON	DURBAN	McFARLAND	MACKAY	McGOVERN	CARLIN	O'HARE	HECTOR	HINTON	NA
VENUE	AWAY O	BEST	CARROLL	MILLS	MORRIS	BAXTER	JEFFERSON	WOODS	VILJOEN	WIGG	O'ROURKE	BROGAN	NA
OPPOS	IPSWICH TOWN												
RESULT	1-0 C	McFARLAND											
ATTND	20551 O	NA											
POS	4-15												
		MILESTONES:											
DATE	16.8.69	GREEN	WEBSTER	ROBSON	DURBAN	McFARLAND	MACKAY	McGOVERN	CARLIN	O'HARE	HECTOR	HINTON	NA
VENUE	AWAY O	GLAZIER	COOP	CATTLIN	HILL	CURTIS	BLOCKLEY	GOULD	GIBSON	MARTIN	CARR	CLEMENTS	NA
OPPOS	COVENTRY CITY												
RESULT	1-1 C	McFARLAND											
ATTND	41036 O	MARTIN											
POS	8-5												
		MILESTONES:											
DATE	20.8.69	GREEN	WEBSTER	ROBSON	DURBAN	McFARLAND*	MACKAY	McGOVERN	CARLIN	O'HARE	HECTOR	HINTON	WIGNALL
VENUE	HOME C	BEST	CARROLL	MILLS	MORRIS	BAXTER	JEFFERSON	VILJOEN	COLLARD	WIGG*	O'ROURKE	BROGAN	WOODS
OPPOS	IPSWICH TOWN												
RESULT	3-1 C	HINTON (2) (1P), CARLIN											
ATTND	31467 O	BROGAN											
POS	6-22												
		MILESTONES:											
DATE	23.8.69	GREEN	WEBSTER	ROBSON	DURBAN	RHODES	MACKAY	McGOVERN	CARLIN	O'HARE	HECTOR*	HINTON	WIGNALL
VENUE	HOME C	BANKS	MARSH	ELDER	SKEELS	SMITH	ALLEN	CONROY	DOBING	RITCHIE	EASTHAM	BURROWS	NA
OPPOS	STOKE CITY												
RESULT	0-0 C	NA											
ATTND	36170 O	NA											
POS	5-11												
		MILESTONES:											
DATE	27.8.69	GREEN	WEBSTER	ROBSON	DURBAN	McFARLAND	MACKAY	McGOVERN	CARLIN	O'HARE	HECTOR	HINTON	NA
VENUE	AWAY O	PARKES	WILSON	PARKIN	BAILEY	HOLSGROVE	MUNROE	McCALLIOG	KNOWLES	DOUGAN	CURRAN	WALKER*	McALLE
OPPOS	WOLVERHAMPTON WANDERERS												
RESULT	1-1 C	HINTON											
ATTND	45025 O	DOUGAN											
POS	5-3												
		MILESTONES:											

Match 1

DATE	VENUE	OPPOS	RESULT	ATTND	POS
30.8.69	AWAY	WEST BROMWICH ALBION	2-0	34173	3-20

GREEN	WEBSTER	ROBSON	DURBAN	McFARLAND	MACKAY	McGOVERN	CARLIN	O'HARE	HECTOR	HINTON	NA
CUMBES	FRASER	MERRICK	BROWN	TALBUT	KAYE	SUGGETT	HUGHES	KRZYWICKI	HOPE	HARTFORD	NA

MILESTONES: HECTOR, MACKAY / NA

Match 2

DATE	VENUE	OPPOS	RESULT	ATTND	POS
6.9.69	HOME	EVERTON	2-1	37708	3-2

GREEN	WEBSTER	ROBSON	DURBAN	McFARLAND	MACKAY	McGOVERN	CARLIN	O'HARE	HECTOR	HINTON	NA
WEST	WRIGHT	BROWN	KENDALL	LABONE	HARVEY	HUSBAND	BALL	ROYLE	HURST	MORRISSEY	NA

MILESTONES: O'HARE, HECTOR / KENDALL / NA

Match 3

DATE	VENUE	OPPOS	RESULT	ATTND	POS
10.9.69	HOME	SOUTHAMPTON	3-0	35826	2-16

GREEN	WEBSTER	ROBSON	DURBAN	McFARLAND	MACKAY	McGOVERN	CARLIN	O'HARE	HECTOR	HINTON	NA
MARTIN	KIRKUP	JONES	KEMP	McGRATH	GABRIEL	PAINE	CHANNON	DAVIES	WALKER	FISHER	NA

MILESTONES: DURBAN, CARLIN, HECTOR / NA

Match 4

DATE	VENUE	OPPOS	RESULT	ATTND	POS
13.9.69	AWAY	NEWCASTLE UNITED	1-0	39382	1-12

GREEN	WEBSTER	ROBSON	DURBAN	McFARLAND	MACKAY	McGOVERN	CARLIN	O'HARE	HECTOR	HINTON	NA
McFAUL	CRAGGS	CLARK	GIBB	BURTON	MONCUR	SCOTT*	ROBSON	DAVIES	SMITH	FOGGON	ARENTOFT

MILESTONES: McFARLAND

Match 5

DATE	VENUE	OPPOS	RESULT	ATTND	POS
20.9.69	HOME	TOTTENHAM HOTSPUR	5-0	41826	2-8

GREEN	WEBSTER	ROBSON	DURBAN*	McFARLAND	MACKAY	McGOVERN	CARLIN	O'HARE	HECTOR	HINTON	WIGNALL
JENNINGS	BEAL	KNOWLES	MULLERY	ENGLAND	COLLINS	PEARCE	GREAVES	GILZEAN	PRATT	MORGAN*	WANT

MILESTONES: DURBAN (2), CARLIN, O'HARE, HECTOR

Match 6

DATE	VENUE	OPPOS	RESULT	ATTND	POS
27.9.69	AWAY	SHEFFIELD WEDNESDAY	0-1	44332	3-19

GREEN	WEBSTER	ROBSON	DURBAN	McFARLAND	MACKAY	McGOVERN	CARLIN	O'HARE	HECTOR	HINTON	NA
SPRINGETT	SMITH	BRANFOOT	YOUNG	ELLIS	CRAIG	PUGH	EUSTACE	WARBOYS	FORD	WOODHALL*	PRENDERGAST

MILESTONES: WARBOYS

Match 7

300TH OVERALL LEAGUE GAME FOR HECTOR

DATE	VENUE	OPPOS	RESULT	ATTND	POS
4.10.69	HOME	MANCHESTER UNITED	2-0	40724	2-12

GREEN	DANIEL	ROBSON	DURBAN	McFARLAND	MACKAY	McGOVERN	CARLIN	O'HARE	HECTOR	HINTON	NA
STEPNEY	FITZPATRICK	DUNNE	BURNS	URE	SADLER	MORGAN*	KIDD	CHARLTON	ASTON	BEST	SARTORI

MILESTONES: HECTOR, FITZPATRICK (OG)

	C/O	GREEN	DANIEL	ROBSON	DURBAN	McFARLAND	MACKAY	McGOVERN	CARLIN	O'HARE	HECTOR	HINTON	NA
DATE 8.10.69	C	GREEN	DANIEL	ROBSON	DURBAN	McFARLAND	MACKAY	McGOVERN	CARLIN	O'HARE	HECTOR	HINTON	NA
VENUE HOME	O	GLAZIER	COOP	BRUCK	SETTERS	CURTIS	BLOCKLEY	HUNT	GIBSON	MARTIN	CARR*	CLEMENTS	JOICEY
OPPOS COVENTRY CITY													
RESULT 1-3													
ATTND 39880													
POS 3-5													

MILESTONES: DURBAN / MARTIN, BLOCKLEY, McFARLAND (OG)

	C/O	GREEN	DANIEL	ROBSON	DURBAN	McFARLAND	MACKAY	McGOVERN	CARLIN	O'HARE	HECTOR	HINTON	NA
DATE 11.10.69	C	GREEN	DANIEL	ROBSON	DURBAN	McFARLAND	MACKAY	McGOVERN	CARLIN	O'HARE	HECTOR	HINTON	NA
VENUE AWAY	O	BONETTI	WEBB	HARRIS	HOLLINS	DEMPSEY*	HINTON	BOYLE	HOUSEMAN	BIRCHENALL	HUDSON	COOKE	OSGOOD
OPPOS CHELSEA													
RESULT 2-2													
ATTND 51421													
POS 2-12													

MILESTONES: O'HARE, HECTOR / HOUSEMAN, HOLLINS

	C/O	GREEN	DANIEL	ROBSON	DANIEL	McFARLAND	MACKAY	McGOVERN	CARLIN	O'HARE	HECTOR	HINTON	NA
DATE 18.10.69	C	GREEN	WEBSTER	ROBSON	DANIEL	McFARLAND	MACKAY	McGOVERN	CARLIN	O'HARE	HECTOR	HINTON	NA
VENUE HOME	O	CORRIGAN	BOOK	PARDOE	DOYLE	BOOTH	OAKES	SUMMERBEE	BELL	LEE	YOUNG	BOWYER	NA
OPPOS MANCHESTER CITY													
RESULT 0-1													
ATTND 40788													
POS 3-7													

MILESTONES: NA / LEE

	C/O	GREEN	WEBSTER	DANIEL	DURBAN	McFARLAND	MACKAY	McGOVERN	CARLIN	O'HARE	HECTOR	HINTON	NA
DATE 25.10.69	C	GREEN	WEBSTER	DANIEL	DURBAN	McFARLAND	MACKAY	McGOVERN	CARLIN	O'HARE	HECTOR	HINTON	NA
VENUE AWAY	O	SPRAKE	REANEY	MADELEY	BREMNER	CHARLTON	HUNTER	LORIMER	CLARKE	JONES	BATES	GRAY*	HIBBITT
OPPOS LEEDS UNITED													
RESULT 0-2													
ATTND 44183													
POS 3-4													

MILESTONES: NA / CLARKE (2) / 100TH RAMS LEAGUE GAME FOR O'HARE

	C/O	GREEN	WEBSTER	DANIEL	DURBAN	McFARLAND	MACKAY	McGOVERN	CARLIN	O'HARE	HECTOR	HINTON	NA
DATE 1.11.69	C	GREEN	WEBSTER	DANIEL	DURBAN	McFARLAND	MACKAY	McGOVERN	CARLIN	O'HARE	HECTOR	HINTON	NA
VENUE HOME	O	LAWRENCE	LAWLER	STRONG	SMITH	YEATS	HUGHES	CALLAGHAN	HUNT	GRAHAM	ST JOHN	THOMPSON	NA
OPPOS LIVERPOOL													
RESULT 4-0													
ATTND 40993													
POS 4-3													

MILESTONES: HECTOR (2), McGOVERN, O'HARE / NA / FIRST GOAL FOR McGOVERN / CLOUGH'S 100TH LEAGUE GAME IN CHARGE

	C/O	GREEN	WEBSTER	ROBSON	DURBAN	McFARLAND	MACKAY	McGOVERN	CARLIN	O'HARE	HECTOR	HINTON	NA
DATE 8.11.69	C	GREEN	WEBSTER	ROBSON	DURBAN	McFARLAND	MACKAY	McGOVERN	CARLIN	O'HARE	HECTOR	HINTON	NA
VENUE AWAY	O	BARNET	STOREY	McNAB	COURT	NEIL*	SIMPSON	ROBERTSON	SAMMELS	RADFORD	GRAHAM	ARMSTRONG	GEORGE
OPPOS ARSENAL													
RESULT 0-4													
ATTND 49763													
POS 4-11													

MILESTONES: SAMMELS (2), GEORGE, ARMSTRONG / NA

	C/O	GREEN	WEBSTER	ROBSON	DURBAN	McFARLAND	MACKAY	McGOVERN	CARLIN	O'HARE	HECTOR	HINTON	NA
DATE 15.11.69	C	GREEN	WEBSTER	ROBSON	DURBAN	McFARLAND	MACKAY	McGOVERN	CARLIN	O'HARE	HECTOR	HINTON	NA
VENUE HOME	O	MONTGOMERY	IRWIN	ASHURST	TODD	HESLOP	McGIVEN	KERR	HARRIS	BAKER	HUGHES	PARK*	SYMM
OPPOS SUNDERLAND													
RESULT 3-0													
ATTND 31918													
POS 5-22													

MILESTONES: DURBAN (2), ASHURST (OG) / NA / DURBAN SCORES TWICE IN 300TH OVERALL LEAGUE GAME / 100TH RAMS LEAGUE GAME FOR McFARLAND

Match details

DATE	VENUE	OPPOS	RESULT	ATTND	POS	Goalscorers	MILESTONES	Notes
22.11.69	AWAY (C/O)	WEST HAM UNITED	0-3	32485	6-14	HURST (2), PETERS	NA	
29.11.69	HOME (C/O)	NOTTINGHAM FOREST	0-2	38225	7-14	MOORE, LYONS	NA	
6.12.69	AWAY (C/O)	CRYSTAL PALACE	1-0	20883	6-20	HECTOR	NA	250TH RAMS LEAGUE GAME FOR DURBAN
13.12.69	HOME (C/O)	NEWCASTLE UNITED	2-0	30057	5-14	McGOVERN, HINTON	NA	
20.12.69	AWAY (C/O)	EVERTON	0-1	44914	6-1	BALL	NA	250TH RAMS LEAGUE GAME FOR WEBSTER
26.12.69	AWAY (C/O)	STOKE CITY	0-1	37787	8-6	BURROWS (P)	NA	
27.12.69	HOME (C/O)	WEST BROMWICH ALBION	2-0	35581	5-15	O'HARE (2)	NA	

Line-ups (Derby player / opponent), shirts 1–12

Match	1	2	3	4	5	6	7	8	9	10	11	12
West Ham	GREEN / FERGUSON	WEBSTER / BONDS	ROBSON* / LAMPARD	DURBAN / HOWE	McFARLAND / STEPHENSON	MACKAY / MOORE	McGOVERN / REDKNAPP	CARLIN / PETERS	O'HARE / BROOKING	HECTOR / HURST	HINTON / BEST	STEWART / NA
Nott'm Forest	GREEN / HILL	WEBSTER / HINDLEY	ROBSON / WINFIELD	DURBAN / CHAPMAN	McFARLAND / HENNESSEY	MACKAY / NEWTON	McGOVERN / REES	CARLIN / LYONS	O'HARE / HILLEY	HECTOR / HALL	HINTON / MOORE	NA / NA
Crystal Palace	GREEN / JACKSON	WEBSTER / SEWELL	ROBSON / LOUGHLAN	DURBAN / PAYNE	McFARLAND / McCORMICK	MACKAY / HYND	McGOVERN / KEMBER	CARLIN / HOADLEY	O'HARE / QUEEN	HECTOR / TOMKINS	HINTON / DAWKINS	NA / NA
Newcastle	GREEN / McFAUL	WEBSTER / CRAIG	ROBSON / CLARK	DURBAN / GIBB	McFARLAND / BURTON	MACKAY / MONCUR	McGOVERN / SCOTT	CARLIN / ROBSON	O'HARE / DAVIES	HECTOR / FOGGON	HINTON / HINDSON	NA / NA
Everton	GREEN / WEST	WEBSTER / WRIGHT	ROBSON / NEWTON	DURBAN / KENDALL	McFARLAND / LABONE	MACKAY / JACKSON	WALKER / HUSBAND*	CARLIN / BALL	O'HARE / ROYLE	HECTOR / HURST	HINTON / MORRISSEY	/ BROWN
Stoke City	GREEN / BANKS	WEBSTER / MARSH	ROBSON / PEJIC	DURBAN / STEVENSON	McFARLAND / SMITH	MACKAY / BLOOR	McGOVERN* / EASTHAM	WALKER / GREENHOFF	O'HARE / CONROY	HECTOR / DOBING	HINTON / BURROWS	WIGNALL / NA
West Bromwich Albion	GREEN / OSBORNE	WEBSTER / WILLIAMS	ROBSON / WILSON	DURBAN / BROWN	McFARLAND / POTTER	MACKAY / HUGHES	McGOVERN / HEGAN	WIGNALL / SUGGETT	O'HARE / ASTLE	HECTOR / HARTFORD	HINTON / MARTIN*	NA / KRZYWICKI

203

TOTTENHAM HOTSPUR

GREEN	WEBSTER	DANIEL	DURBAN	McFARLAND	MACKAY	McGOVERN	CARLIN	WIGNALL	HECTOR	HINTON	NA
JENNINGS	KINNEAR	KNOWLES	MULLERY	ENGLAND	BEAL	PEARCE	GREAVES	GILZEAN	PERRYMAN	MORGAN	NA

- DATE: 10.1.70
- VENUE: AWAY — C / O
- OPPOS: TOTTENHAM HOTSPUR
- RESULT: 1-2
- ATTND: 38645
- POS: 6-12
- MILESTONES: CARLIN — GREAVES, MORGAN

SHEFFIELD WEDNESDAY

GREEN	WEBSTER	ROBSON	DURBAN	McFARLAND	MACKAY	McGOVERN	CARLIN	O'HARE	HECTOR	HINTON	NA
SPRINGETT	WILCOCKSON	MEGSON	ELLIS	PROPHETT	PUGH	SINCLAIR	SMITH	WARBOYS	DOWNES	COLEMAN	NA

- DATE: 17.1.70
- VENUE: HOME — C / O
- OPPOS: SHEFFIELD WEDNESDAY
- RESULT: 1-0
- ATTND: 32991
- POS: 5-12
- MILESTONES: O'HARE / NA

MANCHESTER UNITED

GREEN	WEBSTER	ROBSON	STEWART*	McFARLAND	MACKAY	McGOVERN	CARLIN	O'HARE	HECTOR	HINTON	WIGNALL
STEPNEY	EDWARDS	BURNS	CRERAND	URE	SADLER	MORGAN	SARTORI	CHARLTON	KIDD	ASTON	NA

- DATE: 31.1.70
- VENUE: AWAY — C / O
- OPPOS: MANCHESTER UNITED
- RESULT: 0-1
- ATTND: 59315
- POS: 9-8
- MILESTONES: NA — CHARLTON; LAST APPEARANCE FOR STEWART

CHELSEA

GREEN	WEBSTER	ROBSON	HENNESSEY	McFARLAND	MACKAY	DURBAN	CARLIN	O'HARE	HECTOR	HINTON	NA
BONETTI	WEBB	McCREADIE	HOLLINS	MULLIGAN	HINTON	BALDWIN	HUDSON	OSGOOD	HUTCHINSON	HOUSEMAN	NA

- DATE: 11.2.70
- VENUE: HOME — C / O
- OPPOS: CHELSEA
- RESULT: 2-2
- ATTND: 35109
- POS: 10-3
- MILESTONES: DURBAN, HECTOR — OSGOOD, HUDSON; DEBUT FOR HENNESSEY

BURNLEY

GREEN	WEBSTER	ROBSON	HENNESSEY	McFARLAND	MACKAY	DURBAN	CARLIN	O'HARE	HECTOR	HINTON	NA
MELLOR	ANGUS	THOMPSON	O'NEIL	DOBSON	MERRINGTON*	CASPER	COATES	WILSON	THOMAS	KINDON	TODD

- DATE: 14.2.70
- VENUE: AWAY — C / O
- OPPOS: BURNLEY
- RESULT: 1-1
- ATTND: 18470
- POS: 9-16
- MILESTONES: O'HARE — CASPER

ARSENAL

GREEN	WEBSTER	ROBSON	HENNESSEY	McFARLAND	MACKAY	DURBAN	CARLIN	O'HARE	HECTOR	HINTON	NA
WILSON	STOREY	McNAB	McLINTOCK	ROBERTS	KELLY	MARINELLO	GEORGE	RADFORD	SAMMELS	GRAHAM	NA

- DATE: 21.2.70
- VENUE: HOME — C / O
- OPPOS: ARSENAL
- RESULT: 3-2
- ATTND: 35284
- POS: 5-14
- MILESTONES: O'HARE, HECTOR, MACKAY — RADFORD, ROBERTS; 100TH RAMS LEAGUE GAME FOR HINTON

LIVERPOOL

GREEN	WEBSTER	ROBSON	HENNESSEY	McFARLAND	MACKAY	DURBAN	CARLIN*	O'HARE	HECTOR	HINTON	McGOVERN
CLEMENCE	LAWLER	WALL	SMITH	STRONG	HUGHES	CALLAGHAN	LIVERMORE	EVANS	THOMPSON	GRAHAM	NA

- DATE: 28.2.70
- VENUE: AWAY — C / O
- OPPOS: LIVERPOOL
- RESULT: 2-0
- ATTND: 43594
- POS: 4-9
- MILESTONES: O'HARE — HENNESSEY; FIRST GOAL FOR HENNESSEY

Date	Venue	Opponents	Result	Attnd	Pos	Derby County (1–11, sub)	Opponents (1–11, sub)	Derby Scorers	Opp. Scorer	Milestones
7.3.70	HOME	WEST HAM UNITED	3-0	35615	4-17	GREEN, WEBSTER, ROBSON, HENNESSEY, McFARLAND, MACKAY, DURBAN, CARLIN, O'HARE, HECTOR, HINTON; sub NA	GROTIER, BONDS, LAMPARD, CUSHLEY, STEPHENSON, MOORE, BEST, PETERS, HURST, EUSTACE, HOWE; sub NA	DURBAN, O'HARE, HINTON (P)	NA	NA
14.3.70	AWAY	NOTTINGHAM FOREST	3-1	42074	3-13	GREEN, WEBSTER, ROBSON, HENNESSEY, McFARLAND, MACKAY, DURBAN, CARLIN, O'HARE, WIGNALL, HINTON; sub NA	HOLLINS, HINDLEY, WINFIELD, CHAPMAN, O'KANE, NEWTON, LYONS, RICHARDSON, INGRAM, REES*, HILLEY; sub McCAFFEREY	DURBAN, O'HARE, O'KANE (OG)	NEWTON	
21.3.70	HOME	CRYSTAL PALACE	3-1	30198	4-21	GREEN, WEBSTER, ROBSON, HENNESSEY, McFARLAND, MACKAY, DURBAN, CARLIN, O'HARE, HECTOR, HINTON; sub NA	JACKSON, SEWELL, HOADLEY, PAYNE, McCORMICK, BLYTH, SCOTT, KEMBER, HOY, QUEEN, JACKSON; sub NA	CARLIN, HECTOR, HINTON (P)	JACKSON	
27.3.70	AWAY	MANCHESTER CITY	1-0	42316	4-21	GREEN, WEBSTER, ROBSON, DURBAN, McFARLAND, HENNESSEY, McGOVERN, CARLIN, O'HARE, HECTOR, HINTON; sub NA	CORRIGAN, BOOK, MANN, DOYLE, BOOTH, OAKES, JEFFRIES, LEE, GLENNON, YOUNG, PARDOE; sub NA	McFARLAND	NA	
28.3.70	AWAY	SUNDERLAND	1-1	18818	4-12	GREEN, WEBSTER, ROBSON, DURBAN, McFARLAND, HENNESSEY, McGOVERN*, CARLIN, O'HARE, HECTOR, HINTON; sub WIGNALL	MONTGOMERY, IRWIN, HARVEY, TODD, HESLOP, McGIVEN, PARK, KERR, HUGHES, HARRIS, TUEART; sub NA	McGOVERN	HARRIS	150TH RAMS LEAGUE GAME FOR HECTOR
30.3.70	HOME	LEEDS UNITED	4-1	41011	3-2	GREEN, WEBSTER, ROBSON, DURBAN, McFARLAND, HENNESSEY, WIGNALL, CARLIN, O'HARE, HECTOR, HINTON; sub NA	HARVEY, DAVEY, PETERSON, LUMSDEN, KENNEDY, YORATH, GALVIN, BATES, BELFITT, HIBBITT, JOHANNESON; sub NA	McFARLAND, CARLIN, O'HARE, WIGNALL	KENNEDY	
4.4.70	HOME	WOLVERHAMPTON WANDERERS	2-0	33585	3-11	GREEN, WEBSTER, ROBSON, DURBAN, DANIEL, MACKAY, WIGNALL, CARLIN, O'HARE, HECTOR, HINTON; sub NA	PARKES, TAYLOR, PARKIN, WILSON, HOLSGROVE, MUNROE, BAILEY, McCALLOIG, DOUGAN, CURRAN, O'GRADY*; sub WALKER	WIGNALL, HENNESSEY	NA	300TH OVERALL LEAGUE GAME FOR CARLIN

League

DATE: 15.4.70 **VENUE:** AWAY (C) **OPPOS:** SOUTHAMPTON **RESULT:** 1-1 (C) **ATTND:** 21229 (O) **POS:** 3-18

Team												SUB
Derby	GREEN	WEBSTER	ROBSON	DURBAN	DANIEL	MACKAY	McGOVERN	CARLIN	O'HARE	HECTOR	HINTON	NA
Southampton	MARTIN	KIRKUP	BYRNE	FISHER	GABRIEL	WALKER	O'BRIEN	CHANNON	DAVIES	PAINE	JENKINS	NA

Scorers: McGOVERN / BYRNE

MILESTONES: 350TH OVERALL LEAGUE GAME FOR HENNESSEY / GREEN AND HINTON BOTH EVER-PRESENT

AFTER ALL TEAMS HAD PLAYED 42 GAMES DERBY FINISHED IN 4TH PLACE

LEAGUE CUP

DATE: 3.9.69 **VENUE:** AWAY (C) **OPPOS:** HARTLEPOOL UNITED **RESULT:** 3-1 (C) **ATTND:** 7700 (O) **ROUND:** 2ND

Team												SUB
Derby	GREEN	WEBSTER	ROBSON	DURBAN	McFARLAND	MACKAY	McGOVERN	CARLIN	O'HARE	HECTOR	HINTON	NA
Hartlepool United	SMITH	BIRCUMSHAW	DOBBING	SHERIDAN	GILL	GOAD	PARRY	BELL	THOMPSON	WRIGHT	YOUNG	NA

Scorers: McFARLAND, CARLIN, HINTON (P) / BELL

MILESTONES:

DATE: 24.9.69 **VENUE:** HOME (C) **OPPOS:** HULL CITY **RESULT:** 3-1 (C) **ATTND:** 31603 (O) **ROUND:** 3RD

Team												SUB
Derby	GREEN	WEBSTER	ROBSON	DURBAN	McFARLAND*	MACKAY	McGOVERN	CARLIN	O'HARE	HECTOR	HINTON	WIGNALL
Hull City	McKECHNIE	BANKS	BUTLER	PETIT	BARKER	SIMPKIN	WILKINSON	WAGSTAFF*	CHILTON	HOUGHTON	BUTLER	JARVIS

Scorers: O'HARE, HECTOR, HINTON / CHILTON

MILESTONES:

DATE: 14.10.69 **VENUE:** AWAY (C) **OPPOS:** CRYSTAL PALACE **RESULT:** 1-1 (C) **ATTND:** 30399 (O) **ROUND:** 4TH

Team												SUB
Derby	GREEN	WEBSTER	ROBSON	DURBAN	McFARLAND*	MACKAY	McGOVERN	CARLIN	O'HARE	HECTOR	HINTON*	WIGNALL
Crystal Palace	JACKSON	PAYNE	LAUGHLAN	HOADLEY	McCORMICK	HYND	KEMBER	WOODRUFF	JACKSON	QUEEN	TAYLOR	NA

Scorers: CARLIN / JACKSON

MILESTONES:

DATE: 29.10.69 **VENUE:** HOME (C) **OPPOS:** CRYSTAL PALACE **RESULT:** 3-0 (C) **ATTND:** 33059 (O) **ROUND:** 4TH R

Team												SUB
Derby	GREEN	WEBSTER	DANIEL	DURBAN	McFARLAND	MACKAY	McGOVERN	CARLIN	O'HARE	HECTOR	HINTON	NA
Crystal Palace	JACKSON	LAUGHLAN	HOADLEY	PAYNE	McCORMICK	HYND	KEMBER	TAYLOR	WOODRUFF*	QUEEN	DAWKINS	JACKSON

Scorers: HINTON (2), HECTOR / NA

MILESTONES:

DATE: 12.11.69 **VENUE:** HOME (C) **OPPOS:** MANCHESTER UNITED **RESULT:** 0-0 (C) **ATTND:** 38893 (O) **ROUND:** 5TH

Team												SUB
Derby	GREEN	WEBSTER	ROBSON	DURBAN	McFARLAND	MACKAY	McGOVERN	CARLIN	O'HARE	HECTOR	HINTON	NA
Manchester United	STEPNEY	BRENNAN	DUNNE	BURNS	URE	SADLER	SARTORI	BEST	CHARLTON	LAW	ASTON	JACKSON

Scorers: NA / NA

MILESTONES:

DATE	VENUE	OPPOS	RESULT	ATTND	ROUND													
19.11.69	AWAY	MANCHESTER UNITED	0-1	57393	5TH R	GREEN	WEBSTER	ROBSON	DURBAN	McFARLAND	MACKAY	McGOVERN	CARLIN	O'HARE	HECTOR	HINTON	NA	
						STEPNEY	FITZPATRICK	DUNNE	BURNS	URE	SADLER	BEST	KIDD	CHARLTON	LAW*	ASTON	SARTORI	
			MILESTONES:			NA												
						KIDD												

FA CUP

DATE	VENUE	OPPOS	RESULT	ATTND	ROUND													
3.1.70	AWAY	PRESTON NORTH END	1-1	21479	3RD	GREEN	DANIEL	ROBSON	DURBAN	McFARLAND	MACKAY	McGOVERN	CARLIN	WIGNALL	HECTOR	HINTON	NA	
						KELLY	ROSS	RITCHIE	HIPPOLETTE	CRANSTON	McNAB	LYALL	SPAVIN	HAWKINS	GEMMILL	TEMPLE	NA	
			MILESTONES:			DURBAN												
						LYALL												

DATE	VENUE	OPPOS	RESULT	ATTND	ROUND													
7.1.70	HOME	PRESTON NORTH END	4-1	25201	3RD R	GREEN	WEBSTER	ROBSON	DURBAN	McFARLAND	MACKAY	McGOVERN	CARLIN	WIGNALL	HECTOR	HINTON	NA	
						KELLY	ROSS	RITCHIE	HIPPOLETTE	CRANSTON	McNAB	SPARK	SPAVIN	HAWKINS	GEMMILL*	TEMPLE	LLOYD	
			HECTOR (2), DURBAN (2)			HAWKINS												
			MILESTONES:															

DATE	VENUE	OPPOS	RESULT	ATTND	ROUND													
24.1.70	HOME	SHEFFIELD UNITED	3-0	41705	4TH	GREEN	WEBSTER	ROBSON	DURBAN	McFARLAND	MACKAY	McGOVERN	CARLIN	O'HARE	HECTOR	HINTON	NA	
						HODGKINSON	BADGER	HEMSLEY	BARLOW	COLQUHOUN	FLYNN	WOODWARD	CURRIE	ADDISON	SALMONS	REECE	NA	
			O'HARE (2), DURBAN			NA												
			MILESTONES:															

DATE	VENUE	OPPOS	RESULT	ATTND	ROUND													
7.2.70	AWAY	QUEENS PARK RANGERS	0-1	27685	5TH	GREEN	WEBSTER	DANIEL	DURBAN	McFARLAND	MACKAY	McGOVERN	CARLIN	O'HARE	HECTOR	HINTON	NA	
						KELLY	CLEMENT	GILLARD	WATSON	MOBLEY	HAZELL	BRIDGES	VENABLES	CLARKE	MARSH	FERGUSON	NA	
			NA															
			CLARKE															
			MILESTONES:															

DIVISION 1		1	2	3	4	5	6	7	8	9	10	11	12
DATE	15.8.70	GREEN	WEBSTER	ROBSON	DURBAN	McFARLAND	MACKAY	McGOVERN	CARLIN	O'HARE	HECTOR	HINTON*	WIGNALL
VENUE	AWAY	C											
OPPOS	CHELSEA	BONETTI	MULLIGAN	HARRIS	HOLLINS	DEMPSEY	HINTON*	WELLER	HUDSON	OSGOOD	HUTCHINSON	HOUSEMAN	COOKE
RESULT	1-2	O											
ATTND	46969	O'HARE											
POS	19-1	HUTCHINSON (2)											
		MILESTONES:											
DATE	19.8.70	GREEN	WEBSTER	ROBSON	DURBAN*	McFARLAND	MACKAY	McGOVERN	CARLIN	O'HARE	HECTOR	HINTON	WIGNALL
VENUE	AWAY	C											
OPPOS	WOLVERHAMPTON WANDERERS	OLDFIELD	TAYLOR	PARKIN	BAILEY	HOSLSGROVE	WILSON	McCALLIOG	DOUGAN	GOULD	CURRAN	WAGSTAFFE	NA
RESULT	4-2	O											
ATTND	29910	McGOVERN (2), DURBAN, O'HARE											
POS	8-22	DOUGAN, CURRAN											
		MILESTONES:											
DATE	22.8.70	GREEN	WEBSTER	ROBSON	HENNESSEY*	McFARLAND	MACKAY	McGOVERN	CARLIN	O'HARE	HECTOR	HINTON	WIGNALL
VENUE	HOME	C											
OPPOS	STOKE CITY	BANKS	MARSH	PEJIC	BERNARD	SMITH*	BLOOR	EASTHAM	GREENHOFF	RITCHIE	DOBING	BURROWS	STEVENSON
RESULT	2-0	O											
ATTND	35461	HINTON (P), WIGNALL											
POS	5-10	NA											
		MILESTONES:			350TH OVERALL LEAGUE GAME FOR MACKAY								
DATE	26.8.70	GREEN	WEBSTER	ROBSON	DURBAN*	McFARLAND	MACKAY	McGOVERN	CARLIN	O'HARE	HECTOR	HINTON*	WIGNALL
VENUE	HOME	C											
OPPOS	IPSWICH TOWN	BEST	MILLS	HARPER	MORRIS	BAXTER	JEFFERSON	ROBERTSON	VILJOEN	CLARKE	WOODS	LAMBERT*	WHYMARK
RESULT	2-0	O											
ATTND	30869	HECTOR, HARPER (OG)											
POS	5-22	NA											
		MILESTONES:											
DATE	29.8.70	GREEN	WEBSTER	ROBSON	McGOVERN	McFARLAND	MACKAY	WIGNALL	CARLIN	O'HARE	HECTOR	HINTON	NA
VENUE	AWAY	C											
OPPOS	HUDDERSFIELD TOWN	POOLE	CLARKE	HUTT	NICHOLSON	ELLAM	CHERRY	SMITH	LAWSON	WORTHINGTON	McGILL	KRZYWICKI	NA
RESULT	0-0	O											
ATTND	27997	NA											
POS	4-10	NA											
		MILESTONES:											
DATE	2.9.70	GREEN	WEBSTER	ROBSON	WIGNALL	McFARLAND	MACKAY	McGOVERN	CARLIN	O'HARE	HECTOR	HINTON	NA
VENUE	HOME	C											
OPPOS	COVENTRY CITY	GLAZIER	COOP	CATTLIN	SMITH*	BLOCKLEY	STRONG	JOICEY	CARR	MARTIN	MACHIN	CLEMENTS	HUNT
RESULT	3-4	O											
ATTND	31621	McGOVERN, HECTOR, HINTON											
POS	7-10	MARTIN (2), CLEMENTS, CARR											
		MILESTONES:											

5.9.70 — HOME v NEWCASTLE UNITED — Result 1-2 — Attendance 30466 — Pos 8-14

Derby	Opposition
GREEN	McFAUL
WEBSTER	CRAIG
ROBSON	CLARKE
DURBAN	GIBB
McFARLAND	BURTON
MACKAY	MONCUR
McGOVERN	DYSON
CARLIN	ROBSON
O'HARE	DAVIES
HECTOR*	SMITH
HINTON	YOUNG
WIGNALL	NA

MILESTONES: O'HARE / DYSON, YOUNG

12.9.70 — AWAY v SOUTHAMPTON — Result 0-4 — Attendance 19429 — Pos 13-6

Derby	Opposition
GREEN	MARTIN
WEBSTER	KIRKUP
ROBSON	HOLLYWOOD
DURBAN*	FISHER
RHODES	McGRATH
MACKAY	GABRIEL
McGOVERN	PAINE
CARLIN	CHANNON
O'HARE	DAVIES
HECTOR	O'NEIL
HINTON	JENKINS
WIGNALL	NA

MILESTONES: NA / DAVIES (2), CHANNON (2)

19.9.70 — HOME v BURNLEY — Result 1-0 — Attendance 26749 — Pos 11-22

Derby	Opposition
GREEN	WAITERS
RICHARDSON	ANGUS
ROBSON	MERRINGTON
DURBAN*	DOCHERTY
RHODES	WALDRON
MACKAY	THOMSON
WALKER	THOMAS
CARLIN	COATES
O'HARE	CASPER
HECTOR	COLLINS
HINTON	NULTY
WIGNALL	NA

MILESTONES: HINTON / NA

26.9.70 — AWAY v WEST BROMWICH ALBION — Result 1-2 — Attendance 31216 — Pos 14-16

Derby	Opposition
GREEN	CUMBES
RICHARDSON	MERRICK
ROBSON	WILSON
DURBAN	BROWN
RHODES	TALBOT
MACKAY	KAYE
GEMMILL	McVITIE
CARLIN	SUGGETT
O'HARE	ASTLE
HECTOR	HOPE
HINTON	HARTFORD
NA	NA

MILESTONES: O'HARE / McVITIE, BROWN

HINTON SCORES IN 350TH OVERALL LEAGUE GAME

DEBUT FOR GEMMILL / LAST APPEARANCE FOR RHODES

3.10.70 — HOME v TOTTENHAM HOTSPUR — Result 1-1 — Attendance 36007 — Pos 13-4

Derby	Opposition
GREEN	JENNINGS
WEBSTER	KINEAR
ROBSON	KNOWLES
DURBAN	MULLERY
DANIEL	ENGLAND
MACKAY	BEAL
GEMMILL	PEARCE
CARLIN	PERRYMAN
O'HARE	CHIVERS
HECTOR	PETERS
HINTON	MORGAN
NA	NA

MILESTONES: HINTON (P) / PETERS

350TH OVERALL LEAGUE GAME FOR HECTOR

10.10.70 — AWAY v EVERTON — Result 1-1 — Attendance 44614 — Pos 13-11

Derby	Opposition
GREEN	RANKIN
WEBSTER	NEWTON
ROBSON	BROWN
McGOVERN	KENDALL
McFARLAND	KENYON
MACKAY	HARVEY
GEMMILL	WHITTLE
CARLIN	JACKSON
O'HARE	ROYLE
HECTOR	HURST
HINTON	MORRISSEY
NA	NA

MILESTONES: McGOVERN / MORRISSEY, NA

17.10.70 — HOME v CHELSEA — Result 1-2 — Attendance 35166 — Pos 14-6

Derby	Opposition
GREEN	BONETTI
WEBSTER	MULLIGAN
ROBSON	HARRIS
DANIEL	HINTON
MACKAY	WEBB
McGOVERN	HOLLINS
GEMMILL	WELLER
CARLIN	HUDSON
O'HARE	OSGOOD
HECTOR	BALDWIN
HINTON	HOUSEMAN
NA	NA

MILESTONES: O'HARE / WELLER (2)

LAST APPEARANCE FOR CARLIN.

24.10.70 — HOME v LEEDS UNITED — 0-2 — Att: 32797 — Pos: 18-1

Team	1	2	3	4	5	6	7	8	9	10	11	Sub
Derby (C)	GREEN	WEBSTER	ROBSON	HENNESSEY	McFARLAND	MACKAY	GEMMILL	McGOVERN	O'HARE	HECTOR	HINTON	NA
Leeds (O)	SPRAKE	DAVEY	COOPER	BREMNER	CHARLTON	HUNTER	LORIMER	CLARKE	JONES	BELFITT	MADELEY	NA

Scorers: CLARKE, LORIMER
MILESTONES:

31.10.70 — AWAY v ARSENAL — 0-2 — Att: 43013 — Pos: 20-2

Team	1	2	3	4	5	6	7	8	9	10	11	Sub
Derby (C)	GREEN	WEBSTER	ROBSON	HENNESSEY	McFARLAND	MACKAY	GEMMILL	DURBAN	O'HARE	HECTOR	HINTON	NA
Arsenal (O)	WILSON	RICE	McNAB	KELLY	McLINTOCK	ROBERTS	ARMSTRONG	STOREY	RADFORD	KENNEDY	GRAHAM	NA

Scorers: KELLY, RADFORD
MILESTONES:

7.11.70 — HOME v LIVERPOOL — 0-0 — Att: 33004 — Pos: 18-8

Team	1	2	3	4	5	6	7	8	9	10	11	Sub
Derby (C)	GREEN	WEBSTER	ROBSON	DURBAN	McFARLAND	MACKAY	GEMMILL	McGOVERN	O'HARE	HECTOR	HINTON	NA
Liverpool (O)	CLEMENCE	LAWLER	LINDSAY	SMITH	LLOYD	HUGHES	HALL	BOERSMA	HEIGHWAY	McLAUGHLIN	THOMPSON	NA

MILESTONES: 100TH RAMS LEAGUE GAME FOR ROBSON

14.11.70 — AWAY v MANCHESTER CITY — 1-1 — Att: 31817 — Pos: 19-6

Team	1	2	3	4	5	6	7	8	9	10	11	Sub
Derby (C)	GREEN	WEBSTER	ROBSON	HENNESSEY	McFARLAND	MACKAY	McGOVERN	GEMMILL	O'HARE	HECTOR	HINTON	NA
Man City (O)	CORRIGAN	BOOK	MANN	DOYLE	HESLOP	OAKES	SUMMERBEE	BELL	LEE	HILL	TOWERS	NA

Scorers: O'HARE / BELL
MILESTONES: 100TH RAMS LEAGUE GAME FOR GREEN - CONSECUTIVE APPEARANCES

21.11.70 — HOME v BLACKPOOL — 2-0 — Att: 28237 — Pos: 16-21

Team	1	2	3	4	5	6	7	8	9	10	11	Sub
Derby (C)	GREEN	WEBSTER	ROBSON	HENNESSEY	McFARLAND	MACKAY	GEMMILL	DURBAN	O'HARE	HECTOR	HINTON	NA
Blackpool (O)	THOMSON	ARMFIELD	BENTLEY	JOHNSTON	JAMES	ALCOCK	PICKERING	GREEN	CRAVEN	WANN*	HUTCHINSON	BURNS

Scorers: McFARLAND, HECTOR
MILESTONES:

28.11.70 — AWAY v NOTTINGHAM FOREST — 4-2 — Att: 30539 — Pos: 14-20

Team	1	2	3	4	5	6	7	8	9	10	11	Sub
Derby (C)	GREEN	WEBSTER	ROBSON	DURBAN	HENNESSEY	MACKAY	McGOVERN	WIGNALL	O'HARE	HECTOR	GEMMILL	NA
Forest (O)	BARRON	HINDLEY	WINFIELD	CHAPMAN	O'KANE	JACKSON	LYONS	RICHARDSON	CORMACK	REES	MOORE	NA

Scorers: McGOVERN, O'HARE, WIGNALL, GEMMILL / CHAPMAN, MOORE
MILESTONES: FIRST GOAL FOR GEMMILL

5.12.70 — HOME v WEST HAM UNITED — 2-4 — Att: 30806 — Pos: 16-19

Team	1	2	3	4	5	6	7	8	9	10	11	Sub
Derby (C)	GREEN	WEBSTER	ROBSON	DURBAN	HENNESSEY	MACKAY	McGOVERN	WIGNALL	O'HARE	HECTOR	GEMMILL	NA
West Ham (O)	FERGUSON	BONDS	LAMPARD	EUSTACE	TAYLOR	MOORE	LINDSAY	BROOKING	BEST	HURST	GREAVES	NA

Scorers: DURBAN, WIGNALL / BEST(2), GREAVES, BROOKING
MILESTONES: 100TH RAMS LEAGUE GAME FOR MACKAY

12.12.70 — AWAY — CRYSTAL PALACE — Result 0-0 — Attnd 24218 — Pos 15-7

Derby	Crystal Palace
GREEN	JACKSON
WEBSTER	SEWELL
ROBSON	WALL
HENNESSEY*	PAYNE*
McFARLAND	McCORMICK
MACKAY	BLYTH
DURBAN	TAYLOR
WIGNALL	KEMBER
O'HARE	HOADLEY
HECTOR	BIRCHENALL
GEMMILL	SCOTT
DANIEL	HUMPHRIES

MILESTONES: NA, NA
250TH OVERALL LEAGUE GAME FOR WIGNALL

19.12.70 — AWAY — STOKE CITY — Result 0-1 — Attnd 21906 — Pos 17-13

Derby	Stoke City
GREEN	BANKS
WEBSTER	MARSH
ROBSON	PEJIC
HENNESSEY	SKEELS
McFARLAND	SMITH
MACKAY	BLOOR
DURBAN	HASELGRAVE
BUTLIN*	BERNARD
O'HARE	CONROY
HECTOR	EASTHAM
GEMMILL	BURROWS
McGOVERN	NA

MILESTONES: NA, BURROWS

26.12.70 — HOME — MANCHESTER UNITED — Result 4-4 — Attnd 34068 — Pos 17-18

Derby	Manchester United
GREEN	RIMMER
WEBSTER	FITZPATRICK
DANIEL	DUNNE
HENNESSEY	CRERAND
McFARLAND	URE
MACKAY	SADLER
DURBAN	MORGAN
WIGNALL	BEST
O'HARE	CHARLTON
HECTOR	KIDD
GEMMILL	LAW
NA	NA

MILESTONES: MACKAY, HECTOR, WIGNALL, GEMMILL — LAW (2), BEST, KIDD
LAST APPEARANCE FOR GREEN – ENDED SEQUENCE OF 129 CONSECUTIVE LEAGUE/CUP GAMES

9.1.71 — HOME — WOLVERHAMPTON WANDERERS — Result 1-2 — Attnd 34243 — Pos 18-6

Derby	Wolverhampton Wanderers
BOULTON	PARKES
WEBSTER	SHAW
DANIEL	PARKIN
HENNESSEY	BAILEY
McFARLAND	MUNROE
MACKAY*	McALLE
McGOVERN	McCALLIOG
WIGNALL	HIBBITT
O'HARE	GOULD
HECTOR	DOUGAN
GEMMILL	RICHARDS
DURBAN	NA

MILESTONES: GEMMILL (P) — SHAW, GOULD

16.1.71 — AWAY — IPSWICH TOWN — Result 1-0 — Attnd 20332 — Pos 16-18

Derby	Ipswich Town
BOULTON	SIVELL
WEBSTER	HAMMOND
ROBSON	MILLS
HENNESSEY	MORRIS
McFARLAND	BAXTER
MACKAY	McNEIL
McGOVERN	ROBERTSON
DURBAN	VILJOEN
O'HARE	CLARKE
HECTOR	COLLARD*
GEMMILL	HILL
NA	WOODS

MILESTONES: O'HARE, NA

6.2.71 — AWAY — WEST HAM UNITED — Result 4-1 — Attnd 26606 — Pos 15-20

Derby	West Ham United
BOULTON	GROTIER
WEBSTER	McDOWALL
ROBSON	LAMPARD
DURBAN	BONDS
McFARLAND	TAYLOR
MACKAY	HOWE*
McGOVERN	REDKNAPP
GEMMILL	LINDSAY
O'HARE	HURST
HECTOR	BROOKING
HINTON	EUSTACE
NA	MOORE

MILESTONES: HECTOR (2), HINTON (2) — EUSTACE
150TH RAMS LEAGUE GAME FOR O'HARE

17.2.71 — HOME — CRYSTAL PALACE — Result 1-0 — Attnd 23521 — Pos 15-9

Derby	Crystal Palace
BOULTON	JACKSON
WEBSTER	SEWELL
ROBSON	WALL
DURBAN	DAWKINS
McFARLAND	HUADLEY
MACKAY	BLYTH
McGOVERN	WHARTON
GEMMILL	KEMBER
O'HARE	QUEEN
HECTOR	BIRCHENALL
HINTON	PAYNE
NA	NA

MILESTONES: MACKAY, NA

DATE 20.2.71 — VENUE AWAY — OPPOS BLACKPOOL — RESULT 1-0 — ATTND 17892 — POS 15-21

Derby (C)	Opposition (O)
BOULTON	RAMSBOTTOM
WEBSTER	ARMFIELD
ROBSON	BENTLEY*
DURBAN	SUDDABY
McFARLAND	JAMES
MACKAY	HATTON
McGOVERN	GREEN
GEMMILL	KEMP
O'HARE	PICKERING
HECTOR	CRAVEN
HINTON	HUTCHINSON
NA	JOHNSTON

O'HARE
NA
MILESTONES:

DATE 27.2.71 — VENUE HOME — OPPOS ARSENAL — RESULT 2-0 — ATTND 35775 — POS 13-2

Derby (C)	Opposition (O)
BOULTON	WILSON
WEBSTER	RICE*
RICHARDSON	McNAB
TODD	STOREY
McFARLAND	McLINTOCK
MACKAY	SIMPSON
McGOVERN	ARMSTRONG
GEMMILL	SAMMELS
O'HARE	RADFORD
HECTOR	KENNEDY
HINTON	GEORGE
NA	GRAHAM

McFARLAND, HECTOR
NA
DEBUT FOR TODD
MILESTONES:

DATE 6.3.71 — VENUE AWAY — OPPOS LEEDS UNITED — RESULT 0-1 — ATTND 36647 — POS 14-1

Derby (C)	Opposition (O)
BOULTON	HARVEY
WEBSTER	DAVEY
ROBSON	REANEY
TODD	BATES
McFARLAND	CHARLTON
MACKAY	HUNTER
McGOVERN	LORIMER
GEMMILL	BELFITT
O'HARE	JONES
HECTOR	GILES
HINTON	MADELEY
NA	NA

NA
LORIMER
MILESTONES:

DATE 13.3.71 — VENUE HOME — OPPOS MANCHESTER CITY — RESULT 0-0 — ATTND 31987 — POS 13-8

Derby (C)	Opposition (O)
BOULTON	HEALEY
WEBSTER	BOOK*
RICHARDSON	TOWERS
TODD	DOYLE
McFARLAND	BOOTH
MACKAY	OAKES
McGOVERN	SUMMERBEE
GEMMILL	BELL
O'HARE	LEE
HECTOR	DOYLE
HINTON	JEFFERIES
NA	BRENNAN

NA
NA
MILESTONES:

DATE 20.3.71 — VENUE AWAY — OPPOS LIVERPOOL — RESULT 0-2 — ATTND 40940 — POS 14-6

Derby (C)	Opposition (O)
BOULTON	CLEMENCE
WEBSTER	LAWLER
RICHARDSON	LINDSAY
TODD	SMITH
McFARLAND	LLOYD
MACKAY	HUGHES
McGOVERN	CALLAGHAN
GEMMILL	EVANS
O'HARE*	HIGHWAY*
HECTOR	TOSHACK
HINTON	HALL
ROBSON	THOMPSON

NA
MACKAY (OG), LAWLER
MILESTONES:

DATE 27.3.71 — VENUE AWAY — OPPOS NEWCASTLE UNITED — RESULT 1-3 — ATTND 26052 — POS 14-12

Derby (C)	Opposition (O)
BOULTON	McFAUL
WEBSTER	CRAGGS*
ROBSON	CLARKE
TODD	GIBB
McFARLAND	McNAMEE
MACKAY	MONCUR
McGOVERN*	FOGGON
WIGNALL	TUDOR
O'HARE	DYSON
HECTOR	SMITH
GEMMILL	YOUNG
DURBAN	NATTRASS

HECTOR
MACKAY (OG), WEBSTER (OG), FOGGON
MILESTONES:

DATE 31.3.71 — VENUE HOME — OPPOS NOTTINGHAM FOREST — RESULT 1-2 — ATTND 34857 — POS 14-18

Derby (C)	Opposition (O)
BOULTON	BARRON
WEBSTER	HINDLEY
RICHARDSON	WINFIELD
TODD	CHAPMAN
McFARLAND	OKANE
MACKAY	FRASER
GEMMILL	LYONS
WIGNALL	RICHARDSON*
O'HARE	MARTIN
HECTOR	CORMACK
HINTON	MOORE
NA	REES

HECTOR
RICHARDSON, MOORE
MILESTONES:

	1	2	3	4	5	6	7	8	9	10	11	Sub
DATE 3.4.71 — VENUE HOME — OPPOS HUDDERSFIELD TOWN — RESULT 3-2 — ATTND 24194 — POS 13-17	BOULTON	WEBSTER	RICHARDSON	TODD	McFARLAND	MACKAY	GEMMILL	WIGNALL	O'HARE	HECTOR	HINTON	NA
	LAWSON	CLARKE	HUTT	NICHOLSON	ELLAM	CHERRY	SMITH	MAHONEY	WORTHINGTON	BARRY	LAWSON	NA

MILESTONES: HINTON (2) (1P), CLARKE, ELLAM

	1	2	3	4	5	6	7	8	9	10	11	Sub
DATE 7.4.71 — VENUE AWAY — OPPOS TOTTENHAM HOTSPUR — RESULT 1-2 — ATTND 25627 — POS 14-6	BOULTON	WEBSTER	RICHARDSON	TODD	McFARLAND	MACKAY	McGOVERN	GEMMILL	O'HARE	HECTOR	HINTON	NA
	JENNINGS	KINNEAR	WANT	MULLERY	COLLINS	BEAL	GILZEAN	PERRYMAN	CHIVERS	PETERS	PEARCE	NA

MILESTONES: HINTON, PEARCE, CHIVERS
300TH RAMS LEAGUE GAME FOR WEBSTER

	1	2	3	4	5	6	7	8	9	10	11	Sub
DATE 10.4.71 — VENUE AWAY — OPPOS MANCHESTER UNITED — RESULT 2-1 — ATTND 44203 — POS 12-11	BOULTON	WEBSTER	ROBSON	DURBAN	McFARLAND	MACKAY	McGOVERN	GEMMILL	O'HARE	HECTOR	HINTON	NA
	STEPNEY	DUNNE	BURNS	CRERAND	EDWARDS	STILES	MORGAN	BEST	CHARLTON	LAW	ASTON*	GOWLING

MILESTONES: O'HARE (2), LAW
150TH RAMS LEAGUE GAME FOR McFARLAND

	1	2	3	4	5	6	7	8	9	10	11	Sub
DATE 12.4.71 — VENUE HOME — OPPOS SOUTHAMPTON — RESULT 0-0 — ATTND 26420 — POS 12-11	BOULTON	TODD	ROBSON	DURBAN	McFARLAND	MACKAY	McGOVERN	GEMMILL	O'HARE	HECTOR	HINTON	NA
	MARTIN	KIRKUP	HOLLYWOOD	FISHER	McGRATH	GABRIEL	PAINE	CHANNON	DAVIES	O'NEIL	JENKINS	NA

MILESTONES: NA, NA

	1	2	3	4	5	6	7	8	9	10	11	Sub
DATE 17.4.71 — VENUE HOME — OPPOS EVERTON — RESULT 3-1 — ATTND 28793 — POS 12-13	BOULTON	TODD	ROBSON	DURBAN	McFARLAND	MACKAY	McGOVERN	GEMMILL	O'HARE	HECTOR	HINTON	NA
	RANKIN	WRIGHT	NEWTON	KENDALL	KENYON	HARVEY	WHITTLE	BALL	ROYLE	HURST	JOHNSON	NA

MILESTONES: O'HARE (2), HECTOR, WHITTLE

	1	2	3	4	5	6	7	8	9	10	11	Sub
DATE 24.4.71 — VENUE HOME — OPPOS BURNLEY — RESULT 3-1 — ATTND 28793 — POS 10-21	BOULTON	TODD	ROBSON	DURBAN	McFARLAND	MACKAY	McGOVERN	BOURNE	O'HARE	HECTOR	HINTON	NA
	MELLOR	ANGUS	LATCHAM	PROBERT	DOBSON	NULTY	COATES	BELLAMY	WILSON	CASPER	COLLINS	NA

MILESTONES: McGOVERN, DURRAN, CASPER
DEBUT FOR BOURNE

	1	2	3	4	5	6	7	8	9	10	11	Sub
DATE 27.4.71 — VENUE AWAY — OPPOS COVENTRY CITY — RESULT 0-0 — ATTND 22051 — POS 9-11	BOULTON	TODD	ROBSON	DURBAN	McFARLAND	MACKAY	McGOVERN	BOURNE*	O'HARE	HECTOR	HINTON	WEBSTER
	GLAZIER	SMITH	CATTLIN	MACHIN	BLOCKLEY	PARKER	MORTIMER	CARR	RAFFERTY	HUNT	CLEMENTS	NA

MILESTONES: NA, NA
CLOUGH'S 200TH COMPETITIVE GAME IN CHARGE

WEST BROMWICH ALBION

	BOULTON	TODD	ROBSON	DURBAN	McFARLAND	MACKAY	McGOVERN	GEMMILL	O'HARE	HECTOR	HINTON	NA
C	CUMBES	WILSON	MERRICK	CANTELLO	WILE	KAYE	SUGGETT	BROWN	ASTLE	HARTFORD	McVITIE	NA
O												

DATE: 1.5.71 — VENUE: HOME — RESULT: 2-0 — ATTND: 33661 — POS: 8-17

MILESTONES: HINTON, DURBAN — NA

LAST GAME FOR MACKAY - AS AN EVER-PRESENT - ALONG WITH O'HARE AND HECTOR

AFTER ALL TEAMS HAD PLAYED 42 GAMES DERBY FINISHED IN 9TH PLACE

LEAGUE CUP

HALIFAX TOWN

	BOULTON	TODD	ROBSON	DURBAN	McFARLAND	MACKAY	McGOVERN	GEMMILL	O'HARE	HECTOR	HINTON	NA
C (GREEN)	SMITH	BURGIN	BUXTON	ROBERTSON	PICKERING	WALLACE	CHADWICK	ATKINS	BRIERLEY	LENNARD	McCARTHY*	HOLMES
O	WEBSTER	ROBSON	DURBAN	McFARLAND*	RHODES	WIGNALL	CARLIN	O'HARE	HECTOR	HINTON	DANIEL	

DATE: 8.9.70 — VENUE: HOME — RESULT: 3-1 — ATTND: 20029 — ROUND: 2ND

MILESTONES: DURBAN, HECTOR — McCARTHY

MILLWALL

	BOULTON	TODD	ROBSON	DURBAN	McFARLAND	MACKAY	McGOVERN	GEMMILL	O'HARE	HECTOR	HINTON	NA
C	GREEN	WEBSTER	ROBSON	McGOVERN	McFARLAND	MACKAY	WIGNALL	CARLIN	O'HARE	HECTOR	HINTON	NA
O	KING	BROWN	CRIPPS	DORNEY	KITCHENER	BURNETT	BROWN	DUNPHY	BOLLAND	POSSEE	ALLDER	NA

DATE: 7.10.70 — VENUE: HOME — RESULT: 4-2 — ATTND: 25537 — ROUND: 3RD

MILESTONES: HINTON (P), McGOVERN, MACKAY, O'HARE — POSSEE, BOLLAND

COVENTRY CITY

	BOULTON	TODD	ROBSON	DURBAN	McFARLAND	MACKAY	McGOVERN	GEMMILL	O'HARE	HECTOR	HINTON	NA
C	GREEN	WEBSTER	ROBSON	HENNESSEY	McFARLAND	MACKAY	McGOVERN	DURBAN	O'HARE	HECTOR	HINTON	NA
O	GLAZIER	COOP	SMITH	CLEMENTS	BLOCKLEY	STRONG	HUNT	CARR	MARTIN	O'ROURKE	ALDERSON	NA

DATE: 27.10.70 — VENUE: AWAY — RESULT: 0-1 — ATTND: 26557 — POS: 4TH

MILESTONES: NA — MARTIN

FA CUP

CHESTER CITY

	BOULTON	TODD	ROBSON	DURBAN	McFARLAND	MACKAY	McGOVERN	GEMMILL	O'HARE	HECTOR	HINTON	NA
C	BOULTON	WEBSTER	DANIEL	HENNESSEY	McFARLAND	MACKAY	McGOVERN	WIGNALL	O'HARE	HECTOR	GEMMILL	NA
O	CARLING	CHEETHAM	BIRKS	BRADBURY	TURNER	POUNTNEY	McHALE	TARBUCK	LOYDEN	DRAPER*	GROVES	WEBBER

DATE: 2.1.71 — VENUE: AWAY — RESULT: 2-1 — ATTND: 15882 — ROUND: 3RD

MILESTONES: WIGNALL, GEMMILL — WEBBER

	C/O												
DATE	23.1.71	C	BOULTON	WEBSTER	ROBSON	DURBAN	McFARLAND	MACKAY	McGOVERN	GEMMILL	O'HARE	HECTOR	HINTON	NA
VENUE	HOME	O	PARKES	SHAW	PARKIN	BAILEY	MUNROE	McALLE	McCALLIOG	HIBBITT	GOULD*	DOUGAN	WAGSTAFFE	RICHARDS
OPPOS	WOLVERHAMPTON WANDERERS													
RESULT	2-1	C	HINTON (P), O'HARE											
ATTND	40567	O	RICHARDS											
ROUND	4TH		MILESTONES:											

	C/O												
DATE	13.2.71	C	BOULTON	WEBSTER	ROBSON	DURBAN	McFARLAND	MACKAY	McGOVERN	GEMMILL	O'HARE	HECTOR	HINTON	NA
VENUE	AWAY	O	WEST	WRIGHT	NEWTON	KENDALL	KENYON	HARVEY	HUSBAND	BALL	ROYLE	HURST	JOHNSON	NA
OPPOS	EVERTON													
RESULT	0-1	C	NA											
ATTND	53490	O	JOHNSON											
ROUND	5TH		MILESTONES:											

DIVISION 1

Manchester United

		1	2	3	4	5	6	7	8	9	10	11	12
DATE	14.8.71												
VENUE	HOME												
OPPOS	MANCHESTER UNITED												
RESULT	2-2												
ATTND	35386												
POS	7-10												
C		BOULTON	WEBSTER	ROBSON	McGOVERN	HENNESSEY	TODD	GEMMILL	WIGNALL	O'HARE	HECTOR	HINTON	NA
O		STEPNEY	O'NEIL	DUNNE	GOWLING	JAMES	SADLER	MORGAN	KIDD	CHARLTON	LAW	BEST	NA

Scorers: WIGNALL, HECTOR / LAW, GOWLING
MILESTONES:

West Ham United

		1	2	3	4	5	6	7	8	9	10	11	12
DATE	18.8.71												
VENUE	HOME												
OPPOS	WEST HAM UNITED												
RESULT	2-0												
ATTND	30783												
POS	6-22												
C		BOULTON	WEBSTER	ROBSON	McGOVERN	HENNESSEY	TODD	GEMMILL	WIGNALL	O'HARE	HECTOR	HINTON	NA
O		FERGUSON	McDOWELL	LAMPARD	BONDS	STEPHENSON	MOORE	AYRIS*	BEST	HURST	TAYLOR	ROBSON	HOWE

Scorers: WIGNALL, O'HARE / NA
MILESTONES:

Leicester City

		1	2	3	4	5	6	7	8	9	10	11	12
DATE	21.8.71												
VENUE	AWAY												
OPPOS	LEICESTER CITY												
RESULT	2-0												
ATTND	35460												
POS	3-12												
C		BOULTON	WEBSTER	ROBSON	McGOVERN	HENNESSEY	TODD	GEMMILL	WIGNALL	O'HARE	HECTOR	HINTON	NA
O		SHILTON	WHITWORTH	NISH	KELLARD	SJOBERG	CROSS	FARRINGTON	BROWN	FERN	SAMMELS	GLOVER	NA

Scorers: HECTOR, HINTON(P) / NA
MILESTONES:

Coventry City

		1	2	3	4	5	6	7	8	9	10	11	12
DATE	24.8.71												
VENUE	AWAY												
OPPOS	COVENTRY CITY												
RESULT	2-2												
ATTND	27759												
POS	3-15												
C		BOULTON	WEBSTER	ROBSON	McGOVERN	HENNESSEY	TODD	GEMMILL	WIGNALL	O'HARE	HECTOR	HINTON	NA
O		GLAZIER	SMITH	CATTLIN	MORTIMER	BLOCKLEY	BARRY	YOUNG	CARR	JOICEY	HUNT	McGUIRE	NA

Scorers: WIGNALL, O'HARE / JOICEY, HUNT (P)
MILESTONES: 50TH RAMS LEAGUE GOAL FOR O'HARE

Southampton

		1	2	3	4	5	6	7	8	9	10	11	12
DATE	28.8.71												
VENUE	HOME												
OPPOS	SOUTHAMPTON												
RESULT	2-2												
ATTND	28498												
POS	4-7												
C		BOULTON	TODD	ROBSON	McGOVERN	McFARLAND	McGOVERN	GEMMILL	DURBAN	O'HARE	HECTOR	HINTON	NA
O		MARTIN	KIRKUP	FRY	FISHER	McGRATH	GABRIEL	PAINE	CHANNON	STOKES	O'NEIL	JENKINS	NA

Scorers: McGOVERN, HECTOR / STOKES, GABRIEL (P)
MILESTONES: HECTOR SCORES IN 200TH RAMS LEAGUE GAME / 350TH OVERALL LEAGUE GAME FOR DURBAN

Ipswich Town

		1	2	3	4	5	6	7	8	9	10	11	12
DATE	31.8.71												
VENUE	AWAY												
OPPOS	IPSWICH TOWN												
RESULT	0-0												
ATTND	18687												
POS	2-10												
C		BOULTON	TODD	ROBSON	McGOVERN	McFARLAND	McGOVERN	GEMMILL	DURBAN	WIGNALL	HECTOR	HINTON	NA
O		BEST	HAMMOND	HARPER	MORRIS	BELL	JEFFERSON	ROBERTS	MILLS	CLARK	HAMILTON	MILLER	NA

Scorers: NA / NA
MILESTONES:

EVERTON — DATE 4.9.71 · VENUE AWAY · RESULT 2-0 · ATTND 41024 · POS 3-18

	1	2	3	4	5	6	7	8	9	10	11	12
C	BOULTON	WEBSTER	ROBSON	TODD	McFARLAND	McGOVERN	GEMMILL	DURBAN	WIGNALL	HECTOR	HINTON	NA
O	WEST	SCOTT	NEWTON	KENDALL*	KENYON	DARRACOTT	HUSBAND	BALL	JOHNSON	HURST	MORRISSEY	ROYLE

MILESTONES: WIGNALL, HECTOR

STOKE CITY — DATE 11.9.71 · VENUE HOME · RESULT 4-0 · ATTND 32545 · POS 2-12

300TH RAMS LEAGUE GAME FOR DURBAN / 150TH RAMS LEAGUE GAME FOR HINTON

	1	2	3	4	5	6	7	8	9	10	11	12
C	BOULTON	WEBSTER	ROBSON	TODD	McFARLAND	GEMMILL	DURBAN	DURBAN	O'HARE	HECTOR	HINTON	NA
O	BANKS	MARSH	PEJIC	BERNARD*	SMITH	LEES	MAHONEY	GREENHOFF	RITCHIE	DOBING	HASELGRAVE	STEVENSON

MILESTONES: TODD, GEMMILL, O'HARE, HINTON

CHELSEA — DATE 18.9.71 · VENUE AWAY · RESULT 1-1 · ATTND 42872 · POS 3-5

FIRST GOAL FOR TODD

	1	2	3	4	5	6	7	8	9	10	11	12
C	BOULTON	WEBSTER	ROBSON	TODD	McFARLAND	McGOVERN	GEMMILL	WIGNALL	O'HARE	HECTOR	HINTON	NA
O	BONETTI	BOYLE	HARRIS	HOLLINS	WEBB	HINTON	COOKE	BALDWIN	OSGOOD	HUDSON	HOUSEMAN	NA

MILESTONES: McFARLAND, BALDWIN

WEST BROMWICH ALBION — DATE 25.9.71 · VENUE HOME · RESULT 0-0 · ATTND 30628 · POS 3-19

	1	2	3	4	5	6	7	8	9	10	11	12
C	BOULTON	WEBSTER	ROBSON	TODD	McFARLAND	GEMMILL	DURBAN*	WIGNALL	O'HARE	HECTOR	HINTON	McGOVERN
O	CUMBES	HUGHES	WILSON	CANTELLO	WILE	KAYE	McVITIE	BROWN	GOULD	HOPE	HARTFORD	NA

MILESTONES: NA

NEWCASTLE UNITED — DATE 2.10.71 · VENUE AWAY · RESULT 1-0 · ATTND 32077 · POS 3-18

	1	2	3	4	5	6	7	8	9	10	11	12
C	BOULTON	WEBSTER	ROBSON	HENNESSEY	McFARLAND	TODD	McGOVERN	DURBAN	O'HARE	HECTOR	HINTON	NA
O	McFAUL	CRAIG	ELLISON	GIBB	HOWARD	CLARK	BARROWCLOUGH	TUDOR	MACDONALD	NATTRASS	HIBBITT	NA

MILESTONES: HINTON

TOTTENHAM HOTSPUR — DATE 9.10.71 · VENUE HOME · RESULT 2-2 · ATTND 35744 · POS 4-7

	1	2	3	4	5	6	7	8	9	10	11	12
C	BOULTON	WEBSTER*	ROBSON	HENNESSEY	McFARLAND	McGOVERN	GEMMILL	DURBAN	O'HARE	HECTOR	HINTON	WIGNALL
O	JENNINGS	EVANS	KNOWLES*	MULLERY	COLLINS	BEAL	PEARCE	PERRYMAN	CHIVERS	PETERS	GILZEAN	PRATT

MILESTONES: TODD, McFARLAND, CHIVERS, PEARCE

MANCHESTER UNITED — DATE 16.10.71 · VENUE AWAY · RESULT 0-1 · ATTND 53247 · POS 4-1

	1	2	3	4	5	6	7	8	9	10	11	12
C	BOULTON	TODD	ROBSON	HENNESSEY	McFARLAND	McGOVERN	GEMMILL	DURBAN	O'HARE	HECTOR	HINTON	NA
O	STEPNEY	O'NEIL	DUNNE	GOWLING	JAMES	SADLER	MORGAN	KIDD	CHARLTON	LAW	BEST	NA

MILESTONES: NA, BEST

	BOULTON	WEBSTER*	ROBSON	TODD	McFARLAND	McGOVERN	GEMMILL	DURBAN	O'HARE	HECTOR	HINTON	POWELL

DATE 23.10.71 (C) — VENUE HOME (O) — OPPOS ARSENAL — RESULT 2-1 — ATTND 36480 — POS 3-8

Derby	BOULTON	WEBSTER	ROBSON	TODD	McFARLAND	McGOVERN	GEMMILL	DURBAN	O'HARE	HECTOR	HINTON	POWELL
Arsenal	WILSON	RICE	NELSON	KELLY*	McLINTOCK	ROBERTS	ARMSTRONG	GEORGE	RADFORD	KENNEDY	GRAHAM	SIMPSON

MILESTONES: O'HARE, HINTON (P) / GRAHAM

DATE 30.10.71 (C) — VENUE AWAY (O) — OPPOS NOTTINGHAM FOREST — RESULT 2-0 — ATTND 36480 — POS 3-8

Derby	BOULTON	WEBSTER	ROBSON	POWELL	McFARLAND	TODD	McGOVERN	GEMMILL	O'HARE	HECTOR	HINTON	
Nott'm Forest	HULME	O'KANE	FRASER	CHAPMAN	HINDLEY	RICHARDSON	LYONS	McKENZIE	BUCKLEY	ROBERTSON	MOORE	NA

MILESTONES: ROBSON, HINTON (P) / NA

DATE 6.11.71 (C) — VENUE HOME (O) — OPPOS CRYSTAL PALACE — RESULT 3-0 — ATTND 30358 — POS 2-22

Derby	BOULTON	WEBSTER	ROBSON	TODD	McFARLAND	McGOVERN	DURBAN	WIGNALL	O'HARE	HECTOR	HINTON	
Crystal Palace	JACKSON	PAYNE	WALL	GOODWIN	BELL	BLYTH	TAMBLING	CRAVEN	HUGHES	WALLACE	TAYLOR	NA

MILESTONES: WIGNALL, HECTOR, BELL (OG) / NA

100TH RAMS LEAGUE GAME FOR McGOVERN / WIGNALL SCORES ON LAST APPEARANCE

DATE 13.11.71 (C) — VENUE AWAY (O) — OPPOS WOLVERHAMPTON WANDERERS — RESULT 1-2 — ATTND 32957 — POS 2-12

Derby	BOULTON	WEBSTER	ROBSON	TODD	McFARLAND	HENNESSEY	McGOVERN	WIGNALL	O'HARE	HECTOR	HINTON	
Wolves	PARKES	SHAW	PARKIN	BAILEY	MUNROE	McALLE	McCALLIOG	HIBBITT	RICHARDS	DOUGAN	WAGSTAFFE	NA

MILESTONES: O'HARE / RICHARDS (2)

DATE 20.11.71 (C) — VENUE HOME (O) — OPPOS SHEFFIELD UNITED — RESULT 3-0 — ATTND 35326 — POS 2-5

Derby	BOULTON	WEBSTER	ROBSON	TODD	McFARLAND	HENNESSEY	McGOVERN	WIGNALL	O'HARE	HECTOR	HINTON	
Sheffield Utd	HOPE	BADGER	HEMSLEY	FLYNN	COLQUHOUN	HOCKEY	WOODWARD	SALMONS	REECE	CURRIE	SCULLION	NA

MILESTONES: HINTON (2) (2P), HECTOR / NA

DATE 27.11.71 (C) — VENUE AWAY (O) — OPPOS HUDDERSFIELD TOWN — RESULT 1-2 — ATTND 15329 — POS 3-17

Derby	BOULTON	WEBSTER	ROBSON	TODD	McFARLAND	HENNESSEY	McGOVERN	WIGNALL	O'HARE	HECTOR	HINTON	
Huddersfield	LAWSON	CLARKE	HUTT	JONES	ELLAM	CHERRY	MAHONEY	SMITH	WORTHINGTON	LAWSON	CHAPMAN	NA

MILESTONES: McGOVERN / WORTHINGTON, LAWSON

DATE 4.12.71 (C) — VENUE HOME (O) — OPPOS MANCHESTER CITY — RESULT 3-1 — ATTND 35384 — POS 2-3

Derby	BOULTON	WEBSTER	ROBSON	TODD	McFARLAND	McGOVERN	DURBAN	GEMMILL	O'HARE	HECTOR	HINTON	
Manchester City	CORRIGAN	ROOK	DONACHIE	DOYLE	BOOTH	OATES	SUMMERBEE	BELL	DAVIES	LEE	MELLOR	NA

MILESTONES: WEBSTER, DURBAN, HINTON / LEE (P)

HINTON SCORES 50TH OVERALL GOAL FOR RAMS IN 350TH OVERALL LEAGUE GAME

DATE	VENUE	OPPOS	RESULT	ATTND	POS	BOULTON	TODD*	ROBSON	HENNESSEY	McFARLAND	McGOVERN	DURBAN	GEMMILL	O'HARE	HECTOR	HINTON	WALKER
11.12.71	AWAY	LIVERPOOL	2-3	44601	4-5	BOULTON	TODD*	ROBSON	HENNESSEY	McFARLAND	McGOVERN	DURBAN	GEMMILL	O'HARE	HECTOR	HINTON	WALKER
						CLEMENCE	LAWLER	LINDSAY	SMITH	ROSS	HUGHES	KEEGAN	HALL	HEIGHWAY	WHITHAM	CALLAGHAN	NA
18.12.71	HOME	EVERTON	2-0	27895	3-18	BOULTON	WEBSTER	ROBSON	HENNESSEY	McFARLAND	McGOVERN	DURBAN	GEMMILL	O'HARE	HECTOR	HINTON	WALKER
						WEST	WRIGHT	McLAUGHLIN	KENDALL	KENYON	NEWTON	HUSBAND	BALL	ROYLE	HURST	WHITTLE	NA
27.12.71	AWAY	LEEDS UNITED	0-3	44214	5-3	BOULTON	WEBSTER	ROBSON	BAILEY	McFARLAND	HENNESSEY	McGOVERN	GEMMILL	O'HARE	HECTOR	HINTON	WALKER
						SPRAKE	MADELEY	COOPER	BREMNER	CHARLTON	HUNTER	LORIMER	CLARKE	JONES	GILES	GRAY	NA
1.1.72	HOME	CHELSEA	1-0	33063	4-10	BOULTON	WEBSTER	ROBSON	TODD	McFARLAND	McGOVERN	DURBAN	GEMMILL	O'HARE	HECTOR	HINTON	WALKER
						SHERWOOD	MULLIGAN	HARRIS	HOLLINS	DEMPSEY	WEBB	GARLAND	KEMBER*	OSGOOD	HUDSON	HOUSEMAN	COOKE
8.1.72	AWAY	SOUTHAMPTON	2-1	19321	4-18	BOULTON	WEBSTER	ROBSON	DURBAN	McFARLAND	McGOVERN	TODD	GEMMILL	O'HARE	HECTOR	HINTON	WALKER
						MARTIN	McCARTHY	FRY	STOKES	GABRIEL	BRYNE	PAINE	CHANNON	DAVIES	O'BRIEN	JENKINS	NA
22.1.72	AWAY	WEST HAM UNITED	3-3	31045	4-12	BOULTON	WEBSTER	ROBSON	DURBAN	McFARLAND	TODD	McGOVERN	GEMMILL	O'HARE	HECTOR	HINTON	WALKER
						FERGUSON	McDOWALL	LAMPARD	BONDS	TAYLOR	MOORE	REDKNAPP	BEST	HURST	BROOKING	ROBSON	NA
29.1.72	HOME	COVENTRY CITY	1-0	29385	3-17	BOULTON	WEBSTER	ROBSON	DURBAN	McFARLAND	TODD	McGOVERN	GEMMILL	O'HARE	HECTOR	HINTON	WALKER
						GLAZIER	SMITH	CATTLIN	MACHIN	BLOCKLEY	PARKER	YOUNG	CARR	CHILTON	RAFFERTY	MORTIMER	NA

MILESTONES:
- 11.12.71 LIVERPOOL: O'HARE (2); WHITHAM (3)
- 18.12.71 EVERTON: HINTON (2); NA
- 27.12.71 LEEDS UNITED: LORIMER (2), GRAY; NA — LAST GAME FOR BAILEY
- 1.1.72 CHELSEA: GEMMILL; NA
- 8.1.72 SOUTHAMPTON: O'HARE, DURBAN; O'BRIEN
- 22.1.72 WEST HAM UNITED: HECTOR, HINTON, DURBAN; LAMPARD, ROBSON, BROOKING
- 29.1.72 COVENTRY CITY: ROBSON; NA

DATE	VENUE	OPPOS	RESULT	ATTND	POS		BOULTON	WEBSTER	ROBSON	DURBAN	McFARLAND	TODD	McGOVERN	GEMMILL	O'HARE	HECTOR	HINTON	NA
12.2.72	AWAY	ARSENAL	0-2	52055	3-4	C	BOULTON	WEBSTER	ROBSON	DURBAN	McFARLAND	TODD	McGOVERN	GEMMILL	O'HARE	HECTOR	HINTON	NA
						O	WILSON	RICE	NELSON	KELLY	McLINTOCK	SIMPSON	ARMSTRONG	BALL	GEORGE	KENNEDY	GRAHAM	NA

MILESTONES: GEORGE (2)

DATE	VENUE	OPPOS	RESULT	ATTND	POS		BOULTON	WEBSTER	ROBSON	DURBAN	McFARLAND	TODD	McGOVERN	GEMMILL	O'HARE	HECTOR	HINTON	NA
19.2.72	HOME	NOTTINGHAM FOREST	4-0	31801	3-22	C	BOULTON	WEBSTER	ROBSON	DURBAN	McFARLAND	TODD	McGOVERN	GEMMILL	O'HARE	HECTOR	HINTON	NA
						O	BARRON	GEMMELL	WINFIELD	CHAPMAN	HINDLEY	COTTAM	LYONS	O'NEIL	CORMACK	RICHARDSON	MOORE	NA

MILESTONES: HINTON (2), HECTOR, O'HARE

HECTOR SCORES IN 400TH OVERALL LEAGUE GAME

DATE	VENUE	OPPOS	RESULT	ATTND	POS		BOULTON	WEBSTER	ROBSON	DURBAN	McFARLAND	TODD	McGOVERN	GEMMILL	O'HARE	HECTOR	HINTON	NA
4.3.72	HOME	WOLVERHAMPTON WANDERERS	2-1	33456	3-7	C	BOULTON	WEBSTER	ROBSON	DURBAN	McFARLAND	TODD	McGOVERN	GEMMILL	O'HARE	HECTOR	HINTON	NA
						O	PARKES	SHAW	TAYLOR	HEGAN	MUNROE	McALLE	McCALLIOG	HIBBITT	RICHARDS	DOUGAN	WAGSTAFFE	NA

MILESTONES: HINTON (P), McFARLAND

McCALLIOG (P)

DATE	VENUE	OPPOS	RESULT	ATTND	POS		BOULTON	WEBSTER	ROBSON	HENNESSEY	McFARLAND	TODD	McGOVERN	GEMMILL	O'HARE	HECTOR	HINTON	NA
11.3.72	AWAY	TOTTENHAM HOTSPUR	1-0	36310	3-5	C	BOULTON	WEBSTER	ROBSON	HENNESSEY	McFARLAND	TODD	McGOVERN	GEMMILL	O'HARE	HECTOR	HINTON	NA
						O	JENNINGS	EVANS	KNOWLES	HOLDER	ENGLAND	BEAL	GILZEAN	PERRYMAN	CHIVERS	PETERS	MORGAN	NA

MILESTONES: HINTON (P)

150TH RAMS LEAGUE GAME FOR ROBSON

DATE	VENUE	OPPOS	RESULT	ATTND	POS		BOULTON	WEBSTER	ROBSON	DURBAN	McFARLAND	TODD	McGOVERN	HENNESSEY*	O'HARE	HECTOR	HINTON*	WALKER
18.3.72	HOME	LEICESTER CITY	3-0	34019	2-16	C	BOULTON	WEBSTER	ROBSON	DURBAN	McFARLAND	TODD	McGOVERN	HENNESSEY*	O'HARE	HECTOR	HINTON*	WALKER
						O	WALLINGTON	WHITWORTH	NISH	CROSS	MANLEY	WOOLLETT	FERN*	SAMMELS	WELLER	BIRCHENALL	GLOVER	LEE

MILESTONES: O'HARE, HECTOR, DURBAN

CLOUGH'S 200TH LEAGUE GAME IN CHARGE

DATE	VENUE	OPPOS	RESULT	ATTND	POS		BOULTON	WEBSTER	ROBSON	DURBAN	McFARLAND	TODD	McGOVERN	GEMMILL	O'HARE	HECTOR	HINTON*	WALKER
22.3.72	HOME	IPSWICH TOWN	1-0	26738	2-14	C	BOULTON	WEBSTER	ROBSON	DURBAN	McFARLAND	TODD	McGOVERN	GEMMILL	O'HARE	HECTOR	HINTON*	WALKER
						O	BEST	MILLS	HARPER	MORRIS	HUNTER	JEFFERSON	ROBERTSON	MILLER	HAMMOND	BELFITT	WHYMARK*	LAMBERT

MILESTONES: HECTOR

DATE	VENUE	OPPOS	RESULT	ATTND	POS		BOULTON	WEBSTER	ROBSON	DURBAN	McFARLAND	TODD	McGOVERN	GEMMILL	O'HARE	HECTOR	WALKER	NA
25.3.72	AWAY	STOKE CITY	1-1	33771	2-15	C	BOULTON	WEBSTER	ROBSON	DURBAN	McFARLAND	TODD	McGOVERN	GEMMILL	O'HARE	HECTOR	WALKER	NA
						O	BANKS	MARSH	JUMP	BERNARD	SMITH	BLOOR	CONROY	GREENHOFF	RITCHIE	DOBBING	BURROWS	NA

MILESTONES: DURBAN, GREENHOFF (P)

28.3.72 — CRYSTAL PALACE — AWAY — 1-0 — 21158 — 2-19

Derby	Opponent
BOULTON	JACKSON
WEBSTER	PAYNE
ROBSON	GOODWIN
DURBAN	KELLARD
McFARLAND	McCORMICK
TODD	BELL
HENNESSEY	CRAVEN
GEMMILL	QUEEN
O'HARE	WALLACE
HECTOR	TAYLOR
WALKER	TAMBLING*
NA	WALL

MILESTONES: WALKER — NA — 250TH OVERALL LEAGUE GAME FOR O'HARE

1.4.72 — LEEDS UNITED — HOME — 2-0 — 38611 — 1-3

Derby	Opponent
BOULTON	SPRAKE
WEBSTER	REANEY
ROBSON	COOPER
DURBAN	BREMNER
McFARLAND	CHARLTON
TODD	HUNTER
McGOVERN	LORIMER
GEMMILL	CLARKE
O'HARE	MADELEY
HECTOR	GILES
WALKER	GRAY
NA	NA

MILESTONES: O'HARE, HUNTER (OG) — NA

3.4.72 — NEWCASTLE UNITED — HOME — 0-1 — 38119 — 1-11

Derby	Opponent
BOULTON	McFAUL
WEBSTER	CRAIG
ROBSON	CLARKE
DURBAN	GIBB*
McFARLAND	HOWARD
TODD	MONCUR
McGOVERN	BARROWCLOUGH
GEMMILL	GREEN
O'HARE	MACDONALD
HECTOR	TUDOR
HINTON	REID
NA	CASSIDY

MILESTONES: NA — CASSIDY — O'HARE SCORES IN 200TH RAMS LEAGUE GAME

5.4.72 — WEST BROMWICH ALBION — AWAY — 0-0 — 32439 — 1-11

Derby	Opponent
BOULTON	OSBOURNE
WEBSTER	NISBET
ROBSON	WILSON
DURBAN	SUGGETT
McFARLAND	WILE
TODD	ROBERTSON
McGOVERN	HOPE
GEMMILL	BROWN
O'HARE	ASTLE
HECTOR	BROWN

MILESTONES: NA — NA

8.4.72 — SHEFFIELD UNITED — AWAY — 4-0 — 38238 — 1-10

Derby	Opponent
BOULTON	HOPE
WEBSTER	BADGER
ROBSON	HEMSLEY
DURBAN	MACKENZIE
McFARLAND	COLQUHOUN
TODD	SALMONS
McGOVERN	WOODWARD
GEMMILL	SCULLION
O'HARE	DEARDEN
HECTOR	HOLMES
HINTON	FORD
NA	NA

GEMMILL, O'HARE, HECTOR, DURBAN — MILESTONES: NA

15.4.72 — HUDDERSFIELD TOWN — HOME — 3-0 — 31414 — 1-21

Derby	Opponent
BOULTON	LAWSON
WEBSTER	CLARK
ROBSON	HUTT
DURBAN	SMITH
McFARLAND	ELLAM
TODD	CHERRY
McGOVERN	HOY
GEMMILL	JONES
O'HARE	WORTHINGTON
HECTOR	LAWSON
HINTON	CHAPMAN

McFARLAND, O'HARE, HECTOR — MILESTONES: NA — 200TH OVERALL LEAGUE GOAL FOR HECTOR

22.4.72 — MANCHESTER CITY — AWAY — 0-2 — 55023 — 3-1

Derby	Opponent
BOULTON	CORRIGAN
WEBSTER*	BOOK
ROBSON	DONACHIE
DURBAN	DOYLE
McFARLAND	BOOTH
TODD	JEFFERIES
McGOVERN	LEE
GEMMILL	BELL
O'HARE	SUMMERBEE
HECTOR	MARSH
HINTON	TOWERS
HENNESSEY	NA

MARSH, LEE (P) — MILESTONES: NA

League

	1	2	3	4	5	6	7	8	9	10	11	12
DATE 1.5.72 · VENUE HOME · OPPOS LIVERPOOL · RESULT 1-0 · ATTND 39159 · POS 1												
C (Derby)	BOULTON	POWELL	ROBSON	DURBAN	McFARLAND	TODD	McGOVERN	GEMMILL	O'HARE	HECTOR	HINTON	NA
O (Liverpool)	CLEMENCE	LAWLER	LINDSAY	SMITH	LLOYD	HUGHES	KEEGAN	HALL	HEIGHWAY*	TOSHACK	CALLAGHAN	McLAUGHLIN

Scorer: McGOVERN
MILESTONES: BOULTON AND HECTOR EVER-PRESENTS

LEAGUE CUP

	1	2	3	4	5	6	7	8	9	10	11	12
DATE 8.9.71 · VENUE HOME · OPPOS LEEDS UNITED · RESULT 0-0 · ATTND 36023 · ROUND 2ND												
C (Derby)	BOULTON	WEBSTER	ROBSON	TODD	McFARLAND	GEMMILL	DURBAN	WIGNALL	O'HARE	HECTOR	HINTON	NA
O (Leeds)	HARVEY	REANEY	YORATH	BREMNER	CHARLTON	HUNTER	LORIMER	CLARKE	BELFITT	GILES	MADELEY	NA

MILESTONES: NA

	1	2	3	4	5	6	7	8	9	10	11	12
DATE 27.9.71 · VENUE AWAY · OPPOS LEEDS UNITED · RESULT 0-2 · ATTND 29132 · ROUND 2ND R												
C (Derby)	BOULTON	WEBSTER	ROBSON	TODD	McFARLAND	GEMMILL	McGOVERN	WIGNALL	O'HARE	HECTOR	HINTON	NA
O (Leeds)	SPRAKE	REANEY	COOPER	BREMNER*	CHARLTON	HUNTER	LORIMER	YORATH	BELFITT	GILES	MADELEY	MANN

Scorers: LORIMER (2)
MILESTONES:

FA CUP

	1	2	3	4	5	6	7	8	9	10	11	12
DATE 3.1.72 · VENUE HOME · OPPOS SHREWSBURY TOWN · RESULT 2-0 · ATTND 33463 · ROUND 3RD												
C (Derby)	BOULTON	WEBSTER	ROBSON	DURBAN	McFARLAND	TODD	McGOVERN	GEMMILL	O'HARE	HECTOR	HINTON	NA
O (Shrewsbury)	MULHEARN	BROWN	FELLOWS	MOORE	HOLTON	BRIDGWOOD	ROBERTS	ANDREWS	WOOD	MOIR	GROVES	NA

Scorers: HECTOR (2)
MILESTONES: NA

	1	2	3	4	5	6	7	8	9	10	11	12
DATE 5.2.72 · VENUE HOME · OPPOS NOTTS COUNTY · RESULT 6-0 · ATTND 39450 · ROUND 4TH												
C (Derby)	BOULTON	WEBSTER	ROBSON	DURBAN	McFARLAND	TODD	McGOVERN	GEMMILL	O'HARE*	HECTOR	HINTON	POWELL
O (Notts County)	BROWN	BRINDLEY	WORTHINGTON	CARLIN	STUBBS	JONES	NIXON	BRADD	HATELEY	MASSON	COZENS	NA

Scorers: DURBAN (3), ROBSON, HECTOR, HINTON (P)
MILESTONES:

	1	2	3	4	5	6	7	8	9	10	11	12
DATE 26.2.72 · VENUE HOME · OPPOS ARSENAL · RESULT 2-2 · ATTND 39622 · ROUND 5TH												
C (Derby)	BOULTON	WEBSTER	ROBSON	DURBAN	McFARLAND	TODD	McGOVERN	GEMMILL	O'HARE	HECTOR	HINTON	NA
O (Arsenal)	WILSON	RICE	NELSON	KELLY*	McLINTOCK	SIMPSON	ARMSTRONG	BALL	GEORGE	KENNEDY	GRAHAM	STOREY

Scorers: DURBAN, HINTON (P); GEORGE (2)
MILESTONES:

DATE	VENUE	OPPOS	RESULT	ATTND	ROUND		1	2	3	4	5	6	7	8	9	10	11	12
29.2.72	AWAY	ARSENAL	0-0	63077	5TH R	C	BOULTON	WEBSTER	ROBSON	DURBAN	McFARLAND	TODD	McGOVERN	GEMMILL	O'HARE	HECTOR	HINTON	NA
						O	WILSON	RICE	NELSON	STOREY	McLINTOCK	SIMPSON	ARMSTRONG	BALL	GEORGE	KENNEDY*	GRAHAM	RADFORD

MILESTONES: NA / NA

DATE	VENUE	OPPOS	RESULT	ATTND	ROUND		1	2	3	4	5	6	7	8	9	10	11	12
13.3.72	AWAY*	ARSENAL	0-1	40000	5TH 2R	C	BOULTON	WEBSTER	ROBSON	DURBAN	McFARLAND	TODD	McGOVERN*	GEMMILL	O'HARE	HECTOR	HINTON	HENNESSEY
						O	WILSON	RICE	NELSON	STOREY	McLINTOCK	SIMPSON	ARMSTRONG	BALL	GEORGE	KENNEDY	GRAHAM	NA

MILESTONES: NA / KENNEDY

* AT FILBERT STREET LEICESTER

TEXACO CUP

DATE	VENUE	OPPOS	RESULT	ATTND	ROUND		1	2	3	4	5	6	7	8	9	10	11	12
15.9.71	HOME	DUNDEE UNITED	6-2	20059	1ST 1L	C	BOULTON	WEBSTER	ROBSON	TODD	HENNESSEY	McGOVERN	BOURNE	DURBAN*	O'HARE	HECTOR	HINTON	WALKER
						O	MACKAY	GRAY	CAMERON	SMITH	HENRY	WATSON	REID	GORDON	ROLLAND	COPELAND*	DEVLIN	

MILESTONES: DURBAN, HECTOR, WALKER, O'HARE, HINTON, ROBSON / GORDON, ROLLAND

DATE	VENUE	OPPOS	RESULT	ATTND	ROUND		1	2	3	4	5	6	7	8	9	10	11	12
29.9.71	AWAY	DUNDEE UNITED	2-3	6000	1ST 2L	C	BOULTON	DANIEL	ROBSON	HENNESSEY	BAILEY	GEMMILL	McGOVERN	WIGNALL	BUTLIN	WALKER	HINTON	NA
						O	McALPINE	ROLLAND	CAMERON	MARKLAND	GRAY	HENRY	TRAYNOR	REID	COPELAND	DEVLIN*	WHITE	SMITH

MILESTONES: HINTON, BUTLIN / COPELAND (2), DEVLIN

FIRST GOAL FOR BUTLIN / DEBUT FOR BAILEY

DATE	VENUE	OPPOS	RESULT	ATTND	ROUND		1	2	3	4	5	6	7	8	9	10	11	12
20.10.71	HOME	STOKE CITY	3-2	21487	2ND 1L	C	BOULTON	DANIEL	LEWIS	HENNESSEY*	McFARLAND	TODD	WIGNALL	POWELL	O'HARE	HECTOR	HINTON	BAILEY
						O	BANKS	MARSH	PEJIC	BERNARD	SMITH	BLOOR	MAHONEY	STEVENSON	GREENHOFF	JUMP*	HASELGRAVE	JACKSON

MILESTONES: O'HARE (2), HECTOR / MAHONEY, SMITH

DEBUTS FOR POWELL AND LEWIS

DATE	VENUE	OPPOS	RESULT	ATTND	ROUND		1	2	3	4	5	6	7	8	9	10	11	12
3.11.71	AWAY	STOKE CITY	1-1	23461	2ND 2L	C	BOULTON	WEBSTER	ROBSON	TODD	HENNESSEY	McGOVERN	DURBAN	WIGNALL	O'HARE	HECTOR	HINTON	NA
						O	BANKS	MARSH	PEJIC	BERNARD	SMITH	BLOOR	HASELGRAVE	MAHONEY	CONROY	EASTHAM*	JUMP	STEVENSON

MILESTONES: WIGNALL / SMITH

DATE	24.11.71	C
VENUE	HOME	O
OPPOS	NEWCASTLE UNITED	
RESULT	1-0	C
ATTND	20201	O
ROUND	SF 1L	

BOULTON	McFAUL	
WEBSTER	CRAIG	
ROBSON	CLARK	
TODD	NATTRASS	
McFARLAND	BURTON	
HENNESSEY	HOWARD	
McGOVERN	BARROWCLOUGH	
GEMMILL	GREEN*	
O'HARE	MACDONALD	
HECTOR	TUDOR	
HINTON	HIBBITT	
NA	GIBB	

MILESTONES: O'HARE — NA

DATE	8.12.71	C
VENUE	AWAY	O
OPPOS	NEWCASTLE UNITED	
RESULT	3-2	C
ATTND	37000	O
ROUND	SF 2L	

BOULTON	McFAUL	
TODD	CRAIG	
WEBSTER	CLARK	
HENNESSEY	NATTRASS	
BAILEY	BURTON	
DANIEL	HOWARD	
DURBAN	BARROWCLOUGH	
McGOVERN	GREEN	
O'HARE	MACDONALD	
HECTOR	HIBBITT	
HINTON*	COULSON*	
WALKER	GIBB	

MILESTONES: McGOVERN, TODD, WALKER — MACDONALD, BARROWCLOUGH

DATE	26.1.72	C
VENUE	AWAY	O
OPPOS	AIRDRIEONIANS	
RESULT	0-0	C
ATTND	16000	O
ROUND	FINAL 1L	

BOULTON	McKENZIE	
WEBSTER	JONQUIN	
ROBSON	CLARKE	
TODD	MENZIES	
DANIEL	McKINLAY	
HENNESSEY	WHITEFORD	
PARRY	WILSON	
GEMMILL	WALKER	
BUTLIN	BUSBY	
WALKER	JARVIE	
HINTON	COWAN*	
NA	WHITEFORD	

MILESTONES: NA — NA

DATE	26.4.72	C
VENUE	HOME	O
OPPOS	AIRDRIEONIANS	
RESULT	2-1	C
ATTND	25102	O
ROUND	FINAL 2L	

BOULTON	McKENZIE	
POWELL	CALDWELL	
ROBSON	CLARKE	
DURBAN	MENZIES	
DANIEL	McKINLAY	
HENNESSEY	WHITEFORD	
McGOVERN	WILSON	
BUTLIN	WALKER	
DAVIES	BUSBY	
HECTOR	JARVIE	
HINTON	COWAN*	
NA	JONQUIN	

MILESTONES: HINTON (P), DAVIES — WHITEFORD

SCORING DEBUT FOR DAVIES

DIVISION 1

DATE 12.8.72 — **VENUE** AWAY — **OPPOS** SOUTHAMPTON — **RESULT** 1-1 — **ATTND** 20525 — **POS** 9-12

1	2	3	4	5	6	7	8	9	10	11	12
BOULTON	WEBSTER	ROBSON	DURBAN	McFARLAND	TODD	McGOVERN	GEMMILL	O'HARE	HECTOR	HINTON	NA
MARTIN	McCARTHY	BURNS	FISHER	McGRATH	STEELE	O'BRIEN	CHANNON	DAVIES	O'NEIL	JENKINS	NA

MILESTONES: HINTON — NA

DATE 15.8.72 — **VENUE** AWAY — **OPPOS** CRYSTAL PALACE — **RESULT** 0-0 — **ATTND** 23401 — **POS** 11-16

1	2	3	4	5	6	7	8	9	10	11	12
BOULTON	WEBSTER	ROBSON	DURBAN	HENNESSEY	TODD	McGOVERN	GEMMILL	O'HARE	HECTOR	HINTON	NA
JACKSON	PAYNE	WALL	KELLARD	McCORMICK	BLYTH	CRAVEN	PINKNEY	JENKINS	WALLACE	TAYLOR	NA

MILESTONES: NA — NA

DATE 19.8.72 — **VENUE** HOME — **OPPOS** CHELSEA — **RESULT** 1-2 — **ATTND** 31868 — **POS** 15-4

1	2	3	4	5	6	7	8	9	10	11	12
BOULTON	WEBSTER	ROBSON	DURBAN	McFARLAND	TODD	McGOVERN	GEMMILL	O'HARE	HECTOR	WALKER	NA
BONETTI	HARRIS	McCREADIE	HOLLINS	DROY	WEBB	GARLAND	KEMBER	OSGOOD	HUDSON	COOKE	NA

MILESTONES: HECTOR — HARRIS, GARLAND

DATE 23.8.72 — **VENUE** HOME — **OPPOS** MANCHESTER CITY — **RESULT** 1-0 — **ATTND** 31173 — **POS** 12-17

1	2	3	4	5	6	7	8	9	10	11	12
BOULTON	POWELL	LEWIS	HENNESSEY*	McFARLAND	TODD	McGOVERN	GEMMILL	O'HARE	HECTOR	WALKER	NA
CORRIGAN	BARRETT	DONACHIE	DOYLE	BOOTH	TOWERS	SUMMERBEE	BELL	MELLOR	LEE*	JEFFERIES	BOOK

MILESTONES: WALKER — NA

DATE 26.8.72 — **VENUE** AWAY — **OPPOS** NORWICH CITY — **RESULT** 0-1 — **ATTND** 29847 — **POS** 15-9

1	2	3	4	5	6	7	8	9	10	11	12
BOULTON	POWELL	NISH	HENNESSEY*	McFARLAND	TODD	McGOVERN	GEMMILL	O'HARE	HECTOR	WALKER	DURBAN
KEELAN	PAYNE	BUTLER	STRINGER*	FORBES	BRIGGS	LIVERMORE	BONE	CROSS	PADDON	ANDERSON	SELF

MILESTONES: NA — PADDON

DATE 29.8.72 — **VENUE** AWAY — **OPPOS** EVERTON — **RESULT** 0-1 — **ATTND** 39780 — **POS** 16-3

1	2	3	4	5	6	7	8	9	10	11	12
BOULTON	POWELL	NISH	HENNESSEY	McFARLAND	TODD	McGOVERN	GEMMILL	O'HARE	HECTOR	WALKER	NA
LAWSON	WRIGHT	NEWTON	KENDALL	KENYON	WHITTLE	JOHNSON	BERNARD	ROYLE	HARVEY	CONNOLLY	NA

MILESTONES: NA — ROYLE

LIVERPOOL
DATE: 2.9.72 — VENUE: HOME — RESULT: 2-1 — ATTND: 32524 — POS: 13-6

Team	1	2	3	4	5	6	7	8	9	10	11	Sub
Rams	BOULTON	POWELL	NISH	HENNESSEY	McFARLAND	TODD	McGOVERN	GEMMILL	O'HARE	HECTOR	HINTON	NA
Liverpool	LANE	LAWLER	HUGHES	SMITH	LLOYD	CORMACK	KEEGAN	HALL	HIGHWAY	TOSHACK	CALLAGHAN	NA

Scorers — Rams: O'HARE, HINTON / Liverpool: TOSHACK
MILESTONES:

WEST BROMWICH ALBION
DATE: 9.9.72 — VENUE: AWAY — RESULT: 1-2 — ATTND: 17262 — POS: 16-20

Team	1	2	3	4	5	6	7	8	9	10	11	Sub
Rams	BOULTON	POWELL	NISH	HENNESSEY	McFARLAND	TODD	McGOVERN	GEMMILL	O'HARE	HECTOR	HINTON	NA
West Brom	LATCHFORD	NISBET	WILSON	CANTELLO	WILE	ROBERTSON	SUGGETT	BROWN	GOULD	BROWN	HARTFORD	NA

Scorers — Rams: McFARLAND / West Brom: GOULD, BROWN
MILESTONES: McFARLAND SCORES IN 200TH RAMS LEAGUE GAME

BIRMINGHAM CITY
DATE: 16.9.72 — VENUE: HOME — RESULT: 1-0 — ATTND: 33753 — POS: 13-18

Team	1	2	3	4	5	6	7	8	9	10	11	Sub
Rams	BOULTON	POWELL	NISH	HENNESSEY	McFARLAND	TODD	McGOVERN	GEMMILL	O'HARE	HECTOR	HINTON	NA
Birmingham	LATCHFORD	CARROLL	PENDREY	CAMPBELL	HYND	PAGE	BURNS	FRANCIS	LATCHFORD	HOPE	HATTON	NA.

Scorers — Rams: HECTOR / Birmingham: NA
MILESTONES:

MANCHESTER UNITED
DATE: 23.9.72 — VENUE: AWAY — RESULT: 0-3 — ATTND: 48255 — POS: 16-21

Team	1	2	3	4	5	6	7	8	9	10	11	Sub
Rams	BOULTON	POWELL	NISH	HENNESSEY	McFARLAND	TODD	McGOVERN	GEMMILL	O'HARE	HECTOR	HINTON	NA
Man Utd	STEPNEY	DONALD	DUNNE	YOUNG	JAMES	BUCHAN	MORGAN	DAVIES	CHARLTON	BEST	MOORE	NA.

Scorers — Rams: NA / Man Utd: MOORE, MORGAN, DAVIES
MILESTONES:

TOTTENHAM HOTSPUR
DATE: 30.9.72 — VENUE: HOME — RESULT: 2-1 — ATTND: 32133 — POS: 14-4

Team	1	2	3	4	5	6	7	8	9	10	11	Sub
Rams	BOULTON	POWELL	NISH	HENNESSEY*	McFARLAND	TODD	McGOVERN	GEMMILL	O'HARE	HECTOR	HINTON	DURBAN
Tottenham	JENNINGS	KINNEAR	KNOWLES	PRATT	ENGLAND	BEAL	GILZEAN*	PERRYMAN	CHIVERS	NAYLOR	COATES	PEARCE

Scorers — Rams: HECTOR, HINTON (P) / Tottenham: PERRYMAN
MILESTONES: 100TH OVERALL LEAGUE GOAL FOR HINTON

LEEDS UNITED
DATE: 7.10.72 — VENUE: AWAY — RESULT: 0-5 — ATTND: 36477 — POS: 16-5

Team	1	2	3	4	5	6	7	8	9	10	11	Sub
Rams	BOULTON	ROBSON	NISH	DURBAN	McFARLAND	TODD	DANIEL	GEMMILL	O'HARE	HECTOR	HINTON	NA
Leeds	HARVEY	MADELEY	CHERRY	BREMNER	CHARLTON	HUNTER	LORIMER	CLARKE	JONES	GILES*	GRAY	BATES

Scorers — Rams: NA / Leeds: GILES (2), BREMNER, CLARKE, LORIMER
MILESTONES:

LEICESTER CITY
DATE: 14.10.72 — VENUE: HOME — RESULT: 2-1 — ATTND: 31841 — POS: 13-16

Team	1	2	3	4	5	6	7	8	9	10	11	Sub
Rams	BOULTON	ROBSON	NISH	HENNESSEY	McFARLAND	TODD	McGOVERN	POWELL	O'HARE	HECTOR	HINTON	NA
Leicester	SHILTON	WHITWORTH	ROFE	SAMMELS	SJOBERG	CROSS	FARRINGTON	BIRCHENALL*	WELLER	WORTHINGT	GLOVER	STRINGFELLOW

Scorers — Rams: HINTON (P), HENNESSEY / Leicester: WELLER
MILESTONES: 250TH RAMS LEAGUE GAME FOR HECTOR

21.10.72 — AWAY — IPSWICH TOWN — Result 1-3 — Attnd 16948 — Pos 16-7

	1	2	3	4	5	6	7	8	9	10	11	Sub	Sub
C	BOULTON	ROBSON	NISH	HENNESSEY	McFARLAND	TODD	POWELL	McGOVERN	HINTON	HECTOR	DURBAN	NA	
O	BEST	MILLS	HARPER	MORRIS	HUNTER	BEATTIE	VILJOEN	HAMILTON	BELFITT	WHYMARK	LAMBERT	NA	

MILESTONES: HINTON (P) / BELFITT, BEATTIE, WHYMARK / 100TH RAMS LEAGUE GAME FOR BOULTON

28.10.72 — HOME — SHEFFIELD UNITED — Result 2-1 — Attnd 30929 — Pos 14-12

	1	2	3	4	5	6	7	8	9	10	11	Sub	Sub
C	BOULTON	POWELL	ROBSON	HENNESSEY	McFARLAND	TODD	McGOVERN	NISH	O'HARE	HECTOR	HINTON	NA	
O	McALISTER	GOULDING	HEMSLEY	FLYNN	COLQUHOUN	HOCKEY	WOODWARD	BADGER	DEARDEN	CURRIE	STAINFORTH	NA	

MILESTONES: TODD, O'HARE / CURRIE

4.11.72 — AWAY — MANCHESTER CITY — Result 0-4 — Attnd 35829 — Pos 16-15

	1	2	3	4	5	6	7	8	9	10	11	Sub	Sub
C	BOULTON	POWELL	ROBSON	HENNESSEY	McFARLAND	TODD	McGOVERN	NISH	DAVIES	BUTLIN	HINTON*	DURBAN	
O	CORRIGAN	PARDOE	DONACHIE	DOYLE	BARRETT	JEFFERIES	SUMMERBEE	BELL	MARSH	LEE	CARRODUS	NA	

MILESTONES: NA / MARSH (2), BELL, TODD (OG) / LAST GAME FOR BUTLIN / HECTOR ABSENCE BROKE SEQUENCE OF 105 LEAGUE GAMES

11.11.72 — HOME — CRYSTAL PALACE — Result 2-2 — Attnd 26716 — Pos 16-22

	1	2	3	4	5	6	7	8	9	10	11	Sub	Sub
C	BOULTON	WEBSTER	ROBSON	POWELL	McFARLAND	TODD	McGOVERN	NISH	O'HARE	HECTOR	HINTON	NA	
O	JACKSON	MULLIGAN	TAYLOR	PHILLIP*	BELL	BLYTH	HUGHES	PAYNE	CRAVEN	COOK	ROGERS	KELLARD	

MILESTONES: HINTON, POWELL / ROGERS, CRAVEN (P) / LAST GAME FOR ROBSON / FIRST GOAL FOR POWELL

18.11.72 — AWAY — WEST HAM UNITED — Result 2-1 — Attnd 28154 — Pos 15-11

	1	2	3	4	5	6	7	8	9	10	11	Sub	Sub
C	BOULTON	WEBSTER	NISH	HENNESSEY	McFARLAND	TODD	McGOVERN	GEMMILL	O'HARE	HECTOR	HINTON	NA	
O	FERGUSON	CHARLES	LAMPARD	BONDS	TAYLOR	MOORE	TYLER	AYRIS*	HOLLAND	BROOKING	ROBSON	BEST	

MILESTONES: HECTOR (2) / ROBSON

25.11.72 — HOME — ARSENAL — Result 5-0 — Attnd 31034 — Pos 13-3

	1	2	3	4	5	6	7	8	9	10	11	Sub	Sub
C	BOULTON	WEBSTER	NISH	HENNESSEY	McFARLAND	TODD	McGOVERN	GEMMILL	DAVIES	HECTOR	HINTON	NA	
O	WILSON	RICE	McNAB	STOREY	McLINTOCK	SIMPSON	MARINELLO*	BALL	RADFORD	GEORGE	KELLY	ARMSTRONG	

MILESTONES: McFARLAND, McGOVERN, HECTOR, HINTON, DAVIES

2.12.72 — AWAY — WOLVERHAMPTON WANDERERS — Result 2-1 — Attnd 24891 — Pos 10-13

	1	2	3	4	5	6	7	8	9	10	11	Sub	Sub
C	BOULTON	WEBSTER	NISH	HENNESSEY	DANIEL	TODD	McGOVERN	GEMMILL	DAVIES	HECTOR	HINTON	NA	
O	PARKES	SHAW	TAYLOR	BAILEY	MUNROE	McALLE	McCALLIOG	HIBBITT	RICHARDS	DOUGAN	WAGSTAFFE	NA	

MILESTONES: HECTOR, HENNESSEY / RICHARDS

		BOULTON	WEBSTER	NISH	O'HARE	DANIEL	TODD	McGOVERN	GEMMILL	DAVIES	HECTOR	HINTON	NA
DATE	9.12.72		RAMSBOTTOM	COOP	CATTLIN	SMITH	DUGDALE	PARKER	MORTIMER	ALDERSON	STEIN	CARR	HUTCHINSON	NA
VENUE	HOME	C/O												NA
OPPOS	COVENTRY CITY													
RESULT	2-0													
ATTND	31002		GEMMILL, HINTON (P)											
POS	7-12		MILESTONES:											

		BOULTON	WEBSTER	NISH*	O'HARE	McFARLAND	TODD	McGOVERN	GEMMILL	DAVIES	HECTOR	HINTON	SIMS
DATE	16-12.72		McFAUL	CRAIG	CLARKE	NATTRASS	HOWARD	MONCUR	BARROWCLOUGH	SMITH	MACDONALD	TUDOR	HIBBITT	NA
VENUE	HOME		HECTOR											
OPPOS	NEWCASTLE UNITED		TUDOR											
RESULT	1-1		MILESTONES:											
ATTND	28826		DEBUT FOR SIMS											
POS	6-8													

		BOULTON	WEBSTER	LEWIS	HENNESSEY	McFARLAND	TODD	McGOVERN	GEMMILL	O'HARE	HECTOR	HINTON	NA
DATE	23.12.72		FARMER	MARSH	PEJIC	MAHONEY	SMITH	SKEELS	CONROY	GREENHOFF	RITCHIE	HURST	EASTHAM	NA
VENUE	AWAY		NA											
OPPOS	STOKE CITY		RITCHIE (2), HURST, GREENHOFF											
RESULT	0-4		MILESTONES:											
ATTND	25098		350TH RAMS LEAGUE GAME FOR WEBSTER / 250TH OVERALL LEAGUE GAME FOR TODD /											
POS	10-17		200TH RAMS LEAGUE GAME FOR HINTON / LAST GAME FOR LEWIS											

		BOULTON	WEBSTER	DANIEL	HENNESSEY	McFARLAND	TODD	McGOVERN	GEMMILL	DAVIES	HECTOR	HINTON	NA
DATE	26.12.72		STEPNEY	O'NEIL	DUNNE*	KIDD	SADLER	BUCHAN	MORGAN	MACDOUGALL	CHARLTON	DAVIES	MOORE	YOUNG
VENUE	HOME		McFARLAND (2), HINTON											
OPPOS	MANCHESTER UNITED		MOORE											
RESULT	3-1		MILESTONES:											
ATTND	35098													
POS	7-22													

		BOULTON	WEBSTER	DANIEL	HENNESSEY	McFARLAND	TODD	McGOVERN	O'HARE	DAVIES	HECTOR	HINTON	NA
DATE	30.12.72		PHILLIPS	WEBB	HARRIS	HOLLINS	DEMPSEY	HINTON	BALDWIN	HUDSON	OSGOOD	HUTCHINSON*	BOYLE	BRITTON
VENUE	AWAY		O'HARE											
OPPOS	CHELSEA		OSGOOD											
RESULT	1-1		MILESTONES:											
ATTND	29794		250TH OVERALL LEAGUE GAME FOR McFARLAND											
POS	6-8													

		BOULTON	NISH	DANIEL	O'HARE	McFARLAND	TODD	McGOVERN	GEMMILL	DAVIES	HECTOR	HINTON	NA
DATE	6.1.73		KEELAN	BUTLER	BLACK	STRINGER	GOVIER	BRIGGS	LIVERMORE	CHEESLEY*	CROSS	PADDON	ANDERSON	O'DONNELL
VENUE	HOME		HINTON (P)											
OPPOS	NORWICH CITY		NA											
RESULT	1-0		MILESTONES:											
ATTND	27580		150TH RAMS LEAGUE GAME FOR McGOVERN											
POS	5-15													

		BOULTON	WEBSTER	NISH	HENNESSEY	McFARLAND	TODD	McGOVERN	O'HARE	DAVIES	HECTOR	POWELL	NA
DATE	20.1.73		CLEMENCE	LAWLER	LINDSAY	SMITH	LLOYD	HUGHES	KEEGAN	CORMACK	HIGHWAY	TOSHACK	CALLAGHAN	NA
VENUE	AWAY		DAVIES											
OPPOS	LIVERPOOL		TOSHACK											
RESULT	1-1		MILESTONES:											
ATTND	45996		400TH OVERALL LEAGUE GAME FOR HENNESSEY.											
POS	6-1													

27.1.73 — HOME — WEST BROMWICH ALBION — 2-0 — 28833 — POS 5-22

BOULTON	WEBSTER	NISH	HENNESSEY	McFARLAND	TODD	McGOVERN	GEMMILL	DAVIES	HECTOR	HINTON	NA
LATCHFORD	NISBET	WILSON	CANTELLO	WILE	MERRICK	SUGGETT	BROWN	BROWN	HARTFORD	JOHNSTON	NA

MILESTONES: HINTON (P), DAVIES

10.2.73 — AWAY — BIRMINGHAM CITY — 0-2 — 38096 — POS 6-20

BOULTON	WEBSTER	NISH	DURBAN	McFARLAND	PARRY	McGOVERN	SIMS	DAVIES	HECTOR	GEMMILL	NA
LATCHFORD	MARTIN	PENDREY	PAGE	HYND	ROBERTS	CAMPBELL*	FRANCIS	LATCHFORD	HATTON	TAYLOR	BURNS

MILESTONES: LATCHFORD, FRANCIS
250TH OVERALL LEAGUE GAME FOR NISH / DEBUT FOR PARRY

14.2.73 — HOME — STOKE CITY — 0-3 — 22106 — POS 6-18

BOULTON	WEBSTER	NISH	DURBAN	DANIEL	TODD	SIMS	GEMMILL	DAVIES	HECTOR	WALKER*	PARRY
FARMER	MARSH	PEJIC	MAHONEY	BLOOR	SKEELS	ROBERTSON	GREENHOFF	RITCHIE	EASTHAM	CONROY	NA

MILESTONES: MAHONEY, ROBERTSON, GREENHOFF

17.2.73 — HOME — SOUTHAMPTON — 4-0 — 26426 — POS 5-12

BOULTON	WEBSTER	NISH	O'HARE	McFARLAND	TODD	McGOVERN	GEMMILL	DAVIES	HECTOR	HINTON	NA
MARTIN	McCARTHY	KIRKUP	FISHER	BENNETT	STEELE	PAINE	CHANNON	DAVIES	O'NEIL	O'BRIEN	NA

MILESTONES: HECTOR (2) HINTON, McCARTHY (OG)

28.2.73 — AWAY — NEWCASTLE UNITED — 0-2 — 34286 — POS 6-5

BOULTON	WEBSTER*	NISH	O'HARE	McFARLAND	TODD	McGOVERN	GEMMILL	DAVIES	HECTOR	POWELL	DURBAN
BURLEIGH	CRAIG	CLARK	NATTRASS	HOWARD	MONCUR	BARROWCLOUGH	SMITH	MACDONALD	TUDOR	HIBBITT	NA

MILESTONES: MACDONALD, TUDOR
CLOUGH'S 300TH COMPETITIVE GAME IN CHARGE

3.3.73 — HOME — LEEDS UNITED — 2-3 — 38462 — POS 6-3

BOULTON	POWELL	NISH	O'HARE	McFARLAND	TODD	McGOVERN	GEMMILL	DAVIES	HECTOR	DURBAN	NA
HARVEY	REANEY*	CHERRY	BREMNER	MADELEY	HUNTER	LORIMER	CLARKE	JONES	GILES	McQUEEN	BATES

MILESTONES: DURBAN, HECTOR / LORIMER (2) (2P), CLARKE

10.3.73 — AWAY — LEICESTER CITY — 0-0 — 29690 — POS 7-14

BOULTON	WEBSTER*	DANIEL	O'HARE	McFARLAND	TODD	McGOVERN	GEMMILL	DAVIES	HECTOR	POWELL	DURBAN
SHILTON	WHITWORTH	ROFE	SAMMELS	MANLEY	CROSS	FARRINGTON	BIRCHENALL	WELLER	WORTHINGTON	GLOVER	NA

MILESTONES: 100TH RAMS LEAGUE GAME FOR DANIEL

This page records the Rams' (Derby County) 1972/73 end-of-season league fixtures. For each match the twelve shirt positions are headed by the usual Derby player; each cell shows the Derby player (top line) and the opposing player (bottom line). The small letters **C** (against DATE) and **O** (against VENUE) appear for every match.

Match summary

#	DATE	VENUE	OPPONENTS	RESULT	ATTND	POS
1	24.3.73	AWAY	SHEFFIELD UNITED	1-3	24403	9-16
2	31.3.73	AWAY	ARSENAL	1-0	45217	8-2
3	14.4.73	AWAY	COVENTRY CITY	2-0	22762	9-13
4	18.4.73	AWAY	TOTTENHAM HOTSPUR	0-1	22659	9-8
5	21.4.73	HOME	WEST HAM UNITED	1-1	28727	9-5
6	28.4.73	HOME	EVERTON	3-1	24094	9-17
7	30.4.73	HOME	IPSWICH TOWN	3-0	20347	9-4

Line-ups (Derby / Opponent)

1 — SHEFFIELD UNITED (1-3)

Shirt	Derby	Sheffield United
BOULTON	BOULTON	McALISTER
WEBSTER	WEBSTER	BADGER
NISH	NISH	HEMSLEY
POWELL	POWELL	MACKENZIE
McFARLAND	McFARLAND	COLQUHOUN*
TODD	TODD	EDDY
McGOVERN*	McGOVERN*	WOODWARD
GEMMILL	GEMMILL	SACRON
O'HARE	O'HARE	DEARDEN
HECTOR	HECTOR	CURRIE
DURBAN	DURBAN	BONE
DAVIES	DAVIES	SPEIGHT

Scorers: DEARDEN (2), BONE
MILESTONES: NA

2 — ARSENAL (1-0)

Shirt	Derby	Arsenal
BOULTON	BOULTON	WILSON
WEBSTER	WEBSTER	RICE
NISH	NISH	McNAB
POWELL	PARRY	STOREY
McFARLAND	McFARLAND	McLINTOCK*
TODD	TODD	SIMPSON
McGOVERN*	McGOVERN	ARMSTRONG
GEMMILL	O'HARE	BALL
O'HARE	DAVIES	GEORGE
HECTOR	HECTOR	KENNEDY
DURBAN	POWELL	KELLY
DAVIES	NA	NELSON

Scorer: POWELL
MILESTONES: NA

3 — COVENTRY CITY (2-0)

Shirt	Derby	Coventry City
BOULTON	BOULTON	RAMSBOTTOM
WEBSTER	WEBSTER	COOP
NISH	NISH	CATTLIN
POWELL	DURBAN*	SMITH
McFARLAND	McFARLAND	BARRY
TODD	TODD	DUGDALE
McGOVERN*	McGOVERN	MORTIMER
GEMMILL	GEMMILL	ALDERSON
O'HARE	O'HARE	STEIN
HECTOR	HECTOR	CARR
DURBAN	POWELL	HUTCHINSON
DAVIES	PARRY	NA

Scorers: O'HARE, HECTOR
MILESTONES: 100TH RAMS LEAGUE GAME FOR GEMMILL

4 — TOTTENHAM HOTSPUR (0-1)

Shirt	Derby	Tottenham Hotspur
BOULTON	MOSELEY	JENNINGS
WEBSTER	WEBSTER	KINNEAR
NISH	NISH	EVANS
POWELL	PARRY	COATES
McFARLAND	McFARLAND	ENGLAND
TODD	TODD	BEAL
McGOVERN*	McGOVERN*	GILZEAN
GEMMILL	GEMMILL	PERRYMAN
O'HARE	O'HARE	PEARCE
HECTOR	HECTOR	PETERS
DURBAN	POWELL	PRATT
DAVIES	DURBAN	NA

Scorer: PETERS
MILESTONES: DEBUT FOR MOSELEY / 450TH OVERALL LEAGUE GAME FOR HECTOR

5 — WEST HAM UNITED (1-1)

Shirt	Derby	West Ham United
BOULTON	MOSELEY	GROTIER
WEBSTER	WEBSTER	CHARLES
NISH	NISH	LAMPARD
POWELL	PARRY*	BONDS
McFARLAND	McFARLAND	LOCK
TODD	TODD	MOORE
McGOVERN*	McGOVERN	BEST
GEMMILL	GEMMILL	LUTTON
O'HARE	O'HARE	MACDOUGALL
HECTOR	HECTOR	BROOKING
DURBAN	POWELL	ROBSON
DAVIES	DURBAN	NA

Scorers: GEMMILL (P) / LUTTON
MILESTONES: LAST APPEARANCE FOR PARRY

6 — EVERTON (3-1)

Shirt	Derby	Everton
BOULTON	BOULTON	LAWSON
WEBSTER	WEBSTER	DARRACOTT
NISH	NISH	McLAUGHLIN
POWELL	DANIEL	SEARGEANT
McFARLAND	McFARLAND	KENYON
TODD	TODD	BERNARD
McGOVERN*	DURBAN	JONES
GEMMILL	GEMMILL	WILSON
O'HARE	O'HARE	LYONS
HECTOR	HECTOR	HARPER
DURBAN	HINTON	CONNOLLY
DAVIES	DAVIES	MORRIS

Scorers: GEMMILL (P), HINTON, NISH / CONNOLLY
MILESTONES: LAST APPEARANCE FOR DURBAN / FIRST GOAL FOR NISH

7 — IPSWICH TOWN (3-0)

Shirt	Derby	Ipswich Town
BOULTON	BOULTON	BEST
WEBSTER	WEBSTER	MILLS
NISH	NISH	HARPER
POWELL	POWELL	MORRIS
McFARLAND	McFARLAND	HUNTER
TODD	TODD	BEATTIE
McGOVERN*	McGOVERN	HAMILTON
GEMMILL	GEMMILL	VILJOEN
O'HARE	DAVIES	JOHNSON
HECTOR	HECTOR	CLARKE
DURBAN	HINTON	LAMBERT
DAVIES	NA	NA

Scorers: HECTOR (2), DAVIES
MILESTONES: NA

DATE	4.5.73	C									
VENUE	HOME	O									
OPPOS	WOLVERHAMPTON WANDERERS										
RESULT	3-0	C	DAVIES (2), McFARLAND								
ATTND	31590	O	NA								
POS	7-5		MILESTONES:								

BOULTON	WEBSTER	NISH	O'HARE	McFARLAND	TODD	McGOVERN	GEMMILL	DAVIES	HECTOR	HINTON	NA
PARKES	TAYLOR	PARKIN	BAILEY	JEFFERSON	McALLE	POWELL	SUNDERLAND	RICHARDS	DOUGAN	KINDON	NA

AFTER ALL TEAMS HAD PLAYED 42 GAMES DERBY FINISHED IN 7TH PLACED

LEAGUE CUP

DATE	5.9.72	C									
VENUE	AWAY	O									
OPPOS	SWINDON TOWN										
RESULT	1-0	C	HENNESSEY								
ATTND	15730	O	NA								
ROUND	2ND		MILESTONES:								

BOULTON	POWELL	NISH	HENNESSEY	McFARLAND	TODD	McGOVERN	GEMMILL*	O'HARE	HECTOR	HINTON	DURBAN
DOWNSBO	THOMAS	TROLLOPE	BUTLER	BURROWS	POTTER	PEPLOW	BUNKELL	TREACY	HUBBARD	ROGERS	NA

DATE	4.10.72	C									
VENUE	HOME	O									
OPPOS	CHELSEA										
RESULT	0-0	C	NA								
ATTND	28065	O	NA								
ROUND	3RD		MILESTONES:								

BOULTON	POWELL	NISH	DURBAN	McFARLAND	TODD	McGOVERN	GEMMILL	O'HARE	HECTOR	HINTON	NA
BONETTI	LOCKE	McCREADIE	HOLLINS	DROY	HARRIS	GARLAND	KEMBER	OSGOOD	WEBB	HOUSEMAN	NA

DATE	9.10.72	C									
VENUE	AWAY	O									
OPPOS	CHELSEA										
RESULT	2-3	C	HINTON, McGOVERN								
ATTND	26395	O	KEMBER, WEBB, OSGOOD								
ROUND	3RD R		MILESTONES:								

BOULTON	POWELL	NISH	POWELL	McFARLAND	TODD	McGOVERN	GEMMILL	O'HARE	HECTOR	HINTON	NA
BONETTI	LOCKE	McCREADIE	HOLLINS	HINTON	HARRIS	BOYLE	KEMBER	OSGOOD	WEBB	HOUSEMAN	NA

FA CUP

DATE	13.1.73	C									
VENUE	AWAY	O									
OPPOS	PETERBOROUGH UNITED										
RESULT	1-0	C	DAVIES								
ATTND	20855	O	NA								
ROUND	3RD		MILESTONES:								

BOULTON	NISH	DANIEL	DURBAN	McFARLAND	TODD	McGOVERN	GEMMILL	DAVIES*	HECTOR	O'HARE	HENNESSEY
DREWERY	BRADLEY	DUNCLIFFE	OAKES	TURNER	CARMICHAEL	HEATH	COZENS	HALL	YOUNG	ROBSON*	SMITH

DATE	3.2.73	C									
VENUE	HOME	O									
OPPOS	TOTTENHAM HOTSPUR										
RESULT	1-1	C	DAVIES								
ATTND	37895	O	CHIVERS								

BOULTON	WEBSTER	NISH	HENNESSEY	McFARLAND	TODD	McGOVERN	GEMMILL	DAVIES	HECTOR	O'HARE	NA
JENNINGS	KINNEAR	KNOWLES	PRATT	ENGLAND	BEAL	GILZEAN*	PERRYMAN	CHIVERS	PETERS	COATES	PEARCE

1972/73

Tottenham Hotspur

DATE	VENUE	OPPOS	RESULT	ATTND	ROUND
7.2.73	AWAY	TOTTENHAM HOTSPUR	5-3 AET	52736	4TH R

BOULTON	WEBSTER	NISH	HENNESSEY*	McFARLAND	TODD	McGOVERN	GEMMILL	DAVIES	HECTOR	O'HARE	DURBAN
JENNINGS	EVANS	KNOWLES	PRATT	ENGLAND	BEAL	GILZEAN	PERRYMAN	CHIVERS	PETERS	COATES*	PEARCE

MILESTONES: DAVIES (3), HECTOR (2)
CHIVERS, GILZEAN, ENGLAND (P)
LAST GAME FOR HENNESSEY / FIRST HAT TRICK FOR DAVIES

Queens Park Rangers

DATE	VENUE	OPPOS	RESULT	ATTND	ROUND
24.2.73	HOME	QUEENS PARK RANGERS	4-2	38100	5TH

BOULTON	WEBSTER	NISH	O'HARE	McFARLAND	TODD	McGOVERN	GEMMILL	DAVIES	HECTOR	HINTON*	DURBAN
PARKES	CLEMENT	WATSON	VENABLES	MANCINI	HAZELL	THOMAS	FRANCIS	LEACH	BOWLES	GIVENS	NA

MILESTONES: HECTOR (3), DAVIES
LEACH, GIVENS

Leeds United

DATE	VENUE	OPPOS	RESULT	ATTND	ROUND
17.3.73	HOME	LEEDS UNITED	0-1	38350	6TH

BOULTON	WEBSTER	NISH	O'HARE	McFARLAND	TODD	McGOVERN	GEMMILL	DAVIES	HECTOR	POWELL*	DURBAN
HARVEY	REANEY	CHERRY	BREMNER*	MADELEY	HUNTER	LORIMER	CLARKE	JONES	GILES	GRAY	NA

MILESTONES: NA
LORIMER

EUROPEAN CUP

Zeljeznicar

DATE	VENUE	OPPOS	RESULT	ATTND	ROUND
13.9.72	HOME	ZELJEZNICAR	2-0	27350	1ST 1L

BOULTON	POWELL	DANIEL	HENNESSEY	McFARLAND	TODD	McGOVERN	GEMMILL	O'HARE	HECTOR	HINTON	NA
JANUS	KOJOVIC	BECIRSPHATIC	DERAKOVIC	KATALINSKI	BRATIC	JELUSIC	JANKOVIC*	BUCAL	SPRECO	RADOVIC*	KOJOVIC / SARACEVIC

MILESTONES: McFARLAND, GEMMILL

Zeljeznicar

DATE	VENUE	OPPOS	RESULT	ATTND	ROUND
27.9.72	AWAY	ZELJEZNICAR	2-1	60000	1ST 2L

BOULTON	DANIEL	ROBSON	HENNESSEY	McFARLAND	TODD	McGOVERN	GEMMILL	O'HARE	HECTOR	HINTON	NA
JANUS	KOJOVIC	BECIRSPHATIC	BRATIC	SARACEVIC	KATALINSKI	JELUSIC	JANKOVIC*	BUCAL*	SPRECO	DERAKOVIC*	KOJOVIC / RADOVIC

MILESTONES: HINTON, O'HARE

Benfica

DATE	VENUE	OPPOS	RESULT	ATTND	ROUND
25.10.72	HOME	BENFICA	3-0	38100	2ND 1L

BOULTON	ROBSON	DANIEL	HENNESSEY	McFARLAND	TODD	McGOVERN	GEMMILL	O'HARE	HECTOR	HINTON	NA
HENRIQUES	DA SILVA	HUMBERTO	MESSIAS	ADOLFO	J.GRACA	NENE	TONI	BAPTISTA*	EUSEBIO	SIMOES	JORDAO

MILESTONES: McFARLAND, HECTOR, McGOVERN

DATE	VENUE	OPPOS	RESULT	ATTND	ROUND
8.11.72	AWAY	BENFICA	0-0	75000	2ND 2L

	BOULTON	WEBSTER	ROBSON	HENNESSEY	McFARLAND	TODD	McGOVERN	GEMMILL	O'HARE	HECTOR	HINTON	NA
C	BOULTON	WEBSTER	ROBSON	HENNESSEY	McFARLAND	TODD	McGOVERN	GEMMILL	O'HARE	HECTOR	HINTON	NA
O	HENRIQUES	DA SILVA	HUMBERTO	MESSIAS	ADOLFO	J.GRACA	NENE*	TONI	BAPTISTA*	EUSEBIO	SIMOES	JORDAO / RODRIGUES

NA
NA
MILESTONES:

DATE	VENUE	OPPOS	RESULT	ATTND	ROUND
7.3.73	AWAY	SPARTAK TRNAVA	0-1	28000	3RD 1L

	BOULTON	POWELL	NISH	O'HARE	McFARLAND	TODD	McGOVERN	GEMMILL	DAVIES	HECTOR	O'HARE	NA
C	BOULTON	POWELL	NISH	O'HARE	McFARLAND	TODD	McGOVERN	GEMMILL	DAVIES	HECTOR	O'HARE	NA
O	KEKETI	DOBIAS	MAJERNIK	HAGARA	HRUSECKY	MASRNA	ADAMEC	KABAT	VARADIN	FANDEL	HORVATH	NA

HORVATH
MILESTONES:

DATE	VENUE	OPPOS	RESULT	ATTND	ROUND
21.3.73	HOME	SPARTAK TRNAVA	2-0	36472	3RD 2L

	BOULTON	WEBSTER	NISH	O'HARE	McFARLAND	TODD	McGOVERN	GEMMILL	DAVIES	HECTOR	HINTON	NA
C	BOULTON	WEBSTER	NISH	O'HARE	McFARLAND	TODD	McGOVERN	GEMMILL	DAVIES	HECTOR	HINTON	NA
O	KEKETI	DOBIAS	MAJERNIK	HAGARA	KUNA	HRUSECKY	HORVATH*	MASRNA*	FANDEL	ADAMEC	KABAT	VARADIN / MARTINKONOC

HECTOR (2)
NA
MILESTONES:

DATE	VENUE	OPPOS	RESULT	ATTND	ROUND
11.4.73	AWAY	JUVENTUS	1-3	72000	SF 1L

	BOULTON	WEBSTER	NISH	DURBAN	McFARLAND	TODD	McGOVERN	HECTOR	O'HARE	GEMMILL	POWELL	NA
C	BOULTON	WEBSTER	NISH	DURBAN	McFARLAND	TODD	McGOVERN	HECTOR	O'HARE	GEMMILL	POWELL	NA
O	ZOFF	SPINOSI	MARCHETTI	FURINO	MORINI	SALVADORE	CASIO	CUCCEREDDU*	ANASTAL	CAPELLO	ALTAFINI	HALLER

HECTOR
ALTAFINI (2), CASIO
MILESTONES:

DATE	VENUE	OPPOS	RESULT	ATTND	ROUND
25.4.73	HOME	JUVENTUS	0-0	35350	SF 2L

	BOULTON	WEBSTER	NISH	POWELL*	DANIEL*	TODD	McGOVERN	O'HARE	DAVIES	HECTOR	HINTON	DURBAN/SIMS
C	BOULTON	WEBSTER	NISH	POWELL*	DANIEL*	TODD	McGOVERN	O'HARE	DAVIES	HECTOR	HINTON	DURBAN/SIMS
O	ZOFF	SPINOSI	MARCHETTI	FURINO	MORINI	SALVADORE	CASIO	CUCCEREDDU*	ANASTAL	CAPELLO	ALTAFINI	LONGOBUCCO

LAST GAME FOR SIMS
NA
MILESTONES:

DIVISION 1

DATE	VENUE	OPPOS	RESULT	ATTND	POS		1	2	3	4	5	6	7	8	9	10	11	12
25.8.73	HOME	CHELSEA	1-0	31847	8-18	C	BOULTON	WEBSTER	NISH	POWELL	McFARLAND	TODD	McGOVERN	GEMMILL	DAVIES	HECTOR	HINTON	NA
						O	BONETTI	HOLLINS	McCREADIE	BOYLE	WEBB	HARRIS	GARLAND	KEMBER	OSGOOD	HUTCHINSON	HOUSEMAN	NA
MILESTONES: McGOVERN																		
29.8.73	HOME	MANCHESTER CITY	1-0	31295	5-8	C	BOULTON	WEBSTER	NISH	POWELL	McFARLAND	TODD	McGOVERN	GEMMILL	DAVIES	HECTOR	HINTON	NA
						O	CORRIGAN	PARDOE	DONACHIE	DOYLE	BOOTH	OAKES	SUMMERBEE	BELL	LAW	LEE	MARSH	NA
MILESTONES: HINTON																		
1.9.73	AWAY	BIRMINGHAM CITY	0-0	34899	5-20	C	BOULTON	WEBSTER	NISH	POWELL	McFARLAND	TODD	McGOVERN	GEMMILL	O'HARE	HECTOR	HINTON	NA
						O	LATCHFORD	MARTIN*	PENDREY	PAGE	HYND	BURNS	CAMPBELL	FRANCIS	LATCHFORD	HATTON	TAYLOR	ROBERTS
MILESTONES: NA																		
4.9.73	AWAY	LIVERPOOL	0-2	45237	7-5	C	BOULTON	WEBSTER	NISH	POWELL	McFARLAND	TODD	McGOVERN	GEMMILL	O'HARE	HECTOR	HINTON	NA
						O	CLEMENCE	LAWLER	THOMPSON	SMITH	LLOYD	HUGHES	KEEGAN	CORMACK	HEIGHWAY	TOSHACK	CALLAGHAN	NA
MILESTONES: THOMPSON, KEEGAN																		
8.9.73	HOME	EVERTON	2-1	27638	7-11	C	BOULTON	WEBSTER	NISH	POWELL	McFARLAND	TODD	McGOVERN	GEMMILL	DAVIES	HECTOR	HINTON	NA
						O	LAWSON	DARRACOTT	NEWTON	KENDALL	KENYON	HURST	HARVEY*	BERNARD	LYONS	HARPER	CONNOLLY	HUSBAND
MILESTONES: DAVIES, HECTOR / HUSBAND / 400TH OVERALL LEAGUE GAME FOR HINTON / 100TH RAM'S LEAGUE GAME FOR TODD																		
12.9.73	HOME	LIVERPOOL	3-1	32867	5-8	C	BOULTON	WEBSTER	NISH	POWELL	McFARLAND	TODD	McGOVERN	GEMMILL	DAVIES	HECTOR	HINTON	NA
						O	CLEMENCE	LAWLER	THOMPSON	SMITH	LLOYD	HUGHES	KEEGAN	CORMACK	HEIGHWAY	BOERSMA	CALLAGHAN	NA
MILESTONES: McFARLAND, DAVIES, HECTOR / BOERSMA																		

15.9.73 — AWAY — BURNLEY — 1-1 — ATTND 24493 — POS 5-2

	C	O
1	BOULTON	STEVENSON
2	WEBSTER	NOBLE
3	NISH	NEWTON
4	POWELL	DOBSON
5	McFARLAND	WALDRON
6	TODD	THOMPSON
7	McGOVERN	NULTY
8	GEMMILL	HANKIN
9	DAVIES	FLETCHER
10	HECTOR	COLLINS
11	HINTON	JAMES
sub	NA	NA

MILESTONES: DAVIES / HANKIN

18.9.73 — AWAY — COVENTRY CITY — 0-1 — ATTND 26511 — POS 6-3

	C	O
1	BOULTON	GLAZIER
2	WEBSTER	SMITH
3	NISH	HOLMES
4	POWELL*	MORTIMER
5	McFARLAND	CRAVEN
6	TODD	DUGDALE
7	McGOVERN	McGUIRE
8	GEMMILL	ALDERSON
9	DAVIES	STEIN
10	HECTOR	HUNT
11	HINTON	HITCHINSON
sub	O'HARE	NA

MILESTONES: NA / STEIN

22.9.73 — HOME — SOUTHAMPTON — 6-2 — ATTND 25500 — POS 2-16

	C	O
1	BOULTON	MARTIN
2	WEBSTER	McCARTHY
3	NISH	WALKER
4	POWELL	FISHER
5	McFARLAND	BENNETT
6	TODD	BYRNE
7	McGOVERN	PAINE
8	GEMMILL	CHANNON
9	DAVIES	GILCHRIST
10	HECTOR	O'NEIL
11	HINTON	STOKES
sub	NA	NA

MILESTONES: HECTOR (3), DAVIES (2), HINTON (P), O'NEIL (2)

29.9.73 — AWAY — TOTTENHAM HOTSPUR — 0-1 — ATTND 31408 — POS 4-18

	C	O
1	BOULTON	DAINES
2	WEBSTER	EVANS
3	NISH	KNOWLES
4	POWELL	PRATT
5	McFARLAND	ENGLAND
6	TODD	BEAL
7	McGOVERN	GILZEAN
8	NEWTON	PERRYMAN
9	O'HARE	CHIVERS
10	HECTOR	PETERS
11	GEMMILL	COATES
sub	NA	NA

MILESTONES: GILZEAN — DEBUT FOR NEWTON

6.10.73 — HOME — NORWICH CITY — 1-1 — ATTND 25984 — POS 4-20

	C	O
1	BOULTON	KEELAN
2	WEBSTER	PROPHETT
3	NISH	PAYNE
4	POWELL	STRINGER
5	DANIEL	FORBES
6	TODD	BRIGGS
7	NEWTON	LIVERMORE
8	GEMMILL	SUGGETT
9	DAVIES	CROSS
10	HECTOR	PADDON
11	HINTON	MELLOR
sub	NA	NA

MILESTONES: DAVIES / SUGGETT

13.10.73 — AWAY — MANCHESTER UNITED — 1-0 — ATTND 43724 — POS 3-18

	C	O
1	BOULTON	STEPNEY
2	WEBSTER	BUCHAN
3	NISH	FORSYTH
4	NEWTON	GREENHOFF
5	McFARLAND	HOLTON
6	TODD	JAMES
7	McGOVERN	MORGAN
8	GEMMILL	YOUNG
9	DAVIES	KIDD
10	HECTOR	ANDERSON
11	HINTON	GRAHAM
sub	NA	NA

MILESTONES: HECTOR / NA

LAST GAME UNDER THE MANAGEMENT OF CLOUGH/TAYLOR

AFTER ALL TEAMS HAD PLAYED 42 GAMES DERBY, UNDER THE MANAGEMENT OF DAVE MACKAY, FINISHED IN 3RD PLACE

LEAGUE CUP

DATE	8.10.73	C	BOULTON	WEBSTER	NISH	NEWTON	McFARLAND	TODD	McGOVERN	GEMMILL	DAVIES	HECTOR	HINTON	NA
VENUE	HOME	O	MONTGOMERY	MALONE	GUTHRIE	HORSWILL*	WATSON	YOUNG	KERR	HUGHES	HALOM	PORTERFIELD	LATHAN	BOLTON
OPPOS	SUNDERLAND													
RESULT	2-2	C	NISH, DAVIES											
ATTND	29172	O	LATHAN (2)											
ROUND	2ND		MILESTONES:											

NB: THE REPLAY AT ROKER PARK ENDED 1-1 (AET). DERBY EXITED THE COMPETITION 3-0 IN THE SECOND REPLAY, ALSO IN THE NORTH EAST. BOTH GAMES WERE PLAYED UNDER THE MANAGEMENT OF DAVE MACKAY.

BIBLIOGRAPHY

DERBY COUNTY A COMPLETE RECORD 1884-1988
GERALD MORTIMER (BREEDON BOOKS 1988)

THE LEGENDS OF DERBY COUNTY
IAN HALL (BREEDON BOOKS 2001)

DERBY COUNTY FC - THE 25 YEAR RECORD
MICHAEL ROBINSON (SOCCER BOOK PUBLISHING 1995)

CLOUGHIE, WALKING ON WATER - MY LIFE
WITH JOHN SADLER (HEADLINE BOOK PUBLISHING 2002)

VOICES OF THE RAMS
IAN HALL (BREEDON BOOKS 2000)

ARMED WITH A FOOTBALL
ANDREW WARD (CROWBERRY 1994)

CLOUGH THE AUTOBIOGRAPHY
WITH JOHN SADLER (PARTRIDGE PRESS 1996)

HIS WAY - THE BRIAN CLOUGH STORY
PATRICK MURPHY (PAN BOOKS 1994)

FOOTBALL PLAYERS RECORDS 1946-1984
BARRY HUGMAN (NEWNES BOOKS 1984)

1888-1988 LEAGUE FOOTBALL AND THE MEN WHO MADE IT
SIMON INGLIS (WILLOW BOOKS 1988)

THE FA YEAR BOOK 1971/72
(WILLIAM HEINEMANN PUBLISHERS 1972)

THE FA YEAR BOOK 1972/73
(WILLIAM HEINEMANN PUBLISHERS 1973)

THE GUINNESS FOOTBALL ENCYCLOPEDIA
GRAHAM HART (GUINNESS PUBLISHING 1995)

PURNELL'S ENCYCLOPEDIA OF ASSOCIATION FOOTBALL
NORMAN BARNETT (PURNELL BOOKS 1972)

THE FOOTBALL MANAGERS
JOHNNY ROGAN (QUEEN ANNE PRESS 1989)

PETER LORIMER - LEEDS AND SCOTLAND HERO
PHIL ROSTRON (MAINSTREAM PUBLISHING 2002)

SHANKS - THE AUTHORISED BIOGRAPHY OF BILL SHANKLY
DAVE BOWLER (ORION 1996)

GEORGE GRAHAM - THE GLORY AND THE GRIEF
NORMAN GILLER (ANDRE DEUTSCH 1995)

JACK CHARLTON THE AUTOBIOGRAPHY
BYRNE (PARTRIDGE PRESS 1996)

THE JIMMY HILL STORY - MY AUTOBIOGRAPHY
(HODDER & STOUGHTON 1998)

DALGLISH - MY AUTOBIOGRAPHY
HENRY WINTER (HODDER & STOUGHTON 1996)

VARIOUS NEWSPAPERS FROM THE PERIOD

THE DERBY EVENING TELEGRAPH

THE TIMES

THE DAILY TELEGRAPH

THE GUARDIAN

FOR INSPIRATION:
McILVANNEY ON FOOTBALL
HUGH McILVANNEY (MAINSTREAM PUBLISHING 1997)

PHOTOGRAPHIC CREDITS

The pictures shown on the following pages are from the Associated Sports Photography files and are displayed on their **www.sporting-heroes.com** website:

16, 71, 107, 110, 114, 118, 129, 137, 157, 165, 175.

The pictures shown on the following pages are from the Derby Evening Telegraph archive records and the **www.therams.com** website:

8, 9, 10, 20, 41, 48, 49, 54, 57, 59, 60, 63, 67, 68, 70, 72, 77, 84, 88, 89, 90, 93, 96, 97, 98, 99, 105, 116, 117, 119, 122, 123, 124, 126, 127, 128, 134, 140, 142, 145, 146, 149, 152, 160, 163, 169, 176, 181.

The remainder of the pictures shown on the following pages are from the private collections of Neil Hallsworth, Nigel Mercer, Dave Burrows and the author:

19, 30, 33, 35, 39, 44, 45, 46, 47, 65, 86.